Feminist Media

Feminist Media

From the Second Wave to the Digital Age

Claire Sedgwick

ROWMAN & LITTLEFIELD
Lanham • Boulder • New York • London

Published by Rowman & Littlefield
An imprint of The Rowman & Littlefield Publishing Group, Inc.
4501 Forbes Boulevard, Suite 200, Lanham, Maryland 20706
www.rowman.com

6 Tinworth Street, London SE11 5AL, United Kingdom

British Library Cataloguing-in-Publication Information Available

Library of Congress Cataloging-in-Publication Data

Library of Congress Control Number: 2020940085

ISBN 978-1-78661-040-9 (cloth)
ISBN 978-1-78661-041-6 (paperback)
ISBN 978-1-78661-042-3 (electronic)

Contents

Contents

List of Tables

Acknowledgements

Writing a book is hard, and I could not have done it without the practical, intellectual and emotional support of lots of people. The current academic landscape, with increased casualisation, precarity and competitiveness, has undoubtedly had an impact on the writing of this book. As an Early Career Researcher, the network of feminist friends that I have has been especially important to me. Often, especially in the United Kingdom, academia is metricised in a way that discourages mutual support, emphasises individual achievement and obscures the struggles of those not in a permanent academic job. I am incredibly grateful to work with colleagues who do not subscribe to that model. A few years ago, Helen Wood set up the Media and Gender Group at the University of Leicester. The support of the group (now ably convened by the brilliant Jilly Kay, Melanie Kennedy and Jess Bain) has been invaluable in helping me try out ideas, discuss my research and provide a caring and supportive space. Through the group I have met amazing feminist friends. Thank you Jess Martin and Sabrina Moro, Kaity Mendes and Alison Harvey, scholars who have inspired me with their intellect and kindness. Thank you Jilly Kay and Stevie Marsden for being amazingly supportive as we all went through the first book writing process. Daisy Richards, Jenifer Chao, Indrani Lahiri, Vicky Ball, Ellen Wright, Giuliana Tiripelli and Gurvinder Audja Sidhu were brilliant colleagues during my time at De Montfort University (DMU). Heather Savigny has been hugely supportive of my work, giving me a confidence in it that I would not have otherwise. I am incredibly grateful to have so many brilliant women in my life.

Much of the book was written between teaching undergraduate students at De Montfort University and the University of Nottingham. I have been lucky to have been able to share ideas with students at both De Montfort University and the University of Nottingham, and I am grateful for all of the discussions

I have had with them and for the hope they give me when the world seems hopeless. I am grateful for the support of great colleagues at both the institutions.

Thank you to Dhara Snowden and Rebecca Anastasi at Rowman & Little-field International for being great editors, and thank you to the reviewers who gave such helpful suggestions to the proposal and the draft of this book. Thank you Jasti Bhavya for managing the copy-editing and proof-reading of the book.

Thank you to my parents, Margaret and Stephen, who have been the biggest support. This book belongs to them and is dedicated to my auntie Donna and my nana Ada, who were both brilliant role models for what a successful and kind woman looks like.

Foreword

The research for this book started in 2012, two months before the re-election of Barack Obama, when I started my PhD. Even though my PhD aimed to explore the importance of second wave feminism in helping us to understand feminism today, I was at the beginning of the research complacent about feminism's gains and at that point unaware of the stark parallels between the 1970s and 1980s and the present day. As my research developed, it became increasingly clear that although feminism had become much more mainstream, many of the issues that were discussed in *Spare Rib* and *Ms.* continued to be relevant today. Although most of the research was written during a time when the United States had a liberal president, this is also research written wholly within the context of austerity in the United Kingdom. Just as in the 1980s, articles in *Spare Rib* were investigating the impact that austerity has had on women, today, feminist organisations such as Sisters Uncut are similarly challenging the austerity policies that are disproportionately impacting women.

Other similarities can be easily drawn, most specifically the continued debates within feminism about racism and homophobia. Although the term 'white feminism' is more commonly used today, the dominance of white feminists within the feminist movement is not a new phenomenon. The attitude of white feminists towards inclusion of women of colour in the 1980s mirrors that of today. This suggests that as white feminists, we must do more to challenge our own racism, as well as the assumptions that are made about who feminism is for. At this point, it would also be worth explaining my decision to have a chapter that specifically discusses race, as I am aware that this risks looking tokenistic. Put simply, the reason there is a chapter on race is because there was such a paucity of articles written by, or reflecting the experiences of, women of colour when discussing *Spare Rib* and *Ms.* I felt, therefore, that it was important to interrogate further the way that whiteness dominated in the magazines by looking specifically at how *Spare Rib* and *Ms.* represented race.

There are issues that this book does not cover, either because of limitations of space or because my own lack of expertise meant I did not feel I could adequately engage with the complexity of these issues. I do, however, think that these issues are worth reflecting on here. Transphobia within British feminism, in particular, has increasingly become a problem in the past few years. However, there was very little discussion of trans issues in *Spare Rib*. In *Ms.*, articles about transgender tennis player Renée Richards (1977) showed a hostile attitude towards trans women, though in an op-ed for *Advocate* in 2013, Steinem stated that trans 'lives should be celebrated, not questioned'. In *Spare Rib* there was one article from September 1987 written by a transgender woman, and this was clear about the challenges faced by trans women due to a sometimes hostile wider women's movement. Another issue that I have not discussed in detail is the discussion of Israel, Palestine and anti-Semitism. This is a particularly complex issue which I did not feel I had the expertise or experience to discuss in detail.

The final stages of my PhD coincided with the election of Donald Trump, meaning that many of the discussions in this book about the role of feminism in conservative times have new meaning. The rise of anti-feminism discourse is again a threat for feminism. However, as the later chapters of this book show, feminists continue to challenge this. There is so much to learn from the past, in terms of both the strength and community that can be seen through feminist media, and the challenges faced by feminists. It is because of this that it seemed integral to me to view contemporary feminist media in relation to historical feminist media, as a way to understand how feminism can help change the future too.

Introduction: Second Wave Feminist Media and Its Contemporary Relevance

The past decade has seen a resurgence of feminism, both within the media and within political discourse more broadly. Celebrity identification with feminism, alongside events such as the Women's March, has led to an increased visibility within popular culture. Alongside this, the importance of feminist history has been affirmed through the *Sisterhood and After* oral history project (Jolly, 2019) and the digitisation of *Spare Rib*, both in conjunction with the British Library, each acknowledging the importance of maintaining an archive of feminist media and activism. Furthermore, the proposed reboot of *Spare Rib* by the journalist Charlotte Raven in 2014 shows the link between contemporary feminist media and its predecessors, whilst disagreements between Raven and the *Spare Rib* founders over ownership of the iconic title suggest that the relationship between past and present is not straightforward. The current political climate where feminism is 'circulated in popular and commercial media' (Banet-Weiser, 2018, loc 236) means that this is the ideal time to reassess the feminist media of the past, looking at how a feminist media tradition can be drawn between the activism of the 'second wave' and contemporary feminist media production, whilst also identifying how key debates from the 'second wave' reverberate today. The reassessment and drawing of this tradition of feminist media activism is the primary aim of this book.

In her discussion of Women's Liberation Movement Music (2015), Withers explains her desire to understand the history of feminist music to enhance her own experience as a feminist musician. Similarly, the arguments made in this book understand second wave feminist media production as part of a wider tradition of feminist media production that continues today. In addition to this, the project identifies the common issues that feminist media producers have had, namely ensuring that a wide range of feminist perspectives are represented whilst situating themselves within a competitive capitalist marketplace that is often hostile to feminist perspectives that challenged capitalist norms.

Archive material is integral to this project in helping to construct a history of second wave feminism that does not have generational biases (Hemmings, 2011). However, crucially, the book charts a history of feminist media but does not fossilise this history, instead using it to understand feminist media as a continuing way to understand feminism. *Spare Rib* and *Ms*. are the central case studies for the first chapters of this book due to their popularity in the United States and the United Kingdom, respectively. Erdman Farrell (1998, p. 1) describes *Ms*. as 'the popular icon of the women's movement, synonymous for many Americans, with the women's movement itself'. However, despite its popularity, there has been little scholarly analysis of *Ms*. Similarly, Chambers et al. (2004, p. 165) argue that '*Spare Rib* influenced an entire generation of women' and though there has been research on the magazine (Todd, 1999; Hollows, 2012, Forster, 2016; Smith, 2017), there has been little work that has compared the magazines to each other, and there is a lack of research that connects historic feminist media with engagement with the media today. It is particularly important to understand the continued ways capitalism needs to be considered when trying to understand how feminists managed their relationship with the media.

CHARTING THE HISTORY OF FEMINIST MEDIA: SECOND WAVE FEMINIST MEDIA

The importance of feminist media has been emphasised by many scholars. Forster (2016, p. 1) argues that 'the significance of the printed word to the Women's Liberation Movement (WLM) of the 1970s can hardly be overstated', whilst Mendes (2011, p. 6) states that there was an 'incredible amount of feminist publishing taking place in alternative publications'. The importance of feminist media production is noted by Chambers et al. (2004, p. 160), who argue that there was a rise in 'local and national women's liberation newsletters, magazines and journals' in the 1970s and 1980s. Feminist media production was a way to put feminist theory into practice, and Travis (2008, p. 277) suggests that feminist media producers were 'united by common ideological commitments'. Although the research in the first section of this book focuses on two feminist magazines, *Spare Rib* and *Ms*, they are only two of the many feminist publications to come out of the United States and the United Kingdom. In the United States, other feminist magazines included *Off Our Backs* (1970–2008), whilst in the United Kingdom there were a plethora of publications, including *Shrew* (1968–1978), *Red Rag*

(1973–1980), *Shocking Pink* (1981–1982, 1987–1992) and the *WIRES* newsletter (1975–1985).[1]

In her discussion of feminist publishing, Murray (2004, p. 138) suggests that radical feminist media production often featured 'staff consciousness raising, skills sharing and the development of theoretical analysis', whilst a 'leitmotif of the 1970s feminist media theory is a deeply ingrained suspicion of the multinational corporate publishing sector'. For organisations such as *Spare Rib*, editorial collectives provided an alternative to mainstream hierarchical structures, whilst the hierarchies between the reader and the writer were also destabilised. Thomas Flannery (2005, p. 25) argues that feminist media 'sought to break down the traditional lines between reader, expert and novice, teacher and learner' (p. 26). In *Spare Rib* and *Ms.*, there were proactive attempts to engage with readers through letters, whilst *Spare Rib* asked readers to contribute to the magazine, especially about contentious issues. However, despite having a number of authors, magazines still have an editorial process that means that not all submissions are printed. In addition, as this book will demonstrate, attempts to disengage with capitalism were limited due to the need to operate as businesses. This means the ability of the magazines to be wholly representative of all feminism was limited.

Studying Women's Magazines

Scholarship on women's magazines can help us to understand the relationship between feminism and women's magazines, which subsequently helps us to identify the differences between women's magazines and feminist magazines. There have been numerous studies on women's magazines in the United States (White, 1968; Tuchman, 1979; Hunter, 1990; Walker, 1998) and the United Kingdom (Ferguson, 1983; Winship, 1987; Gough-Yates, 2003). McRobbie (1997, p. 190) describes women's magazines as 'commercial sites of intensified femininity and hence rich fields of analysis and critique'. Similarly, Johnson (2007, p. 253) suggests that 'magazines help readers make sense of their world and lives'. These quotes highlight how magazines play an important role in defining how readers understand their role in the world. Ferguson (1983, p. 185) argues that women's magazines provide 'step-by-step instructions' for women to understand their gender roles. Feminists were often highly critical of the role that women's magazines played in inscribing gender roles through their focus on domesticity. Friedan (1963, p. 45) focuses heavily on the retreat to traditional values in the post-war period, arguing that the emphasis on domestic happiness in women's magazines actively undermined women's attempts to succeed in the public sphere. Similarly, White (1970, p. 45) questioned the extent to which women's magazines could be 'innocuous' or be seen as having little impact on women's ambitions and role.[2] Tuchman (1979, p. 533) suggested that women's magazines aimed to 'isolate and undercut' women's participation in the workforce by emphasising their place in the home. Ferguson (1983, pp. 49–58) argues that women's magazines cultivate a 'cult of femininity' which reinforces gender stereotypes that keep women in the domestic sphere. Discussing the representation of Black women in women's magazines, Onwurah (1987, p. 40) addresses the ways Black women are marginalised by being 'consigned to specific areas – entertainment, art, perhaps travel – and kept in their place'.

There have also been analyses of the cultural economies of women's magazines. Walker (1998) and Beetham (1996, p. 2) discuss women's magazines as businesses and highlight the importance of advertising in dictating content and sustaining revenue. McRobbie's (1997, p. 190) description of women's magazines as 'commercial sites of intensified femininity' aptly sums up the relationship between women's magazines, capitalism, the construction of femininity and the messages that women's magazines promote. This is in contrast with feminist magazines such as *Spare Rib*, and to a lesser extent *Ms*. They both reframed the influence of advertisements and commercialisation in magazines, albeit in different ways and to varying levels of success, as the chapter on the magazines as businesses will illustrate.

Although the difference between women's magazines and feminist magazines may appear obvious, the inclusion of feminist content in women's magazines (Hunter, 1990) means that this distinction is not always clear. Hermes (1995, p. 96) states that readers were 'not sure whether or not feminist magazines are women's magazines', suggesting that for the general reader the distinction between the two is not clear. In contrast, Winship (1987, p. 19–20) argues that 'for some, *Spare Rib*'s politics set it apart, unfavourably, from commercial magazines, which have always insisted on their non-political status'. The main difference between women's magazines and feminist magazines is that feminist magazines are explicitly interested with gender equality, and this is a primary concern. In contrast, whilst women's magazines may discuss feminism or women's equality, this is not the primary aim. Winship (1987, p. 184) argues that whilst feminist magazines 'embrace certain aspects of . . . femininity', they are also 'central sites of political struggle'. It is this politicisation that differentiates feminist magazines from women's magazines. Discussing *Ms*. in the 1970s, Phillips (1978, p. 124) compared it with *Family Circle*, a commercial women's magazine. Phillips suggested that 'with less than five percent of *Family Circle*'s readership, *Ms*. represents a minority view of female role models and expected behaviour patterns'. Whilst contemporary women's magazines are generally much more supportive of feminism (this will be discussed in the second half of this book with reference to *Teen Vogue*), their status as capitalist products makes it difficult to regard them as unproblematically feminist.

FEMINIST MAGAZINES

Although there has been recognition of the vibrancy of second wave feminist media production (Chambers et al., 2004; Thomas Flannery, 2005; Mendes, 2011), there has been relatively little discussion of the role of *feminist magazines* specifically. There have also been very few studies of *Spare Rib* or *Ms.*, and none that takes a longitudinal or comparative lens. Feminist magazines are important for helping us understand the relationship between feminist media and capitalism, which is an important theme in this book. In her discussion of Canadian feminist periodicals, Godard (2002, p. 213) argues that although feminist publications have the benefit of editorial independence, they do not have the 'safety net of dominant practices' and thus are often in an insecure place in the market. This is echoed in an influential article by the collective Comedia (1984), which highlight the problems that alternative publications have sustaining themselves financially. The tension between maintaining a sustainable position within the market and practicing feminist principles will be a central theme throughout this book.

Winship (1987) discusses *Spare Rib* within the context of a much larger study of women's magazines, and similarly McCracken (1993) discusses *Ms.* in relation to commercial women's magazines. In both examples feminist magazines are placed in opposition to mainstream women's magazines and the differences *between* feminist magazines are not explored. This is especially significant as magazines such as *Spare Rib* and *Ms.* differ in terms of editorial practices, audience and commercial interests, showing that there was certainly more than one vision for what a feminist magazine could look like, and what it could achieve. We cannot assume that feminist magazines will be like each other, and more research needs to attend to the differences *between* feminist magazines, rather than focusing only on the differences between feminist magazines and commercial women's magazines.

Forster (2016) studies the importance of feminist print culture and includes *Spare Rib* in her analysis. The article is a useful overview of *Spare Rib*'s publication history, its circulation figures and the magazine's approach. Forster (2016, p. 13) suggests that the magazine 'offered a broad church of views'. However, Forster's article does not analyse any articles from *Spare Rib* in depth, as this monograph will. Todd (1999) discussed the magazine in relation to feminism and femininity, whilst Hollows (2012) analysed *Spare Rib* in relation to consumption. Both studies analyse articles from the magazine and are useful for identifying the relationship between *Spare Rib*, feminism and wider culture. *Re-Reading Spare Rib* (2017) provides a range of perspectives on the magazine, including its relationship to advertising and its representation of race. Chapters from this edited collection will be engaged with throughout this book.

Ms. has been the subject of a couple of comprehensive histories. Erdman Farrell (1998) provides a history of the magazine from its inception up until its last issue in 1989 before its relaunch, discussing the impact of *Ms.* on the wider feminist movement. Mary Thom (1997), who was heavily involved in the founding of the magazine, wrote an account of the magazine's origins. Both texts are helpful when understanding the context in which *Ms.* was produced, though neither analyses the content of articles within the magazine. Whilst attention has been paid to *Ms.* and *Spare Rib* separately, scholarly work has not compared them to each other or placed them within a wider feminist publishing tradition. This chapter will now provide a brief history of both magazines.

Spare Rib

The first issue of *Spare Rib* was published in July 1972. The magazine was founded by Rosie Boycott and Marsha Rowe. Rowe and Boycott had both worked in the alternative British press on magazines *Oz* and *Frendz*, and Rowe (1982, p. 13) saw *Spare Rib* as the 'daughter of the underground press'. Rowe described the underground press as a 'more authentic voice for the concerns and mood of the youth movement than the mass media' (p. 14). However, she also describes the sexism she encountered, suggesting that 'women who worked on its magazines and newspapers served the men and did office and production work rather than editorial work' (p. 15). In contrast, *Spare Rib* would be a magazine aimed at women, with most of the content written by women too. Rowe describes the magazine as an 'an activity and consciousness-raising process combined' (p. 19). This can be linked to Travis's (2008) assertion that feminist media production allowed for feminists to practically apply the knowledge learnt through feminist theory and critique of the media. The magazine had a capacity-building role and 'invited contributions from readers, including women not active in the women's movement' (Rowe, 1982, p. 19). Furthermore, as Edmonds and White (2017, p. 27) note, the magazine was 'available in newsagents. It was visible on the shelf'. The ready availability of the magazine further increased the likelihood that it would be consumed by women not already familiar with the women's movement. This research will discuss the ways in which *Spare Rib* and *Ms.* addressed its imagined reader and whether it *was* addressing women not involved in the women's movement.

The focus on politics differed from mainstream women's magazines such as *Women's Own* and *Good Housekeeping*, and Winship (1987, p. 135) compares the 'fragile contentment with women's lot' that can be found in these magazines with the 'critical discontent' displayed by *Spare Rib*. Winship (p. 135) argues that *Spare Rib* provided an outlet for feminists to 'feel neither mad, nor bad, nor alone in [their] beliefs'. Similarly, Chambers et al.

(2004, p. 165) argue that *Spare Rib* 'overturned taken for granted patriarchal assumptions about femininity and women's daily experiences' by providing alternative representations of women than those that can be seen in mainstream women's magazines.

ORGANISATIONAL STRUCTURE

An important change that occurred in *Spare Rib* was the move towards an editorial collective in 1974 (Hollows, 2012, p. 5). Rowe (1982, p. 17) describes the process as resulting from a feeling that there was no 'chance to talk or discuss the content of the magazine democratically' whilst the magazine had 'hierarchical editorial structure'. Within the mainstream magazine industry, traditional hierarchies with an editor in chief are the norm. By choosing a collective structure, *Spare Rib* differentiated itself from mainstream women's magazines. Indeed, Rowe framed the move to an editorial collective as a conscious feminist decision. In her memoir, Rosie Boycott (1984, p. 12) describes how Rowe argued that 'we'll never have a feminist magazine while we have a hierarchy . . . *Spare Rib*'s just a men's magazine without the men'. This is in keeping with other feminist media organisations that were characterised by 'non-hierarchical, collectivist structures' and 'heightened self-consciousness vis a vis the corporate mainstream' (Murray, 2004, p. 128).

However, Boycott (1984, p. 127) critiqued the collective, suggesting that 'it's hopeless when ten people make decisions'. There is a tension between the practicality of producing a magazine and wanting to maintain feminist ideals. This tension and potential for conflict is discussed by former collective member Sue O'Sullivan (2012) in her interview for the British Library *Sisterhood and After* project. O'Sullivan describes the 'divisions and horrible things' in the magazine. Murray (2004, p. 129) suggests that 'an under-examined allegiance to non-hierarchical organizing' led to a 'large share of the failure, self-recrimination and personal animosity that is the unfortunate legacy of much radical women's media activity'. O'Sullivan (2012) confesses to feeling out of her depth and struggling to manage the changes within the collective:

> At one point the *Spare Rib* collective decided that they needed more black women, in the first instance it was a black woman but then more, and we rather, I think, we were rather unprepared, it was almost like come and join us at our table, we will love to welcome you to our table, would you like to sit down here with us at our table, oh excellent you know.

This points to the difficulty of having a more representative collective without engaging in tokenism and dictating the terms in which Black women can engage. The metaphor of asking women of colour to 'come and join us at our table' suggests that women of colour are *invited* into the conversation by white women, who hold authority since it is their decision as to whether to offer this invitation. I will return to look at the ways in which *Spare Rib* discussed issues of race and representation throughout this book.

THE END OF *SPARE RIB*

The last issue of *Spare Rib* was in January 1993, but there was no indication that the last issue would be the final one. In the preceding decade, the magazine found it increasingly difficult to maintain an audience and remain solvent. It was rebranded in the 1980s, though, as Chambers et al. (2004, p. 167) point out, this was not well received by all, and some accused the magazine of 'falling prey to the vacuous "style" that became the trademark of the 1980s'. An editorial from October 1990 highlights some of the issues that the magazine faced in its later years. It discusses the importance of competing in the marketplace and suggests that the magazine has not been 'as good as the right [wing] at marketing our message' (October 1990, p. 4). *Spare Rib* needed to adapt to changing economic and cultural conditions, whilst at the same time remain appealing for long-time readers. O'Sullivan (1996, p. 6) describes *Spare Rib* as walking a 'tightrope between "inside" the movement and "outside" it', suggesting that whilst the magazine was explicitly feminist, it aimed to attract readers who did not yet identify with the women's movement.

The demise of *Spare Rib* can be related to an increasingly post-feminist culture (Gill, 2017), and this will be discussed further in the chapter on politics and the backlash. The magazine market had changed so that 'oppositional ideas had shifted to become mainstream', and this meant that women's magazines were more likely to include articles typically seen within feminist magazines (Chambers et al., 2004, p. 172). Similarly, Milloy and O'Rourke (1991, p. 12) state that '*Woman* and *Woman's Own* now regularly cover topics such as rape, returning to work . . . that five or ten years ago would have been featured in *Spare Rib* and would have been considered extreme'. Once mainstream women's magazines began covering topics that were considered feminist, *Spare Rib*'s unique selling point was less obvious.

MS. MAGAZINE

Ms. was launched as a '"one-shot" sample insert in *New York Magazine* in December 1971' (*Ms.* website) and as a magazine in July 1972. Within eight days of going to press in July 1972, 300,000 copies had been sold. Consolidating this success, there were 26,000 subscriptions and 20,000 letters in the weeks after the launch (*Ms.* website). Whilst the founders of *Spare Rib* were involved in the British alternative press, *Ms.* staffers had extensive experience in mainstream women's magazine publishing and news journalism (Steinem, 2012, p. 4). Founder Gloria Steinem (2012, p. 7) suggests that the aim of the magazine was to provide an alternative to 'all those magazines directed at men [that] were totally male-owned and controlled'. *Ms.* served to widen access for feminist journalists to the magazine publishing industry and in the case of Steinem, allowed her to 'control her own image' (Bradley, 2003, p. 157).

Thom (1997, p. 44) describes *Ms.* as 'a monthly advocate for the women's movement', suggesting that the magazine clearly aimed to complement the activities of the wider feminist movement. This relationship was fostered partly through the letters to the magazine. The extent to which letters to the magazine played an important role has been commented on by Chambers et al. (2004, p. 174), who compare the magazine to a 'mass consciousness raising group'. Erdman Farrell (1998, p. 4) argues that this was achieved through 'downplaying status' and hierarchies between reader and writer. The extent to which the magazine's letters were used as a locus of debate will be seen throughout the book.

MS. AND LIBERAL FEMINISM

The magazine featured long-running campaigns on feminist issues such as the Equal Rights Amendment (ERA) and reproductive rights, predominantly from a liberal feminist perspective. Many criticisms of liberal feminism (Tong, 1997; Arneil, 1999; Bryson, 2003) are applicable here, especially in relation to the ability that the magazine had to represent all women. McCracken (1993, p. 279) criticises *Ms.* by describing it as a 'special interest publication read primarily by relatively privileged women' and argues that the magazine is 'limited by the liberal feminist consciousness of its staff' (p. 282). This is highlighted by Erdman Farrell (1998, p. 9), who argues that 'the *Ms.* staff were by no means representative of the women involved in the movement'.

In contrast, Bradley (2003, p. 178) argues that *Ms.* was concerned with 'female universality' and 'there seemed no one who were not included in the pages in *Ms*'. Bradley is critical of this, suggesting that the 'insistence that there was room at the table of sisterhood for everyone in some sense robbed marginal groups of power' (p. 192). This suggests that *Ms.*'s tendency to universalise women's experience disempowered some women and ignored the inequality that exists between women. The lack of consensus between scholars regarding the relationship that the magazine had with the wider feminist movement is indicative of the complex relationship that feminists had with the magazine.

Ms.'s liberalism was regarded with suspicion by some radical feminists, highlighting the criticism it faced from within the feminist movement. Buchanan (2011, p. 18) states that 'members of the radical group the Redstockings would label Steinem and *Ms.* a CIA front to stop the radical feminist movement'. Furthermore, Buchanan suggests that *Ms.* 'was willing to play ball with the paternalistic capitalistic system which the radical feminists so heartily opposed' (p. 18). It is important to note that as with *Spare Rib*, *Ms.* cannot be viewed as representative of the whole feminist movement; instead it reflected one representation amongst many others.

COMMERCIAL AND WORKING PRACTICES AT *MS.*

In contrast to *Spare Rib*, *Ms.* had an editorial hierarchy and staff were paid differently depending on the seniority of their role. Thom (1997, p. 38) quotes Gloria Steinem, who remembers that:

> The first idea that everyone would make the same salary. But some voice of reason, probably Pat [Carbine, *Ms.* editorial staff member], pointed out that this was not going to work, because people had different needs and expertise and so on.

Whilst the magazine was unusual in that it considered a staff member's practical needs in salary decisions, considering whether a staff member had dependents, for example, the fact that all staff members were not being paid the same reinforces a traditional workplace hierarchy. In some instances, this led to disagreement. Thom (1997, p. 101) describes how one staff member 'Harriet Lyons dared to suggest that beneath the egalitarian *Ms.* exterior, some staff members were being exploited'. Furthermore, Thom suggests that financial issues meant that staff were paid late. Murray (2004, p. 151) states that:

> It remains an open question . . . whether the exploitation of women's unpaid labour in the name of a feminist communications network is any more ideologically defensible than women's utilisation as unpaid labour in the domestic sphere.

There is a tension between maintaining feminist ideals and acknowledging the realities of operating a business, and the potential for these ideals to be compromised. It also meant that women who could not afford to have their income delayed were privileged over less wealthy women. The way in which the staffing of *Ms.* impacted how the magazine could discuss feminism and race will be explored further in the chapter on feminism and race. The importance of commercial practices will also be discussed in relation to *Bitch*, *Bust* and contemporary feminist blogs, since the difficulty of ensuring feminist working practices is one that is still pertinent today.

FEMINIST RESEARCH AND FEMINIST HISTORICISATION: SITUATING SECOND WAVE FEMINISM

How feminism has been historicised impacts how we construct, or fail to construct, a history of feminist media. The analysis of *Spare Rib* and *Ms.* in this book is influenced by a desire to understand the 'multiple and varied histories' of feminism (Deem, 2003, p. 617), and the methods chosen reflect the need for an in-depth analysis of primary texts to do this.

The methodology for this project is based on an understanding that current histories of feminism are not a-political and have privileged some narratives over others. Benjamin (1969, p. 257) discussed the radical potential of 'brush[ing] history against the grain'. This involves not taking for granted that existing histories are universal and acknowledging that forgotten or underrepresented histories exist. A study of feminist media, especially multi-authored feminist media, allows for a richer understanding of feminism and its negotiations with capitalism.

It has been a long-held aim of feminist scholarship to 'restore to hegemonic memory the stories that have been forgotten or erased' (Hirsch and Smith, 2002, p. 11). In the 1970s, feminist historians such as Sheila Rowbotham (1973) claimed women's history as a valid and important object of study within the academy. Although I begin this book in the more recent past than Rowbotham's work did, I situate this text within a wider feminist tradition that acknowledges the importance of women's history. It is important to understand how the women's movement has been historicised, and particularly how contemporary feminism has been theorised in relation to the past. Hemmings' (2011) analysis of the ways in which 'second wave' feminism has been historicised is particularly important. He suggests that second wave feminism has been storied in ways that privilege certain narratives over others, so that the version of the story that is told depends on the temporal position of the teller. The first version of the story assumes that the movement from second to third wave feminism represents a progression – that feminism has evolved through considering a more diverse range of women's experiences. In this framework, third wave feminism can be viewed as a distinct development from second wave feminism, as Mann and Huffman (2005) suggest. In contrast, the second story of feminism sees contemporary feminism as having lost some of the vibrancy of second wave feminism of the 1970s. Post-feminism is understood as something that indicates demise in feminism and a more general understanding of feminism as 'over' (Hemmings, 2011, p. 7).

The story teller's temporal position in relation to second and third wave feminism is important since it has an impact on which narrative is privileged. Hemmings argues that feminists who were active in the 1970s and 1980s were more likely to identify with a loss narrative that presents second wave feminism as vibrant and active, whilst contemporary feminists are more likely to privilege a narrative which views contemporary feminism as progressive. At this point I need to consider my own position as a researcher. I did not directly experience the 'second wave' and therefore my understanding of it has been constructed through histories of the movement. The aim of conducting research that goes back to media from the period is to mitigate against the risk of reinforcing biases, either my own or those of other scholars. Furthermore, the aim of the book is to trace a tradition and understand not only the divergences but also the similarities between feminist media produced in the past and in the present.

In a similar vein, Henry (2004, p. 25) argues that the relationship between second and third wave feminism is portrayed as divisive. He argues that 'in the move from second to third, the naming of a new wave relies upon the connotations of progress implied by the metaphor of the wave' (p. 25). It is worth noting that a feminist history of second wave feminist media must consider the problematic nature of the wave metaphor and how it imposes a progressive view of history that ignores its complexity. Deem (2003, p. 619) argues that 'feminism's past is reclaimed, not for political possibilities within feminism but to measure the growth of feminism'. This tendency to view the history of feminism in relation to a more progressive future means that stereotypes about the second wave are emphasised. The analysis in this book rejects such stereotypes and shows that issues such as pornography were discussed in a much more complex way during the 1970s and 1980s than stereotypes would suggest. Furthermore, as Greene (1991, p. 291) argues, the inability to cultivate feminist memory is a 'major obstacle to change'. The research avoids assuming certain issues were discussed in stereotypical ways and draws out points of conflict and contestation in the discourse that suggest that discussing feminism in a monolithic way is misguided. Furthermore, the book intends to chart a history of feminist media activism and documents the ways in which contemporary feminist media can be understood in relation to its predecessors.

RESEARCHING FEMINIST MEDIA: CONTENT ANALYSIS AND TEXTUAL ANALYSIS

Qualitative content analysis has been used throughout this book. Basic content analysis (Drisko and Maschi, 2015, p. 15) uses 'quantitative analytic techniques that only or predominantly address literal communication content'. The 'frequency of word passage use' is analysed 'to determine the relative importance of specific content'. The researcher identifies 'units of measurement' and 'units of analysis' (Messenger Davies and Mosdell, 2006, p. 100). Units of measurement 'are the things that you are looking for within your unit of analysis' (Messenger Davies and Mosdell, 2006, p. 100). A good example of a feminist content analysis is the Global Media Monitoring Project (2015), which identifies the extent to which women are used as sources, understood as experts and were the writers of stories in newspapers, television and radio news, Twitter and websites.

This research utilised a qualitative form of content analysis called a 'Directed Content Analysis' (Hsieh and Shannon, 2005, p. 1281). Hsieh and Shannon (2005, p. 1281) state that 'the goal of a directed approach to content analysis is to validate or extend conceptually a theoretical framework or theory'. Since *Spare Rib* and *Ms.* will be the focus of the next chapters, I will explain the sample for the magazines here. Brief methodological information will be included at the beginning of each relevant chapter throughout the book.

SPARE RIB AND MS. SAMPLE

Spare Rib was digitised by the British Library in 2015, and 9,882 articles were archived in total between 1972 and 1993. However, this research focuses on five key years: 1972, 1977, 1982, 1987 and 1992, and so only issues from that year are included in the sample. These years were chosen because they allow for an analysis that spans the whole of the magazine's publication history. The digitisation of the magazine means that access to articles is possible by searching by keyword, by type of article and by section. The most prevalent article types were stories, news and reviews. Except for 1972, where reviews only constituted 16 percent of the magazine, in each of the other years at least 30 percent of the articles were reviews. Since reviews were not included in the content analysis for this research, this explains why there are fewer articles in the content analysis than were present in the magazine.

It was difficult to categorise reviews since they could not be easily placed within a topic category and so they are not included within the sample for the content analysis (table I.1). Similarly, fiction and poetry were also excluded.

Table I.1. Articles by Section in *Spare Rib* (Accessed Via The British Library Website)

Story Section	1972	1977	1982	1987	1992	total	% of total overall articles
News	43	209	199	148	102	658	**31.83**
Feature	35	44	103	56	50	400	**19.35**
Reviews	29	136	186	36	130	488	**23.6**
Fiction & Poetry	17	10	22	11	8	51	**2.47**
Man's World	15	N/A	N/A	N/A	N/A	15	**0.73**
What's Up Kids	13	N/A	N/A	N/A	N/A	13	**0.63**
Letters	8	11	11	9	8	47	**2.27**
Spare Parts	7	N/A	N/A	N/A	N/A	7	**0.34**
Spare Time	3	N/A	N/A	N/A	N/A	3	**0.15**
Face Value	2	N/A	N/A	N/A	N/A	2	**0.1**
Garb	2	N/A	N/A	N/A	N/A	2	**0.1**
Cover	1	N/A	N/A	N/A	N/A	1	**0.05**
Whole Earth Foods	1	N/A	N/A	N/A	N/A	1	**0.05**
Short list	N/A	30	14	N/A	N/A	44	**2.13**
Tooth and Nail	N/A	15	N/A	N/A	N/A	15	**0.73**
On the road	N/A	5	N/A	N/A	N/A	5	**0.24**
Children	N/A	1	N/A	N/A	N/A	1	**0.05**
Health	N/A	N/A	6	25	19	50	**2.42**
Cover	N/A	N/A	1	N/A	N/A	1	**0.05**
Editorial	N/A	N/A	1	1	1	3	**0.15**
Subscription	N/A	N/A	1	1	N/A	2	**0.1**
Culture Shock	N/A	N/A	N/A	180	N/A	180	**8.71**
Pulse of the Movement	N/A	N/A	N/A	14	20	34	**1.64**
Parenting	N/A	N/A	N/A	13	21	34	**1.64**
Typical Girls	N/A	N/A	N/A	11	N/A	11	**0.53**
Hersay	N/A	N/A	N/A	7	N/A	7	**0.34**
Turning Points	N/A	N/A	N/A	2	N/A	2	**0.1**
Development	N/A	N/A	N/A	2	N/A	2	**0.1**
Interview	N/A	N/A	N/A	1	9	10	**0.48**
Spare Time	N/A	N/A	N/A	N/A	1	1	**0.05**
Total	176	461	544	516	370	2,067	

Articles that could be clearly identified by theme were included within the sample. Themes include race, education, health, sexuality and so forth. There were a total of 2,067 articles from the sample years. These articles were then manually analysed, and all the articles that could be assigned a theme were included in my analysis. It is more difficult to ascertain the total population for *Ms.* from 1972 to 1992 because the magazine has not been digitised. The total number of articles for *Ms.* was 961 from the years 1972, 1977, 1982,

1987 and 1992. In total, there were 420 articles in *Ms.* and 387 articles in *Spare Rib*, meaning that a total of 807 articles were analysed in the thematic analysis overall. Articles were excluded if they could not be easily placed into a topic category, including reviews, letters, fiction and some news articles. News articles were disqualified if they were very brief or could not be categorised as belonging to a theme due to lack of context. Although access to the *Spare Rib* digital archive undoubtedly made it easier to access material, access to *Ms.* required archival research, which was a time-consuming exercise. Because of this, the decision was made to focus on five sample years since they provided material from across the twenty-year period that was being analysed.

CARRYING OUT THE ANALYSIS

The content analysis indicated the key issues that were being discussed in the magazine. This book focuses on four of these topics: race, pornography, politics and the backlash against feminism. These issues were chosen because they are frequently discussed in histories of the women's movement. Furthermore, as with the case of pornography, there are commonly held assumptions about how second wave feminists viewed the issue, which I argue are inaccurate. It is therefore important to go back to articles that discuss these issues at the time that they were happening. For example, the ERA is regularly brought up in discussions of feminist engagement in politics (Dicker, 2016), and so I will be discussing the prevalence of this in *Ms.* Similarly, the backlash (Faludi, 1991; McRobbie, 2009) has often featured in discussions of feminism in the 1990s, and it is useful to identify whether this was an issue that had a long history within feminist discourse. Pornography was chosen for discussion since it has been understood as a particularly intense site of conflict (Rodgerson and Wilson, 1991), whilst race was chosen as a theme since the issue of inclusiveness in feminism was being discussed in the second wave and continues to be discussed today. This also provides a useful way to discuss the relationship between second wave feminism and contemporary feminist activism.

IDEOLOGICAL TEXTUAL ANALYSIS

Alongside content analysis, the book uses a textual analysis approach (Fairclough, 2003). Textual analysis is used in this thesis to identify the discourses that *Spare Rib* and *Ms.* use to represent feminism and how these may reflect power dynamics within the feminist movement. I am influenced by feminist critical discourse analysis, which aims to 'critiqu[e] discourses which sustain a patriarchal order' (Lazar, 2005, p. 6). In one respect this project is different because most texts analysed are written by feminists who are explicit in their rejection of the patriarchy. However, the research does question the ways that even within an oppressed group, hierarchies still exist, and certain stories are privileged over others, since 'power relations are a struggle over interests, which are reflected, maintained and resisted through a variety of modalities, extents and degrees of explicitness' (Lazar, 2005, p. 9).

IDEOLOGICAL TEXTUAL ANALYSIS OF
SPARE RIB AND *MS.*

Once the content analysis had been carried out, articles that were particularly ideologically rich were selected. The following questions were used as a guide when selecting articles for the textual analysis:

- Mode of address: did the article have a particular mode of address, or was it putting forward a particularly interesting, typical or atypical opinion?
- Was the article positioned prominently in the magazine, or was it part of an ongoing series?
- Was the article particularly timely? For example, did it engage in key debates of the time?
- Did the article strongly relate to one of the issues analysed in the thesis?

Once an article had been selected, in carrying out the analysis the following questions were considered when reading it:

1. How do *Spare Rib* and *Ms.* engage with their readers; that is, what is their tone and mode of address?
2. How can the intended reader be perceived?
3. How do articles understand the role of feminism and strategies of feminist activism?
4. How did the article articulate its position in relation to the issue being discussed?

In the chapters on the representation of race, pornography, politics and the backlash, a table (tables 3.1, 4.1, 5.1 and 5.2) is included at the beginning of the chapter that provides an overview of the number of articles included in the analysis.

OVERVIEW OF THE BOOK

Part I: *Spare Rib, Ms.* and the Political Economies of Feminist Magazines

The first part of this book explores the importance of *Spare Rib* and *Ms.* in shaping our understandings of the relationship between second wave feminism and capitalism. I begin by exploring how capitalism impacted on the way that the magazines did feminism. This part also explores the relationship between the magazines' position within the marketplace, their assumed readership and the extent to which the magazines represented all women. I argue that it is important to understand the relationship the magazines had with their readers, since this had a knock-on effect on content. In the 1970s, both *Spare Rib* and *Ms.* had a white assumed reader, but for *Spare Rib* this did change. Readership surveys in *Spare Rib* in 1975 and 1985 show this change. I argue that the questions the survey in 1975 asked, as well as the questions that were not asked, show that there was no awareness of how sexuality, class or race may be an important consideration when understanding the magazine's readership. In contrast, the survey from 1985 showed growing awareness of the importance of identity. However, the survey also shows the tensions amongst the readership over who the magazine was for.

In contrast, the *Ms.* readership survey (Thom, 1997) supports the argument that the magazine's white middle-class readership, since much was made of the high cultural capital of readers and how this would appeal to advertisers. In the second part of the first chapter I discuss the role of letters to the magazine in creating dialogue between readers and magazine staff. I argue that letters to the editor serve as important para-texts which uncover additional discourses to those that were seen in the editorial content of the magazines.

In the final chapter of this first part, I look at the relationship between *Spare Rib* and *Ms.* and advertising. I argue that *Spare Rib*'s decision to eschew corporate advertising reflects the anti-capitalist nature of the magazine. In contrast, *Ms.* was much more likely to feature advertising for products such as alcohol, cosmetics and cigarettes. This often meant that problematic messages were included within the magazine.

Part II: Feminist Magazines and Historicising the Second Wave

The second part of the book explores how *Spare Rib* and *Ms.* represented race, pornography and politics and the backlash. These issues have been chosen because they have been identified as key feminist issues by scholars and historians (Faludi, 1991; Bradley, 2003; Dicker, 2016). I identify how these issues were represented in *Spare Rib* and *Ms*. to provide an alternative history that challenges existing stereotypical understandings of second wave feminism. Representations of feminism within feminist media were selective and subjective, and neither *Spare Rib* or *Ms*. was beyond critique. McCracken (1993, p. 281) critiqued *Ms*. and argued it 'represents a middle-class feminism' and thus cannot be understood to be universal. Similarly, Bradley (2003) and Buchanan (2011) point to how US feminists viewed the magazine as suspicious. Writing about *Spare Rib*, Milloy and O'Rourke (1991) noted that *Spare Rib* was not necessarily representative of all feminists, whilst Hollows (2012, p. 5) notes that in its early days the magazine was treated with suspicion by some feminists because it was perceived as not radical enough. The ways in which the magazines focused on certain issues can be related to how the magazines understood the aims of feminism. It is therefore important to identify absences within the magazines to understand which issues or perspectives were marginalised. Elaborating on this means that we can more easily see how feminist media presents a selective account of feminism, and we can chart their priorities through the absences that are evident.

In the chapter on representations of race within the magazines, I argue that *Spare Rib* was much more likely to take an intersectional approach to feminism. In contrast, *Ms*. represented race in tokenistic ways. Intersectionality has been defined by Hill Collins and Bilge (2016, p. 2) as 'a way of understanding and analysing the complexity in the world, in people, and in human experiences' since 'the organization of power in a society are better understood as being shaped not by a single axis of social division, be it race, gender or class, but by many axes'. This can be most clearly seen in both *Spare Rib* and *Ms*. in the differing ways that the magazines understood the relationship between race and gender. Whilst *Spare Rib* made a concerted effort to increase the inclusivity of its staff and readership, *Ms*. did not do this, in part because it was more integrated into the capitalist publishing industry. Because of this, it was much more likely to attract a white and middle-class audience who would be attractive to advertisers because of their perceived spending power. However, letters from *Spare Rib* readers demonstrate some of the tensions caused by this shift in assumed readers and how this led to accusations from some white readers that the magazine no longer catered to a feminist audience. I argue that this critique reflected the ways in which some white readers centralised their own experience and understood it as more important.

The chapter on pornography and sex discusses the extent to which *Spare Rib* and *Ms*. discussed an issue that has been presented as contentious. I argue that discussion of pornography was less prevalent in *Spare Rib* and *Ms*. than might be assumed from historicisations of the period and that there were differences in how the magazines discussed it. *Ms*. was much more likely to present a singularly harmful view of pornography, whereas *Spare Rib* presented multiple views. Furthermore, whilst the discourse around pornography has been understood as polarised, *Spare Rib* often presented ambivalent views on the issue, critical both of pornography and of the ways that censorship was proposed as a method to combat it. Although *Ms.* did not cover the issue significantly, letters to the editor provide an important para-text that shows a more complicated understanding of the issue than was presented in the editorial pages. This shows the importance of considering para-textual elements such as letters when analysing the magazines.

In the final chapter of this part, I identify the different relationships that *Spare Rib* and *Ms.* had with politics. *Ms.* was much more amenable to mainstream politics and that engagement with the political system was viewed as an important and worthwhile feminist aim, as seen in the magazine's coverage of the ERA. In contrast, *Spare Rib* was much more critical of mainstream politicians, and this reflects the differing political contexts that the magazines were produced within. In the second half of the chapter, I identify how the magazines engaged with the 'backlash' and neoliberalism in the 1980s. Neither of the magazines capitulated to post-feminism, but *Ms.* was much more likely to include less politicised content to appeal to a wider audience. However, as I will argue, the assumption that the 'backlash' can be situated in the 1980s can be countered by evidence that the magazine was aware of the term long before. Rather than becoming less radical, I argue that there was an increased discussion of radical politics in *Spare Rib* that belied the more commercial aesthetic that the magazine adopted (Chambers et al., 2004), since the magazine became more forthright in its discussions of anti-capitalism and critique of Western democracy.

Part III: Beyond the 'Second Wave'

The final part of the book explores the extent to which a feminist media tradition can be charted from the 1990s onwards. In this chapter I discuss how Riot grrrl followed in a tradition of feminist media, eschewing mainstream media using DIY aesthetics and manifestos (Colman, 2010). After outlining the ways in which Riot grrrl created alternative feminist media, the chapter will focus in depth on two feminist zines which were then established as magazines: *Bitch* (1996–) and *Bust* (1993–). These publications were chosen for analysis because they aimed to reach a wide audience, and therefore to some extent hold similar roles to *Ms.* and *Spare Rib* in earlier periods. In my analysis of these texts, I argue that the complicated relationship between feminism, funding and capitalism is an ongoing concern. Content analysis of the magazines can help us to identify the kinds of issues that were featured, and the ways that these issues were framed. Both *Bitch* and *Bust* published a book based on their work, and each of these was published by a mainstream publisher. This is significant, because it provides an example of how feminist publications have engaged with the mainstream publishing industry, and therefore capitalism. Furthermore, in my discussion of *Bust*, I note the more playful ways in which feminism had begun to be framed, especially through an ironic tone, coupled with an emphasis on pleasure. This playfulness and willingness to engage with popular culture is one way in which the magazine was able to frame itself as approachable, and to distance itself from a second wave feminism that was viewed as more radical, and perhaps less 'fun' as a result. This can be contrasted with *Bitch*, where this was generally not evident.

The final chapter of the book focuses on contemporary feminist digital media. For this chapter, I have again focused on texts which both embrace feminist ideas, whilst working within a capitalist framework, through either being part of capitalist entities themselves or working with them. The chapter begins with a discussion of the impact of feminist blogging. I analyse *xoJane* as my final case study. It is a particularly interesting case study since the site was founded by Jane Pratt, who founded and edited earlier feminist-influenced magazines *Sassy* and *Jane* in the 1990s (Groeneveld, 2016). The site, which ran from 2011 to 2016, also focuses heavily on personal narrative, in a way that can be linked to the increased use of intimate personal narratives in Riot grrrl zines, as well as the second wave focus on the personal as political. The tumultuous history of the site, including controversies over content as well as questions about the influence of capitalism, brings us full circle and shows that issues faced by second wave feminist media producers are still relevant today.

Moving on from that, I discuss recent and important work by Banet-Weiser (2018), which provides a very useful framework for understanding the contemporary relationship between feminism and the popular. *Teen Vogue*, a teen girls blog (and now defunct magazine), is an excellent case study for understanding the relationship between feminism and popular culture. Whilst on the one hand, the site, which is owned by Condé Nast, is clearly a capitalist product, on the other hand, this does not mean that its expressions of feminism are not at times radical and anti-capitalist. *Teen Vogue* helps us to understand the complex and contradictory negotiation between capitalism and social justice, situating this within a broader social and cultural context where feminism is increasingly intertwined with popular capitalist culture.

After the discussion and analysis of *Teen Vogue*, I analyse how mainstream women's magazines have begun to engage with feminism. The book ends with a discussion of *gal-dem*, focusing on the ways in which the magazine and website provide a voice for women of colour. Each part of the book will begin with a brief overview of the context in which the texts need to be read within.

NOTES

1. It is also helpful at this point to acknowledge the Anglo-American focus of this research, which means that a very specific feminism is being mediated in these texts. Although both magazines had a limited focus on international issues, the vast majority of the issues discussed in *Spare Rib* and *Ms.* were approached from a local perspective. As a monolingual researcher, I am limited in the texts that I can analyse, whilst the focus on the relationship between feminism and the mainstream necessitates an analysis of texts that had a relative large audience. However, I am aware that there are a host of alternative texts that could be examined, and that the texts I am looking at reflect my own position as a Western academic.

2. The 1970 Ladies Home Journal sit-in exemplifies feminist attitudes towards the mass media during the period. The magazine was the target of a feminist protest that demanded that the magazine hire a woman as editor and include articles about the women's liberation movement. Other demands included better working conditions for staff members, including childcare provision (Brownmiller, 2000). After an eleven-hour sit-in, LHJ editor John Mack Carter agreed that protestors could edit one issue of the magazine. The debate about the role of the media, feminist journalism and professionalism provides a useful context for thinking about the conflict between the feminist principles of a feminist magazine and the wider capitalist publishing industry. Key to this conflict was the questioning of the role of the professional journalist within the feminist movement. Recalling the period, Brownmiller (2000, p. 99) describes the criticism she received from feminists who suggested that she took part in the protest because of professional self-interest.

3. It should be noted that some work was redacted due to copyright issues, as outlined in a blog post by curator Polly Russell: http://www.womensgrid.org.uk/news/?p=5100

Part I

SPARE RIB, MS. AND THE POLITICAL ECONOMIES OF FEMINIST MAGAZINES

Chapter 1

Constructing the Reader

Magazines, perhaps more than any other textual form, allow for the intervention of the reader into the production of the magazine. However, this still needs to be understood within the context of a capitalist publishing industry. This chapter is about the tension between wanting to foster collaborative and supportive relationships with readers and at the same time appeal to a wide audience. Whilst Chambers et al. (2004, p. 190) suggest that women's media production blurred 'boundaries between professional journalism and non-professional writing', the magazines had overall editorial control. This was certainly the case with *Ms.* and to a lesser degree *Spare Rib*, where there was a tension between the maintenance of a feminist ethos and the acknowledgement that the magazines stood their best chance of being commercially successful if they appealed to a broad audience, meaning that pleasing everyone was not an option. Readership surveys commissioned by both *Spare Rib* and *Ms.* help us understand how these tensions played out. *Ms.* commissioned a readership survey in 1973 (Thom, 1997), whilst readership surveys were carried out by *Spare Rib* in 1975 and 1985. These surveys provide a useful insight into how the readers saw the magazines, how the magazines viewed their readers and how this impacted on the magazines' content.

THE IMAGINED READERSHIP OF *SPARE RIB* AND *MS.*

In her history of *Ms.* former editor Mary Thom (1997, p. 2) notes the 'intense identification between editor and audience', suggesting that 'the distance between the magazine's editors and its readers tended to all but disappear'. A sense of collectivism is invoked between reader and magazine. However, at the same time, the magazine aimed to bring a 'mass audience to the feminist movement' (Erdman Farrell, 1998, p. 100) and therefore an intimate relationship was not possible. Thom's statement must be interrogated since it ignores how *Ms.*'s desire to exist within the mainstream impacted the choices it made in courting specific kinds of readership. This suggests a disconnect between the idealised aims of the magazines' editors and reality. This chapter will focus on how this chasm was negotiated.

In the opening issue of *Ms.*, Gloria Steinem (July 1972, p. 4) discusses why she chose to create a magazine rather than a newsletter, suggesting that 'newsletters were a fine service for people already interested but weren't really meant to reach out in a populist way'. *Ms.* was constructed as a vehicle to reach a wider audience, including those not already involved in the feminist movement. The consequence of this is that there are several different demographics being catered to, with different expectations from a feminist magazine. However, whilst Steinem aimed for mass appeal, her statement that the magazine will set 'aside some of the profits to go back to the Women's Movement' (p. 4) also makes the *Ms.*'s feminist ethos explicit. Jordan (2010, p. 7) argues that 'feminists periodicals were correlates of the women's movement' that 'reach[ed] women who were not already members of feminists groups'. Feminist magazines can therefore be understood as entry points into and representatives of the feminist movement. It is, therefore, especially important to understand how the magazine represented feminism since this was the representation of feminism that would be likely to reach a wider audience.

Spare Rib was also born out of a desire to provide an alternative to existing women's magazines. In the first issue, Rowe and Boycott (July 1972, p. 4) state that the motivation for the magazine was that they 'could not buy any magazine that discussed what we felt were vital issues', suggesting an aim to fill a gap in the market. However, Rowe and Boycott differ from Steinem in that they are careful not to position *Spare Rib* as a way to 'try and explain the Women's Liberation movement' as that would be 'ludicrous and wrong' (p. 4) owing to the movement's complexity. The differences between how the magazines viewed their role in representing the women's movement provide an important context in which to understand the readership surveys. The readership surveys help us understand the concerns, behaviours and desires of the readership. However, as the discussion of the *Ms.* readership survey shows, readers were also constructed as valuable consumers for advertisers, complicating an idealised understanding of the relationship between the reader and the magazine.

GETTING TO KNOW THE READERS: *SPARE RIB* READERSHIP SURVEYS

Readership surveys were used by *Spare Rib* to better understand the readership, and surveys were carried out in 1975 and ten years later in 1985. The

1975 survey was carried out by market research company RSL (latterly Ipsos MORI). The final report is available at the Feminist Archive North, based at the University of Leeds, UK. The aim of the survey was to:

> obtain a demographic profile of the recipients of the magazine, secondly to gain editorial of the likes and dislikes of the readers of this monthly publication.

Interestingly, although the survey was carried out in conjunction with a market research company, there were feminist considerations and 'bearing in mind the philosophy of Women's Lib some questions were reworded'. This reflects the desire for the survey to maintain a feminist sensibility (Readership Survey, 1975). The survey found that the average reader was an employed twenty-something with a 'relatively high paying job' and half of readers had had a holiday abroad in the last twelve months (whilst this may not seem unusual, the survey was commissioned in the mid-1970s before the ubiquity of budget airlines and package holidays). Even though survey respondents are never explicitly asked about their class identity, it can be assumed that the average reader is middle class because they have the disposable income associated with the middle class.

The average reader of *Spare Rib* was not particularly political, and the fact that 15 percent of readers also read *Cosmopolitan* suggests that *Spare Rib* was one magazine amongst many for some readers, and that readers did not totally reject mainstream publications. There is no mention of whether the reader identifies as a feminist, though it is unclear as to whether this is because the assumption was that if a woman is reading *Spare Rib*, then she already identifies with the feminist movement. This is supported by the finding that one of the reasons that the magazine was read was because it kept the reader in touch with the feminist movement and it was non-sexist. The positioning of the magazine as an alternative to women's magazines is stated by Marie-Therese McGivern (2015), who argues that 'we'd *Spare Rib*, we had our own magazine, *Spare Rib* didn't look like a women's magazine'. In contrast, Campbell (2010) describes *Spare Rib* as being 'in the manner of a woman's magazine' but distinguishes it from women's magazines because it was 'highly politicized'.

The survey identified several aspects to the magazine that readers found positive:

1. It kept them in touch with the women's movement
2. It widened knowledge
3. It was non-sexist
4. It reflected their own views (*Readership Survey*, 1975)

There is nothing unexpected about these comments; one would anticipate that a feminist magazine is non-sexist and that it would provide information about the women's movement. The fact that the coverage reflects the readers' own views suggests that readers valued the magazine because it reinforced already held opinions, as is suggested by Winship (1987, p. 135). *Spare Rib* can be understood as a space where feminists found common ground and community. The conflict between the magazine as a source of community and as a commercial product is a theme that I will return to throughout this book.

The critiques of the magazine are more interesting because they connect with common critiques of the feminist movement by society more widely; these criticisms stated that the magazine was:

1. Too London-centric
2. Anti-male
3. Too humourless (*Readership Survey*, 1975)

The description of the magazine as 'humourless' supports a hegemonic discourse that characterised second wave feminists as lacking a sense of humour. Sue O'Sullivan (quoted in Mendes, 2011, p. 35) blames the mainstream media for "'creating the mocked and mythical persona of the humourless, sour, man-hating' feminist'". However, the inclusion of these criticisms within the *Spare Rib* readership survey suggests that this stereotype influenced how feminists viewed others *within* the movement, highlighting the importance of reading feminist media within the wider cultural context that the texts are produced within. In contrast, the magazine was also criticised for lacking in 'theoretical perspective' and being 'too superficial'. This points to the difficulty of producing a magazine that can appeal to a wide audience, since what is understood as a problem for some readers is not necessarily a problem for others. The magazine was also described as 'too left wing'. The left-wing focus of the magazine reflects that British feminism 'took for granted Britain's long term socialist traditions and in the 1970s actively engaged with Marxism' (Humm, 1992, p. 87). This can be contrasted with earlier criticisms of the magazine that it was not radical enough (Hollows, 2012). This highlights the contradictory nature of the criticism, as well as the difficulty of responding to such criticism in a way that pleases everybody. This further illustrates the folly of characterising *Spare Rib* or *Ms.* as representative of the women's movement. The survey suggests that readers often had a range of opinions on how the magazine could be improved that contradicted each other, suggesting that feminists themselves were not monolithic in their aims.

It is worth noting that although the 1975 survey did attempt to establish the readership's age and disposable income (and therefore their socioeconomic class), no further questions were asked about other aspects of the readers' identity such as race or sexuality. This oversight supports Lowell's (1999, p. 103) criticisms that 'Black, minority and migrant women have been on the whole invisible within the feminist movement'. That the magazine did not consider the race, class or sexuality of their readers when trying to establish a demographic profile suggests either that it was considered unimportant or that the editors held normative visions of their readers as white, heterosexual and middle class and did not think to ask if this was actually the case.

1985 SURVEY

In contrast to the 1975 survey, the 1985 survey was more comprehensive in establishing a demographic profile. I accessed the survey via the Feminist Archive North in Leeds too. When I first encountered the 1985 survey, it was by accident. I had originally intended to look at the 1975 survey again but had realised there was another survey that could be accessed. The fortuitous encounter with the survey illustrates the importance of archives in preserving information for researchers. The survey asked fifty quantitative questions, organised into the following sections:

1. Getting *Spare Rib*. This included questions that focused on how the respondent accessed *Spare Rib*. Questions were asked about where the reader was from, where they buy the magazine from and how easy or difficult it was to access the magazine. This section also included a question about how long a respondent had read the magazine for.
2. What you read. This section focused on the other publications the respondent read, including newspapers, women's magazines and other feminist periodicals.
3. About you. This section asked demographic questions, including age, sexuality, gender, class and race. In comparison to the 1975 survey, these questions were much more detailed. This suggests a greater understanding of how the identity of the reader impacts on the way that they read the magazine.
4. Where you go and what you do. This section included questions about travel, other media consumption and alcohol consumption.
5. The final section of the survey asked readers what they thought about how the magazine addressed issues, including the 'third world', Northern Ireland and lesbian rights. Respondents were asked to state how much they agreed or disagreed with a list of statements using a Likert scale. Statements included 'Your articles on the Third World always connected up with my life in some way' and '*Spare Rib* always goes to the heart of any controversial issue' (*Readership Survey*, 1985).

Alongside this data, there was also a free-form section for further comments. The answers to these questions can be used to identify how the magazine constructed their relationship with *Spare Rib*. The readership survey provides an insight into the tensions and conflicts between the magazine and readers. There were many common criticisms that can be identified, and three of these will now be discussed. The aim of looking at these criticisms is to highlight the extent to which *Spare Rib* became a site of contestation. This further highlights the importance of acknowledging the diversity of opinion within the feminist movement.

One of the criticisms that came out of the free-form responses was about the lack of inclusion of a specific question about whether the reader had children. One respondent stated that 'words fail me. How can you have not included children *how???*' There were also other similar responses. Some readers felt that by not including the option to say that they had children, the magazine was suggesting that their position as a parent was not important. This can be related to a much broader ambivalence within feminism about the role of motherhood. Kinser (2010, p. 2) argues that 'the relationship of feminism to motherhood has clearly been a complex one, even an ambivalent one', since there has been contestation about how much motherhood is empowering or oppressive. The lack of a question perhaps reflects a desire not to construct the reader's identity based on whether or not they have children. However, the strength of responses from mothers suggests that this is an important part of their identity that they want to express.

The London focus on the magazine was also criticised in the survey. This was a critique that was identified in the 1975 survey; its inclusion in the 1985 survey suggests that it was an issue that had not been resolved. Many readers questioned the extent to which the magazine disproportionally focused on London. A reader from Leicester suggests that she would 'like to read more about local events outside the classified' whilst a reader from Manchester stated that 'women outside of London find it hard to identify with content' (*Readership Survey*, 1985). The magazine is also strongly criticised by a reader from Hartlepool (an industrial town in North East England) who said that '*Spare Rib* in common with the rest of the London-based media represents an insult to North-Eastern women' because of the lack of coverage it gave Northern women. The reader states that she 'resent[s] . . . the manner in which you assume that British cultural life revolves around London' (*Readership Survey*, 1985). The reader includes a strongly worded letter with her survey response. The letter suggests that the magazine is intentionally marginalising women from the North since she describes the magazine's lack of inclusion as an 'insult'. The letter ends with the statement that 'it seems that the North and South are indeed two different countries', suggesting a sense of alienation and lack of common ground. *Spare Rib* aimed to represent the country, but most of the magazines' content focused on London. This criticism must be tempered against the fact that London did provide a larger base of readers (*Readership Survey*, 1985), and so arguably the emphasis on London reflects this. However, this emphasises a London-centric vision of feminism that alienated readers from outside of the capital. This reflects the difficulty of appealing to a nationwide audience. More broadly, the difficulty that the magazine had in representing feminists outside the capital can be linked to a difficulty that the magazine had in representing working-class women in particular, especially during a time when working-class communities were particularly vulnerable to government cuts and the subsequent poverty caused by this.

The most prevalent criticism was that *Spare Rib* was not for 'ordinary women'. There was a recurring assumption in some of the survey responses that the magazine did not include articles that 'ordinary women' could relate to, and this is an issue that will be returned to throughout this chapter. There was a recurring assumption that an 'ordinary' reader was white and heterosexual. One reader suggests that she 'want[s] practical and everyday issues such as sexism to be discussed far more than 3rd world problems which I can't relate to' (*Readership Survey*, 1985). Another reader argued that '*Spare Rib* is too radical. The average woman is put off by the image'. Common to these discussions was the sense that the magazine focused too heavily on issues affecting lesbians and women of colour. One woman states that 'sometimes feel lesbians and black women dominate to the exclusion of other things', whilst another states that she is 'a fairly ordinary woman . . . and I frequently feel that SR has nothing to do with me'. Another woman writes that 'as a white middle class (not in the left wing) person, I feel a little bit out of place here', whilst another wishes for more coverage of 'ordinary heterosexual feminists' (*Readership Survey*, 1985).

White and middle-class women positioned themselves as 'ordinary' and their issues as the 'everyday'. This highlights how white and heterosexual privilege operates; some readers are upset about their perceived erasures within the magazine but do not acknowledge that this is something that women of colour and lesbians experience more frequently. There is a heteronormative narrative assumption. Heteronormativity can be understood as 'institutions, structures and practices that help normalise dominant forms of heterosexuality as universal and morally righteous' (Lind, 2013, p. 191). This is also evident in a reader's comment that she is an 'ordinary heterosexual feminist'. Alongside this, whiteness is constructed as 'the norm'. Anderson (2002, p. 25) describes whiteness as 'the invisible norm' since it 'maintains its hegemony by seeming natural or just not being questioned'. In the responses to the readership survey this can be seen through the suggestion that a move away from solely focusing on white women is a move away from 'ordinariness'. Furthermore, this criticism of the magazine is an example of 'white feminism'. Aziz (1997, p. 70) defines white feminism as:

> any feminism which comes from a white perspective and universalizes it . . . it is rather a way of seeing, which however inadvertent, leaves identifiable traces. It subsists through a failure to consider both the wider social and political context of power in which feminist utterances and actions take place, and the ability of feminism to influence that context.

The way that this exclusion is constructed as oppressive (e.g. women of colour and lesbians are characterised as dominating white heterosexual women) can be understood within the context of 'middle-class injury' (Tyler, 2008, p. 23). Tyler draws on the work of Wendy Brown (1995) to suggest that 'access to political power is increasingly premised on the ability to define yourself as injured' (p. 23). This 'perverse appropriation of identity politics' (p. 23) is evident in some of the comments from the readership survey; white heterosexual women reassert their power by presenting themselves as marginalised, therefore obscuring their own power and privilege. The use of 'ordinary' and 'everyday' to describe white heterosexual women's experiences further reinforces the idea that feminist concerns should be mediated through white and middle-class experience. Furthermore, another reader suggests that 'sometimes SR feels a bit "unsafe" i.e. I can't find always find myself in it' (*Readership Survey*, 1985). The magazine is considered unsafe for some white feminists because of the inclusion of alternative experiences. This challenges the idea that white feminist perspectives should be paramount.

However, these views are contradicted by other respondents who point to how the magazines don't sufficiently cover issues concerning women of colour or lesbians, or who find the potential 'overrepresentation' of issues concerning women of colour and lesbians as a strength of the magazine. One reader states that she would:

> Like to read *much* more about the struggles of black and white working class women in Britain but this should *not* be at the expense of women's experience in the third world. (*Readership Survey*, 1985, italics in original)

There is a desire to show the experience of all women and an acknowledgement that increasing the focus on one group of women does not necessarily mean that the dominant group becomes marginalised. Similarly, another reader states that as someone who is 'white, middle class, and hopelessly liberal' she would 'support positive discrimination and other women's views' (*Readership Survey*, 1985). This suggests that some of the readers were prepared to read about the experiences of women not like them and could see the benefit of learning about their experiences.

It must also be noted that whilst there were several readers who said that the magazine focused too heavily on women of colour and lesbians, there were *also* comments that suggested that there was not enough focus on issues affecting women of colour and lesbians. One reader, for example, critiques the magazine and argues for 'less tokenism' and suggests that although there are issues that feature race and sexuality, these need to be included in '*all* issues' alongside more 'photos' that show the diversity of the magazine's readership (*Readership Survey*, 1985). Onwurah (1987) critiques mainstream women's magazines for the lack of inclusion of women of colour. However, the comments from the readership survey suggest that this was also an issue for *Spare Rib*. Another reader asks for 'more articles on international' feminism, whilst one reader argues that 'Black British feminists are discriminated against in SR' (*Readership Survey*, 1985). Furthermore, even though a common critique was that there was too much focus on lesbian issues, a reader states that she would 'like to see more coverage of lesbian issues' (*Readership Survey*, 1985). These diverging comments highlight the tension between readers who felt the magazine overemphasised women of colour and lesbians and those who did not feel those groups were represented enough.

The *Spare Rib* readership surveys demonstrated that readers did not universally agree on what they wanted from the magazine. White heterosexual feminists viewed ordinariness and the everyday as synonymous with issues that directly affected them, demonstrating how they were unable to see how the concerns of Black feminists were important. Similarly, criticisms of the amount of coverage given to issues affecting lesbians reinforced heterosexist and homophobic ideas that located heterosexuality as the norm. This shows how white heterosexual feminists often considered themselves the arbiter of what can be understood as an important feminist issue. How certain issues become privileged over others is an issue that this book will return to in the chapter on race and representation. In the meantime, this chapter will now move on to look at the readership survey carried out by *Ms.* in 1973.

MS. READERSHIP SURVEY

The readership survey carried out by *Ms.* in 1973 was sent to 500 readers, and there was a 57 percent response rate (Thom, 1997, p. 123). Thom (1997) suggests that the high response rate is indicative of the extent to which readers were willing to engage with the magazine, and therefore how close they felt to it. However, one key difference between the *Spare Rib* and *Ms.* surveys is that *Ms.* was more explicit in stating that an aim of the survey was to increase advertising revenue. The survey, therefore, cannot just be understood as catering to the readers but must also be seen as a way to capitalise on readership loyalty in order to increase advertising revenue. Thom (1997, p. 124) states that:

> The readers' response would not only help *Ms.* to succeed but would also help change the world of advertising, and by extension the corporate image of women in America.

From the outset there was acknowledgement that advertisers would be interested in how *Ms*'s readers could provide another market for their products. The results of the survey and the language used by Thom (e.g. 'corporate') imagine a relatively wealthy and ambitious reader. The reader is described as a 'decidedly upscaled group' as a 'third of them owned stock' and 'over 80 percent had savings accounts' (Thom, 1997, p. 124). That the reader was relatively wealthy and financially savvy can be seen in the lifestyle features of the magazines in articles such as 'How to start your own restaurant' (January 1977) or on how to build your own home (June 1977) or the experience of being a female executive (March 1982). This suggests an affluent and ambitious audience and again reinforces the idea that women's liberation can be achieved by being successful in a male-dominated private sphere.

Similarly, the women who read the magazine had a high amount of cultural capital (Bourdieu, 1985) since they 'tended to work in schools and universities, government and politics and the arts and media' (Thom, 1997, p. 124). Although there has been much discussion of the extent to which *Ms.* reached a mass audience (Erdman Farrell, 1998; Bradley, 2003; Buchanan, 2011), their audience was a relatively privileged group of women. The fact that readers owned stocks points to a financially literate readership that was likely to be motivated in part by financial interest. This focus on financial interest suggests that an anti-capitalist feminism that does not see individuals benefiting would be less likely within *Ms*.

In terms of the relationship between the magazine and the women's movement, many respondents were not involved with a women's liberation group, though they were involved in wider politics, either belonging to a political party or writing letters to editors. This is in stark contrast to *Spare Rib* readers who did not consider themselves political. Thirty per cent had done some public speaking, again pointing towards a readership that was generally politically savvy (Thom, 1997, p. 125).

It is important to consider how the readership of *Ms.* may have influenced the kind of topics that were discussed in the magazine. Erdman Farrell (2011) argues that *Ms.* was more likely to include content that would attract a middle-class readership since it was those readers who would be more likely to purchase the products that were being advertised in *Ms.* The tension between the need for *Ms.* and *Spare Rib* to balance profitability against feminist principles is a theme I will return to often in this book. Although the magazines were often understood as representative of the feminist movement, the need to appeal to an audience of women who had disposable income to buy advertised products meant that certain groups were liable to be under-represented or excluded. The readership surveys are significant because they help us to understand who the readers were and what they expected from the magazines.

Letters are an equally fruitful but slightly different form of communication between the reader and the magazine. Letters were responses to specific issues discussed in the magazine and were one of the few opportunities for readers to be included in the magazine's content. The chapter will now go on to discuss how letters provided another avenue for understanding the relationship between the reader and the magazines' staff.

WRITING TO THE MAGAZINE: LETTERS IN *SPARE RIB* AND *MS.*

Chambers et al. (2004, p. 174) argued that 'readers write to *Ms.* as if to a sister, lover or comrade who they imagine listening to their stories, being supportive – somewhat like a mass consciousness raising group'. This suggests a mutually supportive relationship between the reader and the magazine. Thom (1997, p. 73) states that 'the *Ms.* audience in letters to the editor and contributions to reader forums, was so exceptionally responsive'. Letters provide a way to understand the relationship between the reader and the magazine, and since there has been a lack of research on the letters, they represented an understudied but valuable resource.

The importance of letters to the editor has been argued by Wahl Jorgenson (2006), who argues that they play an important role in a deliberative democracy. This can be understood as a '"realm of social life where the exchange of information and views on questions of common concern can take place so that public opinion can be formed"' (Dahlgren, 1995, quoted in Wahl Jorgenson, p. 13). Letters to the editor were an opportunity for readers to directly engage with both the magazine and other readers. According to Wahl Jorgenson, the feminist movement has had a long tradition of letter writing, and she references Chambers et al. (2004), who note that feminist magazines had more letters published than other publications. Wahl Jorgenson (2006, p. 60) argues that 'like other institutions of the public sphere [letters pages] have always been male dominated'. The letters pages in *Spare Rib* and *Ms.* therefore have an added significance as they were one of the few places where women were given substantial space to discuss political issues.

In her discussion of feminist letter writing practice, Jolly (2008) argues that letter writing draws upon a tradition of personal correspondence in the private sphere because of women's limited access to the public sphere. Since 'praise as a letter writer carries limited literary authority' (Jolly, 2008, p. 37), letter writing is a communicative form where individual promotion is not the primary aim. Jolly refers to Olga Kenyon's assertion that women's letter writing shows 'women's refusal to be "authorities"' (p. xix). The magazine could publish several women's contributions, and this meant that a wider range of women's opinions were reflected in the magazine. The chapter will now move on to discuss the significance of letters to the editor in *Spare Rib* and *Ms*. Letters are important because they help us identify the alternative and sometimes conflicting perspectives of the readers. This allows us to identify alternative discourses about feminism than those that were represented within the magazine.

THE PURPOSE OF LETTERS IN *SPARE RIB* AND *MS*.

The extent to which *Ms*. understood letters as an important aspect of the magazine can be seen through the publication of an edited collection of letters to the magazine in 1987, *Letters to Ms. 1972–1987*, edited by Mary Thom. In the introduction to the collection, Gloria Steinem suggests that *Ms*. 'give[s] more space to letters than any magazine I'm aware of' (Steinem in Thom, 1987 p. xi). Similarly, in her introduction, Mary Thom (1987, p. xv) describes the 'very special community – mostly sympathetic to us and each other, sometimes querulous, always demanding' and suggests that 'because the editorial material of *Ms*. has so profoundly to do with their own life choices, most letter writers are anything but detached observers'. Since letters were so important, it is necessary to consider them alongside the editorial content of the magazine. *Letters to Ms*. (1987) is used to supplement analysis of letters to *Ms*. that were published during the sample years.

The significance of letters was also declared within the magazine in articles such as 'Your Letters Make History' (Steinem, March 1982). In the article, Steinem notes that a collection of letters had been given to the Schlesinger Library at Radcliffe College, and as a result 'some feminist scholars helped [Steinem] to see that an important forest had grown from what [she] was taking for granted as very personal trees' (p. 71). Letters are the intimate dialogue between the readers and the magazine, but the archiving of them suggests that they also play an important role in helping us to understand feminist history. It is for this reason that letters will be analysed throughout this book. Since Steinem's article is from 1982, it is important to place it within the context of the early 1980s, a time when backlash politics were becoming increasingly prevalent and *Ms.* was criticised for no longer being feminist enough (Faludi, 1991). However, Steinem quotes a letter from a reader who states that 'now, more than ever, we need each other . . . need information . . . we need *Ms.*' (p. 72). *Ms.* is understood as an anchor in the face of anti-feminist backlash. The vitality of letter writing can be seen in Steinem's simile that letter writing is 'like oxygen', suggesting that correspondence is more than just a feature in the magazine and that it provided an important refuge in the 1980s, at a time when feminist discourse was becoming increasingly marginalised.

However, letters were also used to express discontent with the magazine. Steinem describes 'one young woman in Berkeley who made us all feel guilty with a long letter explaining why our cover price would alienate poor women' (p. 72). This is contrasted to responses to an article about welfare where readers wrote to say, 'they know we had to charge to survive, but not to worry' (p. 72). Although criticism of the magazine is recognised, this criticism is undercut by the inclusion of a letter that defends the magazine's position. This demonstrates that the magazine had final editorial control since it could choose to represent the views of the readership in a way that emphasised a narrative that supported *Ms.*'s decisions.

Whilst the final decisions on which letters would be published sat with the editorial staff, Steinem does recognise how letters to the editor were also a space to air grievances. Steinem states that 'because expectations were so high between a feminist magazine and its readers – and vice versa – the relationship might never be serene' (p. 72). This is evident in some of the more explicitly critical letters that were published in the magazine. June Wright's letter from December 1977 is a good example of this. It begins with the statement: 'After seeing a copy of your rag recently, I don't know who are sillier – *Ms's* editors or the emotionally retarded women who follow them' (p. 4). Rag is a derogatory term for a publication, whilst Wright ridicules the 'tear-jerking [letter] from the alleged former prostitute who changed her whole life and the lives of several of her former colleagues as a result of reading *Ms.*' (p. 4). The tone is dismissive and suggests that Wright believes that the letter was a fabrication. The inclusion of such a critical letter suggests a desire for openness and a welcoming of feedback, both positive and negative. However, the letter is positioned directly below a letter from a young feminist who was drawn to *Ms.* because she is 'really interested in equality for girls and women' (December 1977, p. 4). The placement of an earnest and complimentary letter directly below the letter from Wright undercuts her argument. Even when the magazine publishes negative letters, this is balanced out with positivity and reinforces the idea that even if letters did provide a space for readers to share their opinion, the magazine still maintained overall editorial control.

UNPUBLISHED LETTERS IN *SPARE RIB*

So far, this chapter has discussed the use of letters that were published in *Ms.* and how the relationship between the reader and the magazine was fostered through letter writing. I will now move on to focus on the ways in which editorial decisions about what letters were published can be understood within the context of *Spare Rib*. Wahl Jorgenson (2006) suggests that editors can be positioned as the elite, and even within feminist magazines this led to some letters not being published. Editorial staff, therefore, are in a position of power over the reader because they can choose what to publish. Although *Spare Rib* and *Ms.* both published letters that were critical of the magazine, the number of letters that were sent to the magazine was greater than the number that could be published (Steinem in Thom, 1987). It is important to consider the ways in which editors exerted control over the publication of letters, and it is this theme that the chapter will now turn to.

In *Spare Rib* there were ideological discussions about which letters should be published. One particular example helps us to understand how the decisions about which letters to publish were related to political disagreements between the editorial collective. The conflict between Israel and Palestine has often been a contentious issue within the feminist movement in both the United Kingdom and the United States. Hyman (1997) suggests that there was unease from Jewish feminists who felt that anti-Zionist stances were becoming increasingly anti-Semitic. In August 1982, the magazine published 'Women Speak out Against Zionism'. The subtitle to the article stated that 'if a woman calls herself a feminist she should consciously call herself an anti-Zionist' (p. 22). Written in response to the invasion of South Lebanon by Israel in June 1982, collective member Roisin Boyd interviews 'Nidal, a Lebanese woman, Randa, a Palestinian woman and Aliza Khan an Israeli woman' (p. 22). The article aimed to 'explain the importance of recognising the difference between anti-Zionism and anti-Semitism' (p. 22). In contrast, the Israeli woman who was interviewed in 'Women Speak out Against Zionism' argues that 'if we are concerned about anti-Semitism we must fight Zionism' (p. 22), which highlights the conflicting positions on the topic.

This conflict was further exacerbated by *Spare Rib*'s decision not to publish letters from feminists who were seen by the editorial collective to be promoting Zionism (Jolly, 2008, p. 63). This culminated in the 'Open Letter or Anti-Semitism and Racism' by Dena Attar, published in the first issue of *Trouble and Strife* in winter 1983 and in *Spare Rib* (December 1983). The letter is in response to a July 1983 article 'Sisterhood Is Plain Sailing', which addressed the debates that the editorial collective had when deciding which letters to publish in response to the original 'Women Speak out Against Zionism' article. In the letter, Attar critiques the magazine's decision not to publish letters from Jewish feminists, suggesting that the magazine conflates a Jewish identity with Zionism. Attar (1983, p. 14) argues that 'working on *Spare Rib* you have the power to communicate ideas and information', recognising the power dynamic between the writer and the reader in terms of who sets the agenda. Attar states that the magazine was 'wrong to refuse to publish criticisms of those articles and depict *all* women who criticised them as Zionist and/or racist' (p. 16, italics in original). She highlights the extent to which the decision to publish particular letters was linked to a judgement that criticism of articles about Palestine was tantamount to Zionism.

In 'Sisterhood Is Plain Sailing' (July 1983), the editorial collective explains the difficulty they have in formulating a letter policy to decide which letters to publish. Collective member Roisin Boyd notes that the magazine has 'had Zionist and anti-Zionist letters, though the majority have been pro-Zionist' (p. 25). Since the magazine did not have a letter policy, the collective had become 'unstuck' over whether these letters should be published. The discussion by collective members on the topic demonstrates how the decision to publish or not publish a letter had political implications.

There was antipathy towards the readers, as seen through the statement from a collective member that 'the reasons why I don't wish to respond to influx of letters any more is because I have been discussing the issue since I started working on *SR*' (p. 25). In contrast, collective member Sue O'Sullivan states that she was 'in favour of publishing a selection of Jewish feminist letters . . . even though I did not agree with all of them' (p. 25). This demonstrates how even amongst the collective there was conflict, and the article illustrates that when discussing contentious issues such as Israel and Palestine, choices over whose voice can be heard became a source of conflict. It is, however, significant that *Spare Rib* was transparent in discussing these tensions. Whilst Steinem's 'Your Letters Make History' (*Ms.*, December 1982) positioned letter writing as a way to form a relationship with readers, the way letters were discussed in *Spare Rib* shows how they were also a source of tension and conflict between both the readers and the magazine, and amongst the magazine collective. Letters will be a useful source throughout this book and will be used to identify additional and at times competing discourses to those that can be seen in the editorial content of the magazines.

CONCLUSION

Readership surveys and letters to the magazine provided a useful insight into how the magazines constructed an ideal readership and engaged with the readership that they actually had. It is important to consider how the magazine's content was influenced by who the magazine assumed their reader was. In the

Spare Rib surveys, it was clear that the readership was contradictory in the expression of what kind of content they wanted. In contrast, the *Ms.* readership demonstrates how the reader was understood as a commodity to attract advertising revenue and ensure *Ms.*'s sustainability. The influence of capitalism in what the magazines decide to publish will be returned to throughout this book. The discussion of *Bitch* in part II of this book will show how advertising is still a factor for feminist publications in constructing their assumed reader. The construction of a white and middle-class assumed audience meant that issues that disproportionately impacted women of colour and working-class women were less likely to be included.

Alongside readership surveys, letters provided a sense of community for readers and were understood as important both by readers and staff members alike. However, whilst in *Ms.* a sisterly relationship between reader and magazine is evident, in *Spare Rib* it was also a source of conflict and debate. The article 'Sisterhood Is Plain Sailing' identifies the editorial discussions that letters generated, and that even though there was dialogue between magazine and reader, reader helps editorial control.

Chapter 2

Advertising Feminism: Negotiating Economics and Activism

The relationship between feminism and advertising has been described by D'Enbeau (2011, p. 53), who notes, 'For-profit, feminist media organisations today operate within an economic framework that places market value on progressive agenda'. In this chapter I will explore the relationship that *Spare Rib* and *Ms*. had with advertising. I argue that the differing relationship that the magazines had with advertising is indicative of their relationship to capitalism more broadly. Since *Ms*. was much more likely to feature advertising from multinational corporations, it will be used as a case study. *Ms* handily demonstrates the tension between maintaining feminist ideals and operating within a capitalist system. However, to begin with, I will sketch out research on the relationship between feminism and advertising and the magazines' attitudes towards advertising.

SPARE RIB AND ADVERTISING

The feminist aesthetic of *Spare Rib* has been commented on by Chambers et al. (2004, p. 166), who note that the anti-corporate ethos of the magazine can be seen through 'its design, layout and even its non-glossy advertising'. Similarly Hollows (2012, p. 5) states that '*Spare Rib* was a less professionalised and less mainstream operation'. Earlier issues of the magazine did solicit more mainstream advertising (Hollows, 2012; Bazin, 2017); however, this changed over time, and for much of the magazine's history advertisements were for niche products such as independent fashion retailers, ecologically friendly menstrual products and lesbian dating services. The choice to exclude advertising that oppressed women has been described by Hollows (2013, p. 13) as part of the magazine's 'promotion of responsible consumption practices' that 'opened up the possibility of a feminist politics of consumption'. The decision not to solicit advertising from larger companies counters the commercialism seen in the mainstream press.

However, it is also important to note that advertising was still necessary, as Bazin (2017, p. 198) argues:

> The determination of its editors, Marsha Rowe and Rosie Boycott, to remain independent from the pressures that come from advertising, did not, however, mean that they could entirely ignore advertising as an income stream.

The magazine was in a double bind, on the one hand striving for independence, whilst on the other hand needing advertising to remain financially viable. However, in comparison to *Ms.* advertising in *Spare Rib* continued to be for independent or political products such as a '1908 suffrage poster in colour' (April 1977) or an undergraduate history course marketed towards those interested in women's and left political history (May 1977). In comparison to *Ms.* there were no advertisements for cosmetics, and advertisements for clothing tended to be sold by independent companies. Since *Ms.* had advertisements that were much more likely to promote mainstream capitalist companies, I am going to focus on the relationship between advertising and editorial content in *Ms.* specifically in this chapter.

MS. AND ADVERTISING

Although *Ms.* provided a counterpoint to mainstream women's magazines, the intention was always to become a commercially successful venture, and Erdman Farrell (1998, p. 16) suggests that *Ms.* 'explicitly set out to make an alliance with the capitalist system'. Advertising was an important aspect of this, and a range of brands ran advertising in the magazine, as the magazine attempted to 'disrupt cultural hegemony from the inside' (Erdman Farrell, 1998, p. 16). However, the major disadvantage of this approach is that the magazine was caught up in the capitalist system. Murray (2004, p. 138) notes that for many feminists 'women would be deluded in thinking that Madison Avenue corporate giants would promote texts subversive of the capitalist, patriarchal endorsed status quo'. There was often a tension between the feminist ideals of the magazine and the content of the advertisements.

Cunningham and Haley (1990, p. 18) argue that *Ms.* 'explicitly recognized that advertising can be a powerful influence and that advertiser's pressure could threaten the integrity of the magazine's feminist ideology'. Ferguson et al. (1990, p.40) suggested that 'a substantial proportion of *Ms.* advertising promotes products generally considered "harmful"', primarily because of heavy advertising of alcohol and cigarettes. McCracken (1993, p. 282) notes that advertising in the magazine promoted middle-class ideals that were not available to many women.

Although *Ms*. relied on advertising for the first twenty years, it eventually became advertising free in 1990. The magazine was sold to Fairfax in 1987 and temporarily ceased publication in 1989 due to a controversial article about Reagan and reproductive rights, which caused many advertisers to pull out (Erdman Farrell, 1998, p. 1). The magazine was then bought by Lang Communications in 1990 and edited by radical feminist Robin Morgan (*Ms* Letters: A Finding Aid, 2009). The magazine no longer included advertising except for non-profit and non-partisan organisations. Comparing *Ms*. as an advertising-free magazine to its previous incarnation, Cunningham and Haley (1990, p. 26) suggested that '*Ms* editors feel they owe their readers special consideration for making this advertising-free format possible' and that '*Ms* staff members feel an obligation to offer a worthwhile magazine to the readers because the readers are the sole financial support'. Since 2001, the magazine has been owned by the Feminist Majority Foundation and run by Liberty Media for Women, LLC, a consortium of feminists (*Ms.*, 2013). It is ironic that whilst the magazine tried to 'forge a place for itself within Madison Avenue publishing' (Erdman Farrell, 1998, p. 3), it is now run not by a major publishing company but by a feminist non-profit.

The kind of advertising that was included in *Ms*. is reflective of the kind of feminism that was presented in the magazine and the kind of reader that the magazine aimed to attract. *Ms*. editor Mary Thom (1997, p. 80) states:

> Most advertisements in *Ms*. – except for the classified section, and perhaps ads for books or the occasional movie or record – were directed at an upscale audience. The demographics of *Ms*. readers, their level of income and education, attracted that kind of audience.

Although advertising copy was not written by *Ms*. staff, *Ms*. staff allowed the advertisement to be run in the magazine. The advertisements ran alongside the editorial content in the magazine, and so it is important to understand the kind of messages that the advertisements transmit and how they interacted with the editorial content of the magazine.

MS. ADVERTISING CONTENT ANALYSIS

A content analysis demonstrates the way that *Ms*. advertisements often reflected a white middle-class readership within the magazine (table 2.1). The content analysis analysed two issues per year for the years 1972, 1977, 1982 and 1987.

Table 2.1. Volume of Advertising in *Ms.*

Year	Double page	Full page	Two-thirds	Half page	Smaller than half page	Total number of advertisements
1972	4	39	7	0	41	91
1977	7	42	1	0	16	66
1982	3	61	3	12	5	84
1987	4	48	3	2	9	66
Total	18	190	14	14	71	307

There is no advertising included from 1992 as the magazine was already advertising free at that point. As the advertising copy was substantial, it would be impractical to analyse all advertisements from all of the magazines in the sample. Furthermore, due to the volume of advertisements in each issue, an appropriate sample size could be reached without the need to look at all advertisements in the period. Issues from March and April each year were analysed (with the exception of 1972 as the magazine did not begin until later in that year). This mitigates against any differences in advertising content due to the time of year. The content analysis recorded the content of the following:

> Page number: This was to identify placement within the magazine and whether or not particular advertisements were more likely to be placed more prominently within the magazine.
>
> Size of advertisements: This was to identify the size of the advertisement. This was important to measure since a larger advertisement is more noticeable than a smaller advertisement.
>
> Product advertised: There has been research that the magazine focused heavily on advertising for alcohol and cigarettes (Cunningham and Haley, 1990). By counting the amount of times that the magazine advertised a particular product, I am able to identify whether or not the magazine advertised products that contradicted the feminist messages within the magazine's editorial content.
>
> Ethnicity of people featured within advertisements: Erdman Farrell (2011) argues that the need to be appealing to advertisers meant that *Ms.* did not adequately represent women of colour. By analysing the ethnicity of people in the advertisements, I could identify whether or not it is the case that *Ms.* was more likely to feature advertisements that included white women and discuss how this can be seen in relation to the magazine's assumed audience.

It is important to acknowledge the volume of advertising in *Ms.*, since, as has already been argued in this book, the para-textual elements of the magazine are important to consider. The large number of advertisements suggests that advertisements took up a large percentage of the magazine. As this chapter will demonstrate, this becomes particularly significant when considering the images that are presented and the extent to which some women are represented more than others. This chapter will now look at who is represented within the magazine's advertising content, linking this to the ways that feminist issues are represented within the magazine.

PRODUCTS ADVERTISED

A range of products were advertised in *Ms*. If we take 1982 as an example, we can see this range. In 1982, nineteen articles were about alcohol, three were about cars, five were for charities, six were for cigarettes, twenty-one were about fashion and beauty, two were for food and non-alcoholic drinks, ten were for healthcare, three were for home items, eight were for leisure products, five were for menstrual products, two were for sex aids/toys and nine were for utilities. It is significant that alcohol is the second most common category. Cunngingham and Haley (1990) note that the magazine had many advertisements for what might be understood as 'harmful' products. It is also significant that these are products that have been historically advertised to men, and Thom (1997) has acknowledged the extent to which the magazine aimed to develop advertising for products that have not historically been advertised to women. This suggests that the magazine saw the benefit of subverting stereotypes through the advertising that they had within the magazine.

However, it is equally significant that the second more prevalent advertisement category in 1982 is for fashion and beauty products. This is an increase in advertisements from 1977, where there were only two, although there were thirteen in 1972, suggesting that advertising of fashion and beauty products was common. Similarly, in 1987 there were thirteen fashion and beauty advertisements, which represent around 20 percent of the total number of advertisements and is the category that is most represented within the magazine. This chapter will now move on to look at the versions of womanhood that were being represented in the magazine through its advertisements. Alongside discussions of beauty standards, the chapter will also explore the ways in which a neoliberal subject was presented within the advertisements for *Ms.*, especially in the 1980s, where individual success was framed as desirable.

REPRESENTATIONS OF RACE IN *MS*. ADVERTISING

One key finding from the analysis of advertising in *Ms*. is that there is an underrepresentation of women of colour. This supports arguments made by Erdman Farrell (2011), who notes that the magazine underrepresented women of colour and poorer women. In 1972, there were ninety-one advertisements and three included people of colour, whilst in 1977, there were seven advertisements out of sixty-six that had people of colour within them. In 1982, ninety-three advertisements were included in the sample, but only seven included any people of colour, and only one of those included a woman of colour prominently. Similarly, in 1987, there were only two advertisements that only include people of colour, whereas thirty-five articles only include white people and twenty-seven articles include no people at all.

Given the lack of inclusion of women of colour in these two sample years, it is important to analyse how these limited representations presented women of colour. Although there were some advertisements that did not tokenise or stereotype women of colour (most notably in the 1972 preview issue), overall representations of women of colour did reinforce stereotypes. This chapter will now analyse examples of this from *Ms*. The first article, from April 1982, is for Sheer Elegance Tights. The advertisement features an East Asian woman sitting on a sofa. She is gazing directly to the camera, with her legs prominently displayed. What is particularly significant about the advertisement is the text that is included within it. The copy of the advertisement states: 'The look . . . the feel . . . of silk from the Orient. Now yours in a pantyhose'. The assumed audience of the advertisement is white women, since 'The Orient' is being exoticised and othered in a way that assumes that Asian women are different from women reading the magazine. This can be linked to the concept of 'Orientalism' as defined by Said (1979), who notes that Western narratives of 'the east' that emphasise difference and otherness from the west can be seen throughout Western culture. The only representation of women of colour where a woman of colour is prominent reinforces racist attitudes towards Asian women. This is especially problematic as there are so few representations of women of colour that any representation has the potential to influence how women of colour are perceived.

Similarly, one of the few other advertisements from 1982 that features a person of colour is for the charity *Save the Children*. The image included in the advertisement is a photograph of a child of colour alongside a donation form. People of colour are presented as in need of help from white Americans. In his work on representation, Hall (1997) suggests that people in the global south are presented in a way that suggests they are helpless, and this is disempowering. These two examples show how people of colour were often presented in *Ms*. as the other to a predominantly white audience. It reinforces the idea that it is Western, middle-class women who are reading the magazine.

ADVERTISEMENTS THAT CELEBRATES WOMEN'S ACHIEVEMENT

Although women of colour were poorly represented in *Ms*., there were other aspects of advertising within the magazine that did provide alternative representations of women from those that could be seen in the mainstream media. One way that *Ms*. provided an alternative to advertising in mainstream women's magazines was through the focus on high-achieving women, especially those in traditionally male-dominated industries. Furthermore, these advertisements often suggested a specifically liberal feminist aim of increasing women's participation within the public sphere. A 1972 advertisement for Dewar's Whisky is a good example of this. The article features physicist Sheila Ann Tong, challenging the stereotype that women are not interested in science (Hill et al., 2010). The use of a profile that highlights Tong's achievement demonstrates an 'individualistic monied feminism' (Erdman Farrell, 2011, p. 401). The photograph was taken in the workplace, situating women's success as being how well they can succeed within the public sphere (Friedan, 1963). Furthermore, Tong is a young white woman who does not differ wildly from the kind of woman usually portrayed in advertising and reinforces the idea that *Ms*.'s target audience is a middle-class white woman (Erdman Farrell, 2011).

Although the profile primarily focuses on Tong's achievements, the advertisement still refers to the fact that she is 'beautiful', suggesting that even within a feminist magazine, beauty was highlighted. The advertisement also emphasised Tong's youth and how this is related to her success, describing her as 'one of the 26 women who made it big in their twenties'. Success is valued more because Tong is young, illustrating Segal's (2014) argument that youth is often privileged in society. Another example of an advertisement that focuses on women's achievements is for Cutty Sark whisky. Kitty O'Neil was a stunt woman and racer in the 1970s. The advertisement includes the text '"it's never been done before". A terrifying thought to some. Here's to those it inspires'. In the main body of the text, O'Neil's ability to overcome adversity is further highlighted. The advertisement notes that O'Neil has been 'deaf since childhood. But that hasn't slowed her down'. It then goes on to state that 'she's set 26 world speed records on land, 2 on water and on waterskis'. Again, the focus is on an individual woman's success, reinforcing the idea that individual success is a feminist act.

OBJECTIFICATION AND THE BEAUTY INDUSTRY IN *MS*.

Whilst some advertisements in the magazine did counter gender stereotypes, there were still stereotypical representations of women and advertisements that objectified women. In an advertisement for Du Pont with the headline 'Goodbye Loose Pantyhose', a topless woman wearing tights is seen kneeling. The focus on the woman's body suggests an objectification that seems at odds with the sentiments of the magazine. As Mulvey (1989, p. 23) argues, women are 'displayed as sexual object'. Whilst the Du Pont advertisement is obviously aimed at a female audience, the model is also objectified. Mulvey (1989) points to the use of the strip tease, and the fact that the model is wearing only tights suggests the woman in the advertisement is in the process of stripping. The photograph also shows the model as passive since she is not photographed doing anything and is instead only there to be looked at by the camera. The placement of the advertisement in *Ms.* is especially surprising since, as Zimmerman and Dahlberg (2008, p. 71) argue, feminists 'have consistently raged against the way advertising treats women'. Advertisements that objectify women show the ways in which advertising content contradicts the editorial content of the magazine.

This is also evident in advertisements for make-up in the magazine. Advertisements for make-up in *Ms.* often presented a version of femininity that was both empowered and at the same time reinforced the idea that investing in beauty products is part of being a woman. For example, an advertisement for *Max Factor* from 1987 reinforces the sense that wearing make-up can be empowering. The advertisement features a white woman who is gazing confidently at the camera. She is in an office and is holding a phone. This positions her as a working woman, and therefore a neoliberal subject, as argued by McRobbie (2015). The make-up range is called 'Colorfast' with the tag line 'when the look's got to last'. This suggests durability is important for women as they will be working all day. The sense of hard work is reinforced in the advertising copy for the advertisement which asks the rhetorical question: 'Who has time for touch-ups after lunch? (Who has time for lunch?)' Working long hours is viewed as a badge of honour that can be performed through the wearing of a lipstick that will not require regular touch-ups, because women do not have the time to do this. This can further be linked to neoliberal values that emphasise productivity as indicative of value, with a focus on the 'metricized and forensic scrutiny of the female body' (Elias and Gill, 2018, p. 60).

However, what is most interesting is the way in which this performance of durable beauty is framed as an essential part of being a woman. The final tag line in the article asks: 'Don't you love being a woman?' In this advertisement, being a woman is explicitly framed as being a modern office worker, who wears make-up as well. On the one hand, this counters traditional versions of femininity that assume women's place within the home, and which feminist writers such as Friedan (1963) were heavily critical of in the 1960s and 1970s. On the other hand, whilst a version of femininity that is compatible with the public sphere is presented, the linking of this with make-up as an essential aspect of womanhood assumes an interest in this that is by no means universal. It is also significant that advertisements for make-up in *Ms.* exclusively feature white women, who are generally thin. Women of colour, fat women and women who present themselves in ways that are not stereotypically feminine are excluded.

Alongside presentations of stereotypical femininity, there are also advertisements that assume thinness as desirable. This can be most clearly seen in the advertisement for Dexatrim, a slimming aid. The headline for the advertisement tells readers, 'If you can't lose weight, do what these people did'. There is an assumption made that weight loss is a desirable aim, and that pharmaceutical help to lose weight is a common-sense solution to difficulties in dieting. The advertisement includes before and after pictures that are common in diet advertisements. Alongside each of these images is the amount of weight that has been lost, and the pill is described as having the 'most effective weight-loss formula'. The people featured in the before and after are described as 'slimmer, happier people'. This reinforces the notion that being thinner is the same as being happier and means that there is little scope for an understanding of being fat and happy. It is telling that health is not mentioned in the advertisement, and that attractiveness is understood as the most important outcome. Although *Ms.* may not be explicitly reinforcing this in its editorial content, the inclusion of it in the advertising copy is also a choice that has been made by the magazine. This points to the tension within the magazine between accepting advertisements because that is the main source of revenue, whilst at the same time acknowledging that the content of such advertising may reinforce negative beauty standards.

This can also be seen in an advertisement from 1982 for Maybelline. The advertisement features a white man and a white woman in an embrace. The woman is looking to the camera, whilst the man is gazing at her. She is wearing fur, which connotes luxury. The advertisement is for 'Soft Shimmer Brush/ Blush'. Rhetorical questions are again used, with the copy asking the reader, 'Why just blushe when you can shimmer? [*sic*]'. There is an assumption that the reader regularly wears make-up and is therefore going to know the difference between 'blushing' and 'shimmering'. Make-up is framed to 'attract more attention'. The fact that the model in the image is embracing a man suggests that the attention that the reader should aim to attract is that of a heterosexual male, and that the reader is a heterosexual herself. Again, whilst there is nothing inherently problematic about this, the fact that this is the only kind of representation of sexuality that can be seen within the magazine's advertisements means that heteronormativity is reinforced.

The extent to which heteronormativity is presented in the advertisements can also be seen in advertisements for the diamond company De Beers in 1987, two of which were included in the sample. As with the previous example, not only is heteronormativity being presented but this is linked to financial affluence, and we will look at the way that affluence is presented as desirable in this chapter as well. The first advertisement featured a man and a woman sitting closely together in a wood in a romantic scene. The advertisement emphasises the diamond as a status symbol, with the copy noting 'her diamond should make the world take notice'. It is interesting that there is a heterosexual male reader assumed here given that the magazine is aimed at women audience. The valorisation of heterosexual love is seen further in the copy with the imposition to 'let the world know the love you share will last forever'. Furthermore, the advertisement notes that buying a diamond means 'spending about 2 months' salary'. Love is presented as something that can be quantified by buying jewellery, further reinforcing the idea that success can be measured in terms of capital. It is important to note that '2 months' salary' is not an objective figure, and for those with lower incomes, this is not necessarily achievable. This again reinforces the middle-class assumed audience for the magazine.

The second De Beers advertisement again reinforces the relationship between diamonds and relationships lasting forever. Similar to the first advertisement, diamonds are positioned as an affordable luxury, with the rhetorical question posed: 'Is 2 month's salary too much to spend for something that lasts forever?' A heterosexual couple are also featured, with a white man and woman embracing each other. In contrast to the previous advertisement, the copy is presented from the point of view of a woman. The woman in the copy explains that whilst her partner is a 'hopeless romantic' she is 'the ultimate pragmatist'. This subverts traditional understandings of heterosexual relationships (Spence and Helmreich, 1979). However, this pragmatism still involves suggesting that her partner buys her a diamond engagement ring, since 'he found out that today you can get a really nice diamond, without breaking your budget'. Whilst there is some subversion of traditional gender relationships, it is important to note that it is still the man who is buying the diamond, and it is still heterosexual coupling that is reinforced.

ADVERTISING AND CAPITALISM IN *MS.*

As well as presenting a particularly white and heterosexual version of success, the magazine's advertising also reinforces capitalist versions of success. The advertising within the magazine for financial services products and utilities reinforces a neoliberal understanding of the world. This can be seen, for example, in an advertisement for the insurance company 'The Travellers'. The advertisement features the quote '"Women can't manage money"', whilst featuring underneath a version of the women's sign with a dollar at the end, rather than a cross. The copy in the article advertises a free financial planning program called 'Making your Money Work', whilst mentioning the importance of 'financial planning'. Financial independence is framed as an important measure of women's freedom. Similarly, an advertisement for the 'Dreyfus Service Corporation' boasts of the 'high financial yields' that can be gained by women who invest in their products. It is clear, as with the advertisements for De-Beers, that an affluent audience is being advertised to. As Erdman Farrell (2011) notes, there is a risk that the inclusion of advertisements aimed primarily at middle-class women serves to alienate those without the financial means to benefit from them. Furthermore, advertisements for financial products serve to reinforce the idea that capitalism is something that can be sustained in the long run. As will be discussed in relation to *Teen Vogue* in the second half of this book, it is difficult to critique capitalism when you rely upon the products of capitalism to maintain your business model.

All the advertisements that have been analysed in this chapter emphasise the extent to which advertising content in *Ms.* often complicated or even contradicted the feminist editorial content within the magazine. This links to a key tension when discussing the relationship between feminism and activism. On the one hand, as has already been extensively acknowledged in this book, to reach a wide audience as a widely circulated magazine, *Ms.* needed to solicit advertising. As we saw in the first chapter, Steinem aimed for the magazine to be a mass market publication due to the increased impact the magazine could have in contrast to a newsletter.

However, there are also limitations in the message that can be presented within the magazine. As we have seen, advertising took up a significant amount of space within the magazine. Even, if readers did not diligently read every advertisement, their existence within the magazine needs to be considered. This is especially important to consider when looking at the types of women that were included within the magazine. As this chapter has shown, the magazine privileged a white, middle-class and heterosexual version of women. Although that of course is not necessarily reflected in the content of the magazine's articles, it does mean that there are potentially contradictory messages within the magazine. Furthermore, as Thom (1997) notes, the readers were understood as a vital asset to the magazine because of their attractiveness to advertisers. If this is the case, then we can also arguably assume that the readers of the magazine are assumed to be white, middle class and heterosexual. This means that there is a limitation to the kinds of alternative perspectives that are presented. The impact that this had in terms of representation of race will be explored in much more detail in the chapter on race. This chapter identifies the lack of representation of women of colour within the magazine. The chapter will now move on to look at how the magazine reckoned with their relationship to the advertising once it had become advertising free in the 1990s.

AD FREE *MS.*

The early 1980s were a turbulent time for *Ms.* The magazine was sold to Fairfax in 1987 and it temporarily ceased publication in 1989 after publishing a controversial article about Reagan and reproductive rights, leading to many advertisers withdrawing their business. When the magazine was bought by Lang Communications in 1990, it became advertising free for the first time in its history. Cunningham and Haley (1990, p. 26) suggest that '*Ms.* editors feel they owe their readers special consideration for making this advertising-free format possible' and that '*Ms.* staff members feel an obligation to offer a worthwhile magazine to the readers because the readers are the sole financial support'. Attitudes towards advertising became much more critical as the magazine became advertising free. In 'Sex, Lies and Advertising' from 1990, Steinem critiques the influence that advertising has. Erdman Farrell (2011) suggests that *Ms.* was more likely than other women's magazines to avoid using sexist advertising, though as this chapter has shown, this was not always the case. The magazine also, especially in the 1980s, placed advertisements that appealed to a more affluent audience that was appealing to advertisers than the concerns of women who would have been less appealing (Erdman Farrell, 2011).

Steinem frames advertising as a form of control of the press, suggesting that advertising has a 'mediawide influence on most of what we read' (1990, p. 170). Advertising is framed by Steinem as a malevolent force within the press, and one that has been harmful to *Ms.* Steinem (1990, p. 170) states that 'advertisers – not readers – have always been the problem for *Ms.*', pointing to the fact that the magazine didn't provide a 'supportive editorial atmosphere' to the advertisers, which meant it was harder to attract them and revenue was lost as a result.

'Sex, Lies and Advertising' reflects the ambiguity that *Ms.* had towards advertising. Whilst Steinem is intensely critical of the advertising industry and its impact on journalism, she also notes, 'When Ms. began, we didn't consider not taking ads. The most important reason was keeping the price of a feminist magazine low enough for most women to afford' (Steinem, 1995 [1990], p. 181). This points to a paradox that has been central to this book: on the one hand, as Steinem argues, advertising can be harmful to women in the way that it perpetuates negative stereotypes about women. However, by being explicit in its aims to cater to a mainstream audience, advertising was unavoidable for *Ms.* (Erdman Farrell, 1997, 2011).

However, beyond viewing advertising as a necessary evil, Steinem also suggests that 'the second and almost equal reason was providing a forum where women and advertisers could talk to each other and improve advertising itself' (p. 181). This is a liberal attitude towards capitalism that assumes that capitalism can be changed directly through feminism's cooperation with it. Bouchier (1983, p. 64) notes that the aim of liberal feminism is to 'improve what exists' and work within the existing political system, rather than aim to 'transform it into a new utopia order' (Bouchier, 1983, p. 64).

However, as 'Sex, Lies and Advertising' suggests, this was not a successful strategy for *Ms*.

Another way that the magazine worked within the capitalist system was through the way that it viewed its readers. Steinem notes that 'by playing their part in this unprecedented mix of all the things our readers need and use, advertisers would also be rewarded' (Steinem, 1995 [1990], p. 181). Steinem is framing *Ms*.'s feminist readers as a valuable consumer for advertisers. However, whilst this suggests a mutually beneficial exchange, as Erdman Farrell (2011) notes, what happened instead was that *Ms*.'s content was much more likely to appeal to an affluent audience that would be attractive to advertisers, therefore potentially excluding those who are less able to buy the products that the advertisers are selling. It is further noted that *Ms*.'s readers were 'good customers because they're out in the world enough to need several sets of everything' (Steinem, 1995 [1990], p. 181). *Ms*.'s readers' independence is framed as indicative of their positive appeal as consumers. Steinem acknowledges the extent to which this had an impact on the day-to-day running of *Ms*. since she 'spent more time persuading advertisers than editing or writing for *Ms*.'. The necessary evil of advertising ended up having a major impact on the extent to which the magazine could operate successfully.

In many respects, 'Sex, Lies and Advertising' can be read as a mea-culpa where Steinem admits to the extent to which the magazine was hamstrung by its engagement with advertising and the extent to which her idealism did not reflect the realities of existing within a capitalist marketplace. For example, Steinem points to the magazine's 'naiveté in thinking we could decide against taking cigarette ads'. Cunningham et al. (1990) noted *Ms*.'s reliance on advertisements for harmful products such as cigarettes and pointed to this as a problematic aspect of the magazine's advertising strategy. However, arguably, since *Ms*. lacked advertisements in 'so many other categories' (Steinem, 1990 [1995], p. 184) the magazine had little choice but to take those advertisements. This is not to excuse the magazine for including advertisements for harmful products such as cigarettes. Rather, the acknowledgement that the magazine had no choice highlights the compromises that are made when attempting to exist within a capitalist marketplace. Similarly, Steinem notes the extent to which the magazine's advertisements were not racially diverse. She notes that even though '[w]omen of color read Ms. in disproportionate numbers', 'this reality is obscured by ads filled with enough white women to make a reader snowblind' (Steinem, 1995 [1990], p. 185). It is important to consider advertisements as an important para-text that adds to the way that the magazine is read. Even if the content of the magazine was representative of all women (though this book will suggest that this is not actually the case), this will not be recognisable if most of the advertisements show white women. Even though Steinem notes that the magazine is read disproportionately by women of colour, the suggestion from advertisers that inclusion of women of colour in advertisements means that '"your [white] readers won't identify"' points to an assumed white reader.

The conclusion of 'Sex, Lies and Advertising' acknowledges that the need to please both readers and advertisers did have an impact on the magazine. Steinem (1995 [1990], p. 191) acknowledges that she's 'just beginning to realise how edges got smoothed down in spite of all of our resistance'. The image of edges being smoothed suggests that the magazine was not as able as it could be to maintain its edginess as a feminist magazine, whilst also suggesting that it was steamrollered by advertisers and could not put up enough resistance to prevent this. It is telling that this article was written after the magazine became advertising free, as this also reflects the new-found freedom that the magazine's editors had to say what it wanted to about advertising and that was not something that could have been done before.

This is something that could also be seen in other articles in the new, advertising-free *Ms*. In the re-launch issue of *Ms*. in 1990, the magazine included a 'No Comment' section which focused on the problematic advertising that was included in *Ms*. 'No Comment' was a semi-regular section that included problematic news and advertising that was found in other news outlets and submitted to *Ms*. by readers. Readers were asked to send in examples of sexist advertising, but as this article shows, the magazine was also often guilty of including advertising that was harmful to women. The text for the article states 'this feature in the old *Ms*. showcased other people's bad ads. Now we can include some of our own'. The distinction between the 'old' and 'new' *Ms*. further separates the *Ms*., including advertising with the new *Ms*. that does not include advertising. Furthermore, the statement that 'now we can include some of our own' suggests that the magazine acknowledges the constraints that held them back previously and there is a new sense of freedom that comes from no longer having to advertise.

READING ADVERTISING IN *MS*. IN RELATION TO COMMODITY ACTIVISM

The way that brands advertised in *Ms*. can be understood in relation to Banet-Weiser's (2012) work on commodity activism. Banet-Weiser argues that a key feature of such advertising is the focus on empowerment, a feature that can be seen in the Dewars and Cutty Sark advertisements. Banet-Weiser (2012, p. 16) describes how 'commodity activism reshapes and reimagines forms and practices of social (and political) activism into marketable commodities and takes specific form within brand culture'. This can be seen in the advertisements that focus on women's achievement as they aim to create a semantic link between the product being sold and the idea of women's independence. Indeed, Banet-Weiser (2012, p. 33) notes that *Ms.* released its own 'record album and book that focused on issues of individuality, tolerance and gender neutrality'. This suggests that *Ms.* presented a version of feminism that could be branded. However, it bears repeating that if feminism is understood as a product to be sold, there are some who will be more able to afford it than others. As Erdman Farrell (2011) has argued, the need for *Ms.* to appeal to a wide audience had the consequence of affecting the content that could be featured within the magazine. This highlights the importance of understanding how para-textual elements such as advertising can have an impact on the content of the magazine.

CONCLUSION

The advertising in *Ms.* often reinforced a liberal feminist perspective that was amenable to capitalism. In addition to this, the magazine also featured advertisements that actively countered the feminist message of the magazine. However, as the magazine became advertising-free, staff were more critical of the role of advertising in the magazine. This demonstrates the difficulty that *Ms.* had as a feminist magazine which needed to maintain both financial solvency through soliciting advertising and a feminist ethos.

This first part of the book has looked at how feminist magazines *Spare Rib* and *Ms.* operated as businesses, and as a result engaged with capitalism. As the discussion of advertising in *Ms.* demonstrates, the fact that feminist magazines such as *Spare Rib* and *Ms.* attempted to reach a wider audience meant that they needed to accept advertising, and in the case of *Ms.* this advertising was often aimed at a largely white, middle-class audience. The next part of this book will move on to look at the kinds of issues that were included in *Spare Rib* and *Ms.* I begin this part of the book with a discussion of race and further highlight some of the ways that the white and middle-class assumed reader of the magazines had an impact on the kind of discussions about race that were had.

Part II

FEMINIST MAGAZINES AND HISTORICISING THE SECOND WAVE

Chapter 3

Representing Race

Historical accounts of feminism commonly note that women of colour's voices have been underrepresented (Bhavnani and Talcott, 2011). Feminism has not only been historically *understood* as a movement for white middle-class women (hooks, 1987; Carby, 1997) but *represented* as comprising predominantly white, middle-class women as well. This means the ways that women of colour were involved in second wave feminism have largely been unaccounted for in mainstream narratives. The continued dominance of what Aziz (1997, p. 70) describes as 'white feminism' means that the marginalisation of feminists of colour remains an unresolved issue. It is because of this marginalisation that discussions of race warrant a separate chapter in this book; since discussions of the experiences of women of colour were so infrequent in *Ms.*, it is useful to discuss this in depth. Similarly, the changing way that *Spare Rib* included women of colour is so illuminating that it warrants in-depth discussion.

Scholars have argued that the hegemonic narrative that reinforces the centrality of white and middle-class women is one that should be questioned and critiqued (Thompson, 2002). Hemmings (2011, p. 13), for example, argues that 'black feminist and transnational critique has been a consistent component of feminist theory, rather than one initiated in the late 1970s or 1980s'. This chapter takes up Hemming's point that although not always included in mainstream historical accounts, women of colour played an important role in the feminist movement. This chapter will explore the extent to which women of colour were represented and were given space to represent themselves in *Spare Rib* and *Ms*.

The chapter begins by critically examining how *Spare Rib* and *Ms.* represented women of colour in the 1970s, before moving on to explore how these representations changed in the 1980s. The key difference between

Spare Rib and *Ms.* is that *Spare Rib* made a deliberate attempt to increase representations of women of colour in a way that *Ms.* did not. This meant that for *Ms.* the imagined reader remained white, whilst in contrast *Spare Rib* began to address women of colour and white feminists. A central reason for this was that the white and middle-class readership was a useful commodity for *Ms.* in a way that it was not for *Spare Rib.* The assumption that it is white middle-class consumers who were valuable to advertisers meant that issues that primarily impacted on marginalised women were generally ignored or underrepresented. This chapter will explore how engagement with the market affected the extent to which the magazines could be representative in their content and address.

There were 152 articles that discussed race and ethnicity, 129 from *Spare Rib* and 23 from *Ms.* Articles were included in the content analysis if they discussed the following:

- Racism
- Imperialism
- Colonialism
- Black feminism
- Jewish feminism[1]

The extent to which *Spare Rib* increased its discussion of race and racism over time is striking (table 3.1). In its inaugural year, one article discussed race. In contrast, by 1992 this had risen to fifty-seven articles, 63.33 percent of the total. There was no similar increase in articles between 1972 and 1987 in *Ms.* In 1992 there was a higher percentage of articles about race in *Ms.* However, as not all articles from 1992 could be accessed, it is not possible to identify whether this increase can be seen throughout 1992, and for most of the sample race was not discussed frequently in *Ms.*

Table 3.1. Discussions of Race in *Spare Rib* and *Ms.*

Year	1972	1977	1982	1987	1992	Total number of articles in sample
Total number of articles in *Spare Rib*	54	75	79	89	90	387
Total number of articles about race *Spare Rib*	1	7	31	33	57	129
% of total	1.85	9.33	39.24	37.07	63.33	33.33
Total number of articles *Ms.*	68	121	82	134	15	420
Total number of articles about race in *Ms.*	1	6	7	6	3	23
% of total	1.47	4.96	8.54	4.48	20	5.78

It is also important to note that the perspectives of women of colour were rarely heard outside of the context of an article addressing race specifically.

By contrast, I argue that the increase in articles discussing race in *Spare Rib* was in response to an intersectional approach to feminism, and a reflection of a more inclusive collective. Since the collective included more women of colour, there were more articles in the magazine that presented issues from this perspective. In contrast, the assumed reader in *Ms.* was consistently white and this can be linked to the magazine's targeting of a middle-class audience who were attractive to advertisers (Erdman Farrell, 2011). Alongside this, the whiteness of the editorial staff meant that issues were less likely to be understood from the perspective of women of colour. The content analysis suggests that it is fair to characterise *Ms.* as appealing to a white audience, but the same cannot be said of *Spare Rib*. This demonstrates the importance of considering the organisational structure of the magazines, as well as the content.

REPRESENTATIONS OF RACE IN *SPARE RIB* AND *MS.* IN THE 1970S AND EARLY 1980S

Race was addressed in *Spare Rib* and *Ms.* in the 1970s, but often in a way that reinforced whiteness. 'Second Thoughts of a Black Feminist' is one of a small number of articles that addressed race in *Ms* during this period. The article, by poet and activist June Jordan, was published in February 1977 and outlines how the women's movement has inadequately represented Black women. This suggests that even though *Ms.* was poor in representing women of colour, there was some awareness of how women of colour had been represented within feminism. Jordan argues that Black people have been underrepresented in the media since 'Black people are a third of the world's population' and asks, 'where our spokesperson is?' (p. 114). She argues that 'there has bene a woeful lack of agreement, or even goodwill' from white women towards women of colour (p. 113), an exclusion seen more widely within the feminist movement. The extent to which Black women were excluded by white women is described by Echols (1989, p. 105), who describes how one radical feminist 'argued that it would be counterproductive to invite radical black women because they would simply use the opportunity to berate the audience for being white and middle class' (p. 105). For some white feminists, Black feminists were potentially threatening because they would challenge their privilege and provoke feelings of guilt. White women's feelings were privileged over the experience of Black women.

Jordan argues that 'black women continue to occupy the lowest rungs of the labor force' (p. 114), pointing to the extent that Black women were oppressed both as women and because of their race. Bhavnani (2007, p. 35) argues that the emphasis on '"common oppression" by white feminists masked the extent to which they shaped the movement so that it addressed and promoted their class interests'. The emphasis on common oppression meant that white feminists did not need to confront the extent to which they oppressed women of colour. Jordan highlights the ways that Black and white women are oppressed differently. This rebuts the idea that access to the labour market will be a liberating experience for all women (Friedan, 1963).

However, although Jordan's article shows that *Ms.* did feature articles that challenged the dominance of white feminism, 'Second Thoughts of a Black Feminist' should also be read intertextually in relation to other articles in the magazine. Jordan's article was the only one in that issue that discussed race, whilst other articles catered towards an affluent audience (articles included in the same issue included advice on how to go to Greece as a 'traveller and not a tourist', whilst previous issues that year included articles on 'How to start your own restaurant' (January 1977)). In general, the assumed reader remained white and middle class, since the assumed audience had enough disposable income to travel abroad or invest in their own business. In contrast, Jordan argues that many Black women are not afforded these opportunities because they are in low-paid work. The focus on travel and business as sources of female independence presents the victims of sexism as 'college-educated white women who were compelled by sexist conditioning to remain in the home' (Bhavnani, 2007, p. 33). The juxtaposition of these articles demonstrates how even when space was afforded to discussions of race, other articles within the magazine continued to assume a white reader. Challenges to white feminist dominance were always compromised by the magazine's appeal to a mainstream audience, which at the time was translated as a white and middle-class audience (Erdman Farrell, 2011), and the need for *Ms.* to sustain itself through advertising meant that it reflected the aspirations of white middle-class women.

Spare Rib also included articles that were critical of the feminist movement's ability to account for the experiences of Black women. 'Yes But . . . What Do Black and Working Class Women Think' (September, 1982) positions Black and working-class women together, further supporting the idea that the assumed feminist, and therefore the assumed reader of *Spare Rib* was white and middle class; since the title of the article assumes that Black and working-class women are not being given the opportunity to speak. The article discusses a women's conference on race and class in Sheffield, the catalyst for which was a 'general feeling amongst feminists in and around Sheffield that there was a lack of communication on some important issues' and more specifically a lack of discussion of race and class (September 1982, p. 18). However, whilst the conference was initiated by the desire for more discussions of race and class, the article notes that 'the conference was dominated by white middle-class women, despite the presence of working class Black and white women' (p. 18). Even in a space where white middle-class women were clearly not the focus of discussion, they continued to dominate the discussion – negating the point of the debate. The idea that white women dominate the discourse even when explicit attempts have been made to create a more inclusive space is noted by Gilman (2007, p. 120), who states:

> Another notable tendency among white feminists has been to provide ubiquitous references to race or feminist scholarship on race while continuing to place at centre stage their own experiences of oppression, a move that essentially amounts to paying lip service to racial difference.

Conference attendee Jackie's statement in the article that 'she agreed with what the working-class women were saying but wouldn't claim to be working class' (p. 18) demonstrates how white middle-class voices were privileged even within spaces that were explicitly for Black and working-class women, and begs the question of why Black and working-class voices weren't given more space in the article. The article has only a short overview written by a Black woman who says that she 'did not get a feeling either from monthly meetings [she had] been to, or from the conference, of a real solidarity from white middle class feminists for either Black or working class women' (September 1982, p. 18). Despite featuring a Black woman, there is no sense that Black women's voices should be prioritised in discussions of race. This is in sharp contrast to discussions of race in *Spare Rib* in the 1980s where Black women were given much more space to articulate their experiences.

The tensions within the British feminist movement can also be seen in 'Women's Liberation 1977' (May 1977), which discusses the Women's Liberation Conference held in London in April 1977. The article is structured into a series of sections, each one covering a particular feminist issue. An editorial comment at the beginning of the section on race suggested that 'a lot of women clapped when the black women took the mike (inverted racism?)' (p. 9). This implies that white women were not appreciated as much as the Black women when they spoke, and there is an assumption that the Black woman's contribution was more valued and that this means that white women were being unfairly treated. However, the dominance of white women meant that it was harder for Black women to be heard, and an increase in applause could reflect this. The idea of 'inverted racism' assumes that applauding a Black woman speaking is somehow indicative of oppression towards white women. This suggests a lack of understanding by the editorial collective of the ways that Black women are oppressed more than white women. It is not enough to discuss race if white women control the narrative. Chambers and Worrall (2017, p. 175) also note that there was 'limited coverage and awareness or awareness of black women's issues'. Furthermore, they point to the extent to which discussions of race were often 'written by white women who presume to write about and for black women' (p. 175). This can be identified in the articles above, where even when discussing race, white women's experiences were privileged. A more representative editorial collective in *Spare Rib* meant that women of colour were able to represent themselves in the magazine, rather than being discussed *by* white feminists.

So far, this chapter has shown how even when discussing the marginalisation of Black women, white women's opinions were prioritised. The chapter will now go on to discuss the changes that can be seen in the 1980s and how *Spare Rib* and *Ms.* diverged from each other, beginning with a discussion of the role of tokenism in *Ms.*

TOKENISM IN *MS.* AND WHITE FEMINISM

As this chapter has demonstrated, in the 1970s, both *Spare Rib* and *Ms.* assumed a white readership so that even articles that explicitly discussed race did so within the context of a magazine that was dominated by a white feminist discourse. However, in the 1980s *Spare Rib* and *Ms.* diverged. *Spare Rib* made a conscious effort to make the collective more representative, but there is no corresponding evidence of this in *Ms.* The magazine instead treats Black writers, and articles by Black women, in a tokenistic way. Tokenism is an attempt to increase diversity in a way that means that an individual or a small group of people are viewed as representative of a larger group. McIntosh (1990) argues that one indicator of white privilege is that individual white people are not expected to act as representatives of their whole race in the same way that Black people are. Tokenism can be used to appear to be diverse, whilst not attempting real structural change to challenge racism. Hazel V. Carby (1997, p. 52) argues that 'Black women do not want to be grafted onto "feminism" in a tokenistic manner as colourful diversions to "real" problems'. This suggests that Black women's problems should not be perceived as supplementary to those of white women.

The use of Black women in tokenistic roles can be seen in *Ms.* in particular. In contrast, *Spare Rib*'s decision to make the magazine more representative (O'Sullivan, 2012) meant that the magazine was not tokenistic. Alice Walker was a writer for *Ms.* from 1974 until 1986 when she resigned (Thom, 1997). Her resignation protested the lack of coverage of Black women in the magazine. Walker described the 'swift alienation' that she felt reading the magazine and argued that 'a people of color cover once or twice a year is not enough. In real life, people of color occur with much more frequency' (Walker, quoted in Thom, 1997, p. 89). The limited inclusion of women of colour in the magazine was insufficient in fully reflecting the diversity of Black women. Ruth Sullivan, a colleague of Walker's at *Ms.*, speculates that Walker's dissatisfaction was because 'Alice felt the burden of being, as she described it, the token black woman at *Ms.*' (Pogrebin, 2011). Many more white women than Black women wrote for the magazine. The content analysis shows that discussions of race were infrequent; meaning that any time race was discussed it was done so in a tokenistic way and was likely to be the only article by a woman of colour or about race in an issue. In no sample year was there more than seven articles about race in *Ms.* It was therefore unlikely that there would be more than one article that discussed race in an issue. This, combined with the assumption that 'woman' means white, middle class and straight, means that those Black women who were in magazines such as *Ms.* carried the heavy burden of representing not only their gender but also their race, something that was not expected of white women who wrote for the magazine.

When white women engaged in discussions of race, this also often reinforced notions of white supremacy within the magazine. Jane O'Reilly's 'A Global Click' (July 1987) discusses the internationalisation of feminism, focusing on the emergence of feminism in lower-income countries. The title 'A Global Click' calls back to an idea that O'Reilly had first described in the preview issue of the magazine in December 1971. A click is 'a moment of truth. The shock of recognition. Instant sisterhood' (O'Reilly, December 1971, p. 54). The click is the moment of feminist awakening when you first become aware of the prevalence of sexism and the role of feminism in challenging it. The title 'A Global Click' suggests that this experience is now happening to women in countries such as Kenya, Mali and Senegal, mentioned in the article. It is important to note that O'Reilly's article comes sixteen years after the original. This suggests that feminism has taken much longer to arrive in low-income countries, reinforcing a narrative where feminism arrives in the West and is then exported to the rest of the world. Thompson (2002, p. 337) critiques a hegemonic feminism which is 'white led, marginalizes the activism and world views of women of color' and 'focuses mainly on the United States'. The positioning of the Global Click is something that happened much later than in the United States, reinforcing the United States as originator which other nations followed. This ignores how feminism developed in other parts of the world in parallel with the United States, and not necessarily as a response to it. The fact that it is a white woman who is discussing international feminism is important to consider since it shows that even when international feminism was discussed it was white Western women who told the stories.

This chapter has so far identified how *Ms.*'s discussion of race was often tokenistic because the magazine assumed a white reader. In the next section of this chapter, I argue that, in contrast, *Spare Rib* was more proactive in attempting to include a wider range of voices and this can be seen through the increase in content from women of colour that focus on race. To begin this discussion, I will discuss Kum-Kum Bhavnani's three-part series from 1982: 'Racist Acts'. This case study will demonstrate how *Spare Rib* changed its attitude towards representations of race in the 1980s.

'RACIST ACTS' AND INCREASED INCLUSION OF WOMEN OF COLOUR IN *SPARE RIB*

As the content analysis shows, there was an increased discussion of *Spare Rib* in the 1980s so that it was no longer a tokenistic topic. This can be seen both in the frequency of articles about race and also through how the issue was approached. The three-part series 'Racist Acts' (1982) can be understood within this context. The series was published a year before the 'Special Black Women's Issue' in October 1983 but demonstrates how the magazine was beginning to change its representation of race, even if the assumed reader was still white. This is also argued by Chambers and Worrall (2017, p. 175), who argue that by 1982 'the magazine had finally started to listen to black women's voices as a regular occurrence'. However, it is also useful to point out that this article was published in the same year as 'Yes . . . what do black and working class women think'. Even as the magazine began to take race more seriously, it still included articles that centred a white reader.

The series was a response to the 1981 Nationality Act which redefined how British Citizenship was legally defined. New definitions of British citizenship led to increased insecurity for some migrants, since being born in Britain no longer guaranteed citizenship unless a parent was a British citizen (Blake, 1982). The inclusion of a series on the issue suggests a commitment to feature articles about race and racism in detail. Furthermore, as the content analysis shows, there were thirty-one articles discussing race in 1982. In the three months that 'Racist Acts' ran, there were eight additional articles on race, including an editorial to introduce Bhavnani's series (February 1982) and one on racism in the NHS in the same issue. This is in sharp contrast to *Ms.* where articles about race or racism were often isolated to one per issue. This suggests that discussions of race and racism in *Spare Rib* were not necessarily tokenistic.

Despite an increase in articles on race, the assumed reader was still white. This can be seen through the educational tone used in 'Racist Acts' which clarifies and defines key terms. The article describes how 'Black people' and those of 'Afro-Caribbean and South Asian origin (from the Indian subcontinent)' are 'defined as the source and course of "law and order problems"'

(February 1982, p. 49). Beginning the series with a definition of these terms suggests that this is information unfamiliar to a white reader, whilst by needing to define Blackness suggests that Bhavnani is addressing a white audience. Bhavnani also defines 'racism' and 'racialism'; that these terms need to be defined suggests that the reader would not have directly encountered racism. Bhavnani distinguishes between 'racism', which is defined as 'the *institutionalised* practices and patterns which have the overall effect of developing the system which places Black people at a disadvantage', and racialism, which is defined as 'individual acts of *discrimination* that many white people carry out in an attempt to "put down" and harass and humiliate Black people' (p. 49, italics original). Racism is defined as both intentional actions against people of colour and the privileges that white people gain because of the oppression of people of colour.

White women are therefore complicit in racism, and this means that an article on racism is as relevant to white women as it is to women of colour. This counters the perception that feminism and racism are mutually exclusive. hooks (1987, p. 119) argues that 'women of all races are socialized to think of racism solely in the context of race hatred' and are therefore unaware of the unconscious racism that white women are capable of because of their white privilege. In stressing that this is not the case, Bhavnani argues that racism is something that all white people, even those who would identify as anti-racist, are complicit in. However, the tone of the article is not accusatory. The article uses the plural pronoun 'we'; for example, 'we cannot eradicate racialist attitudes without understanding and demolishing the institutionalised forms of racism' (p. 49). This promotes a sense of collective responsibility and deflects from white women's individualised feelings of guilt.

Bhavnani states that 'the white majority has been benefitting extensively from a colonial past and an exploitatively racist present' (March 1982, p. 25). Carby (1997, p. 49) argues that 'all women in Britain benefitted in varying degrees from the economic exploitation of the colonies'. It is important to recognise the role of racism in Britain and specifically within the feminist movement and that this needs to be placed within the wider context of a long colonial history. An intersectional approach can be seen, since Bhavnani argues that 'the ways in which white people have experienced these benefits differ according to class and gender' (Bhavnani, March 1982, p. 25). Levine-Rasky (2011, p. 240) argues that 'intersectionality theory arose from black feminist thought as an incisive critique of mainstream feminism'. Bhavnani's article acknowledges how women are oppressed in different ways and oppress each other, challenging the notion that women can be understood as a homogeneous group.

'Racist Acts' is particularly valuable because it highlights how whiteness is a social construct which must itself be interrogated. Bhavnani notes that 'concentrating on "cultural difference" disguises the fact that British society is itself deeply divided among white people as well' (March 1982, p. 27). The defaulting of whiteness means that it is not understood as a constructed racial identity; this further positions whiteness as the norm and Blackness as other. Aziz (1997, p. 73) argues that 'white-ness is every bit as implicated as black-ness in the working of racism'. In problematising the idea of whiteness Bhavnani further reiterates the extent to which racism is relevant to white people, and more specifically white *Spare Rib* readers. The understanding of white privilege as endemic within feminism can be seen within the context of *Spare Rib*'s increased awareness of race and racism in the 1980s.

Bhavnani moves on to show how the feminist movement is complicit in ignoring racism, using the example of reproductive rights. She notes that 'the National Abortion Campaign had to adapt and adjust its positions and slogans in order to consider that *Black* women sometimes fin it only too easy to be sterilised or given abortions' (italics in original, April 1982, p. 25). This demonstrates how feminist campaigns assumed that women's oppressions were all the same, ignoring the extent to which access to reproductive rights for Black women often meant prioritising campaigns to prevent forced sterilisation, rather than access to contraception and abortion (Nelson, 2003).

THE INTERSECTION OF RACE AND CLASS

'Racist Acts' intersectional approach can also be seen through the discussion of racism within the Labour movement. There is no discussion of these intersections in *Ms.*, further highlighting the different ways that the magazines approached race. This indicates a much broader discussion of race in *Spare Rib*. Bhavnani (1982, p. 25) argues that 'British trade unions do not seem to have been in the forefront of the fight against racism in Britain'. She uses the example of the Imperial Typewriters to support this. The strike was by a group of predominantly Indian women who demanded better pay after discovering that not only were they being paid less in bonuses but were less likely to be promoted than their white peers. Bhavnani argues that 'trade union bureaucracies do not support Black members fighting for basic union rights when that dispute is permeated by and is a result of racist practices' (p. 25). She then goes on to critique initiatives such as the Trade Union Congress (TUC) 'Charter for Equality of Opportunity for Black Workers' as 'rather weak and half hearted' again suggesting that anti-racist work is seen as an afterthought as 'Black struggle gets lost as being part of the overall class struggle' (p. 25).

Amrit Wilson (1997, p. 31) suggests that the Imperial Typewriters strike demonstrated that 'Asian women workers can be strong, resourceful and courageous'. In contrast, Bhavnani suggests that the TUC charter presents women of colour as 'passive victims'. By characterising women of colour as passive, the charter ignores the agency of women of colour. Wilson argues that it was the worker's poverty that meant that they were vulnerable to exploitation as they were perceived by management as prepared to accept a lower rate of pay than their white colleagues. Wilson (1997, p. 35) supports Bhavnani's perception of the trade union management, stating that 'whilst hundreds of trade unionists came day after day . . . they hadn't the courage to confront and defy the handful of men who control the trade union bureaucracy'. Though the unions were obviously concerned with worker's rights, they lacked awareness of how race intersected with class, assuming that they were supporting only a white working-class constituency. Through the focus on racism within the unions, Bhavnani further demonstrates how an understanding of class in Britain must also consider endemic racism. This also suggests a more intersectional approach that takes into consideration both class and race identities.

Bhavnani argues for a broadening of discussions of racism, so that 'tackling racism and racialism must involve questioning issues such as mental health, the penal system, the role of political parties, trade unions and left-wing groups' and not be 'tucked away or put in the end of political publications' (April 1982, p. 26). The idea that racism should be considered relevant when discussing most political issues, rather than simply being a specialist issue, is especially important when considering the differences between the way *Spare Rib* and *Ms.* developed their attitudes towards race in the 1980s. 'Racist Acts' was the beginning of a greater understanding in *Spare Rib* that racism is something that should concern all women. This is in stark contrast to articles in *Ms.*, where race was not understood as intersecting with wider political issues. I will now critically examine how *Spare Rib* and *Ms.* developed their discussion of race in the late 1980s and 1990s.

INCREASING REPRESENTATION OF WOMEN OF COLOUR IN THE 1980S AND 1990S: *SPARE RIB* AND *MS.* COMPARED

In the 1980s, as a result of the editorial collective becoming more representative there was a shift in assumed reader and a greater focus on the intersection of race and gender. 'Racist Acts' demonstrated the beginning of an increased focus on race, and this increased substantially throughout the 1980s. This had an impact on the relationship with readers, with some readers arguing that the magazine no longer represented them. This is indicative of the challenge that attempts to make the magazine more inclusive, whilst a more 'traditional' readership still held ideas about what the magazine should include.

Articles that discussed race in *Spare Rib* had begun to increase in 1982, and similar increases can be seen in 1987 and 1992. In the final year 63 percent of the total number of articles were about race or discussed issues from the perspective of women of colour, emphasising the extent to which it had become a central issue for the magazine. In contrast, there was no significant increase in *Ms*. There was also a change in rhetoric so that there were more reference concepts such as imperialism and anti-colonialism. In 1992, there was an article in *Spare Rib* on the 'Gadhafi Human Rights Award' (July 1992) that was favourable towards Muammar Gaddaf (Colonel) Gadhafi, the Libyan leader widely regarded as a dictator. Similarly, the magazine included a tribute to the wife of Zimbabwean dictator Robert Mugabe after her death (March 1992) and favourable articles about Cuba (April 1992). This is significant because it shows how far away *Spare Rib* was from mainstream news reporting on these figures. There was an increase in anti-colonial arguments and praise for liberation movements in formerly colonised countries. The relationship between *Spare Rib* and mainstream British politics will be discussed in greater depth in a later chapter of this book.

An editorial from July 1992 exemplifies *Spare Rib*'s global outlook. It asserts that 'conditions on this planet are critical. Millions of our people are dying as Imperialism's brutal campaign of genocide continues unabated' (p. 7). The phrase 'our people' assumes that the reader would identify as oppressed by the West and suggests a Black audience since people of colour have most often been victims of Western oppression. This is a shift from earlier in the magazine's history where even when discussing race, the assumed reader was still white. However, as this chapter will show, this shift led to some readers arguing that they felt that the increased emphasis on international issues meant that the magazine no longer served its target audience of (white) British feminists.

An explicit discussion of gender or feminism is absent from the twentieth anniversary editorial and the words 'women', 'female' or 'feminism' are not used, though there is a broadening of the discussion to include race and imperialism. A more intersectional approach is taken. Crenshaw (1989, p. 40) in her influential work on intersectionality argues that 'any analysis that does not take intersectionality into account cannot sufficiently address the particular manner in which black women are subordinated'. *Spare Rib*'s shift in focus suggests an increased awareness of the need to understand the role that Western imperialism plays in the oppression of women of colour.

SHIFT IN THE ASSUMED READER

The increased intersectional understanding of both local and global issues can be read in conjunction with a shift in focus in *Spare Rib*'s articles and a much heavier focus on wider political issues, not only those that would be under-stood exclusively as 'feminist'. The extent to which racism was understood as a relevant issue for feminists, without being framed as an exclusively feminist issue, can be seen in two articles addressing police brutality.

The first article 'War Ina Babylon' (June 1992) was a response to riot-ing in LA after the beating of unarmed Rodney King by police officers and their subsequent acquittal in court. The article criticises the 'Western media', which decided to 'suppress certain facts of the Uprising' (p. 13). Although commenting on events taking place in the United States, the West more gen-erally is disidentified (Muñoz, 1999). The 'West' is configured as a pejora-tive term, associated with white oppression. The article praises the 'serious brothers and sisters' who 'slam Western dictatorships' who have 'fallen into the trap of intellectualising the few as opposed to working together with the masses of people' (p. 14). The article advocates action, arguing that 'time ahead is about a fight for our very survival as People of Colour' (p. 15). The use of 'our' suggests that the reader is also a person of colour. This can be contrasted to 'Racist Acts', which was analysed previously in this chapter. Whilst 'Racist Acts' demonstrated a desire to educate its readership on the impact of racism for Black women in 1980s' Britain, it was still assumed that the core readership was white and did not have first-hand knowledge of the impact of racism. In contrast, 'War Ina Babylon' has a Black writer and a Black assumed reader.

'Babylon Blues' (August–September 1992, p. 36) also focuses on police bru-tality and assumes a Black reader. The author suggests that 'we have borne the brunt of years of repressive police practice' and again the 'we' is assumed to be Black. There is no explicit discussion of gender or feminism here, further high-lighting how *Spare Rib*'s discussion of race moved beyond discussing it only in relation to specifically gendered issues. The article interviews 'survivors' of police brutality. It interviews men and women, but the impact of sexism in rela-tion to police behaviour is not considered. The women who are interviewed are introduced through their relationship to male relatives. Whilst one female inter-viewee describes being called a 'black bitch' by a police officer, the gendered nature of this abuse is not discussed (p. 37) and more men are interviewed than women. This reflects the fact that Black men were more likely to be the victims of police harassment, but the lack of focus on women does seem incongruent in *Spare Rib*. This is reflective of a broader change in focus, where the impact of racism was understood as the key priority for the magazine. Although it would be incorrect to describe *Spare Rib* as post-feminist (McRobbie, 2009) in the 1990s, the decreased focus on sexism does indicate a move away from viewing sexism as the most important oppression to dismantle.

The decreased focus on women's oppression by men coincided with an increase in articles that included male perspectives. The May 1992 issue included a feature article about Malcolm X, including excerpts from his writing. However, the inclusion of a feature article about a man was not without criticism from readers of the magazine. One reader wrote a critical letter questioning if 'S.R magazine is the place to write about men or even worse let them write about themselves' (June 1992, p. 4). Although earlier issues of the magazine featured men, this was at a time when the magazine was forming its identity as a feminist magazine (Hollows, 2013), and *Spare Rib* very rarely introduced contributions from men. The inclusion of an article about Malcolm X therefore represents a shift in policy. The editorial collective responded to the letter, stating that 'we have carried many articles on male oppression and this continues to remain one of our priorities'. There is an acknowledgement that women's oppression by men is not the only form of oppression.

The examination of how *Spare Rib* discussed race and racism in the 1980s suggests that there was a developing critique of racism and imperialism as a primary aim of the magazine. I will now move on to explore the tensions between how long-term readers of the magazine saw the remit of *Spare Rib* and the direction that the magazine's editorial collective was taking the magazine.

READER'S RESPONSE TO *SPARE RIB'S* SHIFT IN FOCUS

The shift in the assumed reader of *Spare Rib* led to criticisms from white readers, who felt that they had become alienated. This reflects the fact that some white readers took for granted the whiteness of the magazine. Waters (2016, p. 14) notes that the magazine announced that '"*Spare Rib* is no longer a white women's magazine"', but at the same time it made 'sure to recognise "the difficulty of all of this for many [white] readers"'. The need for white readers to be reassured highlights the extent to which whiteness is understood as the default, and the insecurity of white women when this is challenged. Gilman (2007, p. 117) states that 'white feminists experience extreme levels of discomfort when an anti-racist perspective is introduced within feminist sites of engagement'. This can certainly be seen in some of the correspondence to *Spare Rib* in response to increased anti-racist and anti-imperialist rhetoric. In one letter an anonymous reader states: 'Yes I will renew my subscription but yet again I must make a protest – as I do regularly, and you regularly ignore it' (July 1992, p. 3). The repetition of 'ignore' and 'ignored' suggests that the reader does not feel listened to, whilst 'yet again' articulates a sense of frustration that this has not been addressed previously. The letter focuses on the reader's perception that the magazine blames 'white middle class women for every problem under the sun', and the defensiveness evident in the letter suggests that these criticisms are taken to be a personal attack (July 1992, p. 4). However, as Coote and Campbell (1982, p. 31) argue:

Many black women felt that white women (even working class socialist feminists) enjoyed racial privilege alongside white men unless white women's politics were organized around eliminating that privilege, they remained part of the problem black women faced.

White women are complicit as oppressors of Black women because of their white privilege, and as I have argued in this chapter, white women can be oblivious to this. The letter writer's defensiveness at the complicity of white women in Black women's oppression reflects the discomfort at being acknowledged as an oppressor. The letter ends with a repetition of the sentiment that the letter writer is being ignored, suggesting:

You'll probably ignore this letter, as you have all my others, and instead will print jubilant letters from someone who thinks *Spare Rib* has really found that after all, White middle class women are the source of all the problems that affect humanity at this time. (p. 4)

This further reinforces the sense of victimisation the letter writer feels because she perceives that she is being held responsible for the oppression of Black women. This links back to the sentiments expressed in the readership survey that the magazine no longer represented 'ordinary' women and white middle-class women constructed themselves as victims (Tyler, 2008).

A response to the anonymous letter writer was published in August 1992. The author, Chloe, states that she 'was really pleased to read the letter from "Anon" in the July issue':

Till I saw that, I really thought I was one of the only readers to be multiply handicapped (sorry, differently abled) by being white, middle aged, middle class and heterosexual). (p. 4)

Chloe uses the language of political correctness to mock the use of such terms and deny the need for such language to be used in the first place. She argues that *Spare Rib* has 'largely abandoned the cause of British and world feminism and become too political', linking this politicisation to 'the ANC, South Africa, the Intifada and similar causes' (p. 4). A distinction is made between explicitly feminist issues and broader political issues, which are viewed as not belonging to *Spare Rib*. The accusation that the magazine is too 'political' is a euphemism for the magazine not focusing exclusively on British women's issues.

In contrast to Chloe's letter, another letter from the same issue supports the magazine's new direction. The letter writer states that she has 'been impressed by *Spare Rib*'s new-found ability to address a Black readership in a way that no other "mixed" magazine has achieved' (August–September 1992, p. 4). The idea of a 'mixed audience' suggests that *Spare Rib* is for both women of colour and white women, rather than assuming a white readership. Sudbury praises the magazine for avoiding 'tokenistic' articles, arguing that it has instead 'fundamentally re-evaluat[ed] what is considered to be relevant material for women's magazines' (p. 4). It is relevant to note that Sudbury is Black and given that the women's movement has been dominated by white women's concerns, she is more likely to be positively impacted by *Spare Rib*'s decreased focus on white women. Sudbury makes the interesting point that the magazine does 'address the pain and oppression of white middle class women' but this is 'part of a spectrum of women's concerns and perspectives' (p. 4). Arguably, the change in focus appears more pronounced to some white readers because their concerns have been centralised in previous discourses.

The discussion of these letters demonstrates how the magazine changed its focus to include more international politics and Black women's perspectives, but that these changes were not universally well received. This demonstrates that some white readers viewed feminism as a movement that predominantly addressed issues that affected them, and that when *Spare Rib* broadened its focus it was accused of ignoring its 'core' readership. However, the final letter from Julia Sudbury suggests that *Spare Rib*'s increased intersectionality meant that some Black readers were more likely to see their concerns addressed in a way that had not happened before. I will now move on to argue that such a change could not be seen in *Ms.* and identify some of the reasons for this.

'MY GLOVES ARE OFF SISTERS – POWER, RACISM AND THAT "DOMINATION THING"': WHITE WOMEN'S COMPLICITY IN *MS.*

Although *Ms.*'s coverage of race was largely tokenistic, there were indeed *some* articles that were more nuanced and addressed white women's complicity in racism. 'My Gloves Are off Sisters – Power, Racism and that "Domination Thing"' is one example, published in April 1987. Eventual editor of *Ms.* Marcia-Ann Gillespie is highly critical of how 'white women use feminism as a disclaimer whenever charges of racism are being made' (p. 19). This suggests that for white feminists identifying as a feminist is synonymous to being anti-racist, and no further examination of their behaviour is needed. The allusion to that 'domination thing' can be linked to hooks' (1987, p. 195) argument 'white females have structured a women's liberation movement that is racist and excludes many non-white women'. Gillespie notes that Black women are 'suspicious and somewhat separate from what most of us still privately refer to as the White Women's Movement' (p. 19) and declares that 'My gloves are off, sisters. I'm coming to the party and saying that racism's been stinking up the women's table for far too long' (p. 20). The imagery of Gillespie taking her gloves off suggests that she has previously been treating white women with 'kid gloves' to spare their feelings, but that she is no longer prepared to do that. However, by addressing white feminists as 'sisters' Gillespie maintains the sense that despite racism within the women's movement she still sees the feminist movement as a sisterhood.

As with Bhavnani's article, Gillespie argues that feminists and progressives are capable of racism, stating that 'every time I hear a white woman use feminism as a disclaimer whenever charges of racism are made, I know I am being sold a ticket' (p. 20). hooks (1987) asserts that white women are conditioned to not see their own racism and therefore they are unlikely to understand how their behaviour oppresses Black women. Gillespie argues that 'oppressions do not automatically lead to sainthood', suggesting that white women cannot be excused of racism because they are oppressed as women' (p. 20). Crenshaw (1989, p. 152) argues that the 'adoption of a single-issue framework for discrimination . . . marginalises black women' because it does not adequately account for how oppressions intersect. Echols (1989, p. 75) refers to Allen, who argues that 'the black analogy' used by white women to suggest that racial and gender oppression are synonymous was used by 'white women [who] were avoiding their own racism' (p. 20). This is further argued by Gillespie in the article, who states that 'white women were either unable or simply unwilling to recognise and confront it as an internal problem' (p. 20). The irony is that this statement was made in *Ms.*, where discussions of race were largely absent. Although Gillespie's article is strongly worded and uncompromising, it must be read within the context of a magazine that still assumed a white reader. The article is the only one in April 1987 which discusses race. Consequently, despite its complex understanding of racism within feminism it was still tokenistic, and the emphasis on the white middle-class reader throughout the rest of the magazine reinforces this and demonstrates how race and racism was not understood as a central concern.

By 1992, discussions of race in the magazine *had* increased. Whereas it would have been unusual to see more than seven articles about race in a year, by 1992, there were issues that had three articles on the topic. It is worth noting that by 1992, *Ms.* no longer included advertising. The new magazine is described by editor Robin Morgan (November/December 1992, p. 1) as 'liberated territory' and a 'challenging publication whose editorial freedom isn't threatened by the censorship of advertisers'. Morgan explicitly notes that the magazine now 'contains a minimum of six pages of Sisterhood is Global international News' (p. 1). If, as Erdman Farrell (2011) notes, Black and poor women were less attractive to advertisers; this indicates that no longer needing advertising may have affected the extent to which the magazine felt it could include discussions of race and international issues. One of the advantages of becoming advertising free was, arguably, that the content did not have to appeal only to white middle-class women who were attractive to advertisers. This suggests that one of the causes of *Ms.*'s lack of inclusivity was the commercial market. This highlights the importance of considering the cultural economies in which the magazines exist within, as well as the editorial decisions of staff. The engagement of capitalism with feminism suggests a feminism that fundamentally benefits white middle-class women, and means that marginalised women are excluded, because they are less likely to be understood as valuable to capitalism. The relationship between the reader and commercial imperatives will come up again in the discussion of neoliberalism and post-feminism in a later chapter.

CONCLUSION

Neither *Spare Rib* nor *Ms.* was inclusive enough in the 1970s, but *Spare Rib*'s content did shift as a result of a more representative collective. In contrast, though *Ms.* did include the work of a few Black writers, the assumed reader remained that of a white middle-class woman. The lack of change in the assumed reader in *Ms.* can be understood in light of Erdman Farrell's (2011) argument that the magazine needed to appeal to a white middle-class audience in order to appeal to advertisers. This was demonstrated by the fact that the magazine did include more discussions of Black and international feminism once the magazine no longer relied on advertising in 1992. This suggests that the capitalist imperative of the magazine was inherently racist since it privileged white middle-class women who could buy consumer products. This posed a problem for *Ms.*, which on the one hand rejected racism, whilst on the other hand it neglected the needs of Black women because they were understood as less attractive to the advertising that *Ms.* was reliant on.

In contrast, articles such as 'Racist Acts' in *Spare Rib* are evidence of the ways that issues affecting Black women were increasingly found in the magazine. An increasingly more diverse collective meant that the magazine could appeal to a more diverse audience. By the time the magazine ceased publication it can be argued that the magazine's assumed reader had shifted to include women of colour in its address. However, the critical letters from some white feminists show that there was discomfort from white readers who felt that the magazine was no longer speaking to 'them' or 'their' issues. Even though *Spare Rib* was not working within such a strict capitalist context, reliance on advertising, racism amongst feminist and the assumption that issues should be understood through a white woman's lens prevented the magazine from being as intersectional as it could be.

NOTES

1. Although Jewish feminism isn't discussed in detail in this chapter, I included it in the analysis since Jewishness can be understood as an ethnic identity and an identity that has been subject to xenophobia and anti-Semitism. I should also note that I use the term 'women of colour' throughout this chapter. I am aware of the different ways that women from different ethnic groups are treated within society. However, this difference is not something that was regularly discussed in the magazines. As such, 'women of colour' seemed like the most appropriate term to use.

Chapter 4

Pornography and the Politics of Sex

Debates around pornography and the sex industry have long been heated, and the 'sex wars' of the 1980s demonstrated the extent to which it was a polarised issue. Rodgerson and Wilson (1991, pp. 9–10) argue that pornography 'divided the American feminist community'. However, despite the polarising nature of the topic, and the way it has been historicised as a dominant feminist issue (Strub, 2011), this is not reflected in the frequency in which the issue was discussed in either *Spare Rib* or *Ms*. This suggests that the way that the issue has been theorised in academic discourse is incongruent with the way that it was represented in feminist media, further demonstrating the importance of studying such media.

As with other issues discussed in this book, there were key differences between the way that *Spare Rib* and *Ms*. approached the issue. In *Ms*. pornography was viewed almost exclusively as harmful to women, and there was a singular editorial line on the issue. The places where feelings of ambivalence were expressed in *Ms*. were in letters from readers. This highlights the importance of looking beyond editorial content to understand public feminist attitudes on an issue. In *Spare Rib*, editorial content was more likely to present pornography as a complex issue with no definitive editorial line, but there was not the same engagement from readers on the issue.

I begin this chapter with an overview of the different ways that pornography and sex work were theorised by second wave feminists. After providing this context, I will then analyse how pornography and the politics of sex were represented in *Spare Rib* and *Ms*., focusing on how *Spare Rib* and *Ms*. represented pornography and the sex industry.

DEFINING PORNOGRAPHY

Lindgren (1993) points to the difficulty in defining pornography and suggests that this is central to feminist conflict on the issue. Andrews (2012, p. 457) refers to the oft-cited statement from 'Justice Potter Stewart', who when asked to define what pornography was said, '"I know it when I see it"'. The difficulty in providing an accurate and universally agreed definition can be seen in relation to feminist debates around pornography. Andrews (2012, p. 459) argues that the dominant definition of pornography is that it is 'explicit material, that it is material intended to arouse' and/or that it is 'material dependent on sexual representations'. However, as will be discussed in this chapter, anti-pornography feminists often understood degradation and objectification as a defining feature of pornography.

THE SEX WARS: PORNOGRAPHY IN THE 1980S

The 'sex wars' focused on feminist attitudes towards pornography and sadomasochism (Mennel, 2010; Duggan and Hunter, 2006). Mennel (2010, p. 255) argues that 'the pairing of sexuality and power is constitutive of the feminist movement'. However, there was fierce debate about the extent to which narratives that focused on domination and control contributed to women's subordination in the real world. Hunter (2006, p. 16) argues that the 'core of the feminist debate occurred during a ten-year bell curve' which began with the 'founding of Women Against Violence Against Women in 1976' and culminated with Andrea Dworkin and Catharine MacKinnon's attempt to legislate against pornography in 1984, before this was deemed unconstitutional in 1986. This must, however, be seen within the context of earlier discussions about the role of sexualisation, as seen in the Miss World Protests in the 1970s (Hunter, 2006).

Andrews' (2012) definition of pornography focuses on its explicitness. In contrast, Sunstein (1986, p. 592) defines pornography in relation to its harm to women. Sunstein (1986, p. 591) argues that pornography must:

a. be sexually explicit, b. depicts women as deserving or enjoying some sort of physical abuse and c. have the purpose and effect of producing sexual arousal.

Furthermore, Sunstein (1986, p. 592) argues that 'pornographic materials feature rape, explicitly or implicitly, as a major theme'. Anti-pornography feminist campaigners such as Catharine MacKinnon and Andrea Dworkin understood pornography as misogynistic and harmful to women. MacKinnon (1985, p. 32) describes pornography as a 'form of forced sex', whilst MacKinnon and Dworkin (1997, p. 321) argue that those who defend pornography are 'defending male supremacy'. Pornography is viewed as something that supports the patriarchy because it treats women as sexual objects.

Rubin (1984, p. 164) argues that 'feminist anti-pornography ideology has always contained an implied and sometimes overt indictment of sadomasochism'. Sadomasochism can be understood as 'the deliberate use of physical or psychological "pain" to produce sexual arousal' (Weinberg et al., 1984). Although it is possible for a woman to be dominant and a man to be submissive, mainstream representations of sadomasochism have focused on the infliction of pain onto a submissive female. Brownmiller (2013 [1975], p. 460) suggests that women are 'indoctrinated into a victim mentality', which is reinforced by the focus on female submission and fantasies of violence against women.

The idea that pornography affects the ways men and women perceive what is desirable can be seen by MacKinnon's (1985, p. 326) statement that pornography cannot be 'harmless fantasy' but instead needs to be seen as 'sexual reality', and in Robin Morgan's statement that 'Pornography is the theory, rape is the practice' (Morgan, quoted in Strub, 2011, p. 186). This assumes a didactic relationship between the consumption of pornography and the carrying out of demeaning and violent acts towards women. This is suggested by Easton (1994), who states that there are a number of harms caused by the 'production and consumption of pornography' (p. 10).

Campaigns against pornography were high profile in the 1980s, and Strub (2011) argues that anti-pornography activists have influenced how feminist attitudes to pornography have been historicised, leading to the assumption that second wave feminists were distinctly anti-sex or anti-pornography. However, this was not a position shared by all feminists. It would also be too simplistic to describe critics of anti-pornography as pro-pornography. The arguments against anti-pornography feminism were often based on a dislike of the tactics of anti-pornography feminists, rather than a fundamental acceptance of pornography as positive. This chapter will now outline the key criticisms of anti-pornography feminism.

One key critique was that legislation against pornography by feminists such as MacKinnon and Dworkin was not supported by 'local feminist groups, but by neighbourhood associations, conservative Republican politicians, rigid right wing fundamentalists, and members of the Moral Majority' (Duggan, 2006, pp. 29–30). There was a concern that many more conservative anti-pornography activists objected to pornography in part because of their regressive attitudes towards women and LGBT people. In *Pornography and Feminism: The Case Against Censorship* (1991) the authors point to the ways that legal action against 'obscene material' has tended to be brought against the LGBT community, citing as an example Operation Tiger, which raided the Gay's the Word bookshop in London in 1984 (see also Watney, 1997).

A further argument from feminists who opposed anti-pornography discourses was that pornography could not be singled out as unusually concerning since it was 'no worse than a great deal of the patriarchal and misogynistic culture that it represents' (Ellis et al., 1990, p. 26–27). Similarly, Duggan (2006, p. 52) asks, 'why is sexual explicitness singled out as a cause for women's oppression', when there are many other causes for women's subordination, suggesting that pornography reflects society rather than constitutes it. Furthermore, Strub (2011, p. 354) argues that before the anti-pornography discourses in the 1980s which focused heavily on prohibition, there had been a 'measured critique of pornography' that allowed for the idea of a 'non-sexist porn' (p. 354).

It is important to acknowledge that women do consume pornography, and because pornography is presented as fundamentally harmful the reason women might consume pornography is likely to be ignored. Celia R Daileader (1997, p. 78) warns that 'we cannot ignore the fact that there are women porn viewers, some of who resent anti-porn feminists'. Through their focus on the harms of pornography, anti-pornography feminists have less to say about how consumption of pornography is part of some women's lives. Similarly, Ellen Willis (1993, p. 352) argues that whilst pornography may negatively represent women, they are 'adept at shaping male fantasies for their own purposes'. This hints at the possibility for women to negotiate their relationship to pornography in ways that can be empowering. Now that this chapter has provided an overview of the ways in which feminists responded to pornography, it will now go on to discuss how pornography and sex work were represented in *Spare Rib* and *Ms*.

SPARE RIB AND *MS.* AND REPRESENTATIONS OF PORNOGRAPHY AND SEX WORK

The content analysis included articles discussing the following:

- Pornography
- Sex work
- The sex industry more generally, including discussion of sex shops and toys
- Sadomasochism

There was relatively little discussion of pornography in either magazine, especially in comparison to other issues discussed in this book (table 4.1).

Table 4.1. Discussions of Pornography and Sex Work in *Spare Rib* and *Ms.*

	1972	1977	1982	1987	1992	Total number of articles in sample
Total number of articles in *Spare Rib*	54	75	79	89	90	387
Number of articles in *Spare Rib* about pornography and the politics of sex	5	3	10	6	4	28
% of total	**9.26**	**4**	**12.66**	**6.74**	**4.44**	**7.24**
Total number of articles *Ms.*	68	121	82	134	15	420
Number of articles in *Ms.* on pornography and the politics of sex	0	3	3	1	0	7
% of total	**0**	**2.48**	**3.66**	**0.75**	**0**	**1.66**

In *Spare Rib* there was an increase in discussions in 1982 compared to the rest of the years. The year 1981 saw the publication of Andrea Dworkin's *Pornography: Men Possessing Women*, and this may have been reflected in an increase in discussion of pornography within feminist media.

There was significantly less discussion of pornography in *Ms.* This is surprising since key figures in the anti-pornography movement were American, and campaigns to legislate against pornography mainly occurred in the United States. Gloria Steinem, founder of *Ms.* and a writer in the magazine, throughout the sample was involved in supporting Linda Lovelace after she wrote the book *Ordeal* (1980), uncovering the abuse she suffered during the making of the famous pornographic film *Deep Throat* (1972). Given this, one may assume that there would have been more discussions of pornography than there were (Steinem, 2012). The discrepancy between the actual prevalence of discussion and the perceived ubiquity of the issue is important to consider for two reasons. Firstly, if we assume that the issue was as prevalent than has been historicised, it is important to consider why this is not reflected in *Spare Rib* and *Ms.* to an extent that reflects this. Conversely, if the lack of representation of the issue in the magazines reflects a lack of concern about the issue more broadly, it would be good to question its prevalence in histories of feminism. This chapter will explore the representation of the issue in *Spare Rib* and *Ms.* through an analysis of articles on pornography and letters from the magazines from readers.

REPRESENTATION OF PORNOGRAPHY IN *SPARE RIB*

Five articles from 1972 discussed sex and the sex industry. Although Hunter (2006, p. 16) argues that the 'core of the feminist debate' began in 1976, it was an issue before then. However, in 1972 pornography was not presented as an issue that was particularly important or one that needed combatting. Even when there was a discussion of pornography it was not seen as damaging as when it was portrayed in later discussions. In 'The Aftermath of the Bosom Boom' (Phillips, July 1972, p. 32) there is a description of the 'pictures outside blue movie houses and in the centre of *Playboy*' but there is no detailed analysis of the effect of pornography on women. The article considers 'why . . . most women [are] so worried about the size and the shapes of their breasts' (p. 32), but pornography is cited as only one reason for this alongside others, including Hollywood and modern fashion. Though the article acknowledges that pornography may have an impact on women's self-esteem, it is suggested as one possibility amongst others.

In contrast, Ruth Wallsgrove's 'Pornography: Between the Devil and the True Blue Whitehouse' (December 1977) looks at the specific impact of pornography on women and highlights some of the debates around pornography's harms. The article provides a nuanced understanding of the issue, alongside an acknowledgement of the extent to which anti-pornography arguments have been co-opted by the right. This contrasts with the 'polarized debate' described by Mennel (2010, p. 255). In 'Pornography: Between the Devil and the True Blue Whitehouse', ambivalence is expressed because of the extent to which anti-pornography arguments reproduced restrictive ideas about female sexuality. The article begins with Wallsgrove stating that she finds 'pornography disturbing, chilling, even sometimes physically disgusting' (p. 44). However, though an anti-pornography position is expressed, Wallsgrove also notes that she sees 'a distance between [her] reactions to pornography and the debates carried out in the press about it' (p. 44). These are not the debates within feminism in response to the work of feminists such as Dworkin and MacKinnon, but instead are the debates within the mainstream press from campaigners such as Mary Whitehouse, who seem 'as opposed to what [Wallsgrove] wants for the world as to pornographers' (p. 44). Wallsgrove's distancing from conservative anti-pornography arguments suggests that even though she may be personally opposed to pornography, she is unwilling to associate herself with conservative activists.

Although Wallsgrove expresses ambivalence about how anti-pornography arguments are co-opted by the right, her argument uses anti-pornography discourse through the suggestion that it is 'more to do with power and violence' than sex (p. 44). She states that she 'like[s] to be sexually aroused but [she doesn't] like pictures of women handcuffed, submissive and inviting the reader to be brutal with them' (p. 44). The association of pornography with male domination was argued by prominent anti-pornography feminists such as Andrea Dworkin (1981) and Catharine MacKinnon (1985). The linguistic linking of sex and power can also be seen in a title of an article by Gloria Steinem in 1977 which describes pornography as an 'absurd abuse of power'

(August 1977, p. 43). Since both articles were published in 1977, this suggests that there was an understanding of pornography's relationship between sex and power in both the United States and the United Kingdom at that time.

Wallsgrove's article does not acknowledge the ways in which some women may themselves use pornography, and as Willis (1993) argues, women may subvert masculinist perceptions of sexuality for their own purposes. Wallsgrove states that 'men must be pretty sick to enjoy fantasising about hurting another human being' ignoring that there is a difference between fantasy and reality, and that women are also consumers of pornography. Although Wallsgrove points that 'perhaps porn is only fantasy; perhaps men do not act on it' (p. 44), the use of 'perhaps' suggests that she is unconvinced. Whilst Wallsgrove acknowledges that 'incidence of rape seems unaffected by trends in pornography' (p. 44), this is then undermined in the assertion that pornography and rape are 'linked in spirit' (p. 44), echoing the arguments of anti-pornography feminists such as Dworkin, Morgan and MacKinnon.

Despite this, the article is ambivalent about the ways in which opposition to pornography has been used by the right to oppress women and LGBT people. Wallsgrove addresses this ambivalence by distancing herself from campaigners such as Mary Whitehouse, who focuses her attacks on 'things that are not to my mind pornographic at all' (p. 45). As an example, Wallsgrove points to the fact Mary Whitehouse was responsible for *Gay News* being banned for blasphemy, whilst stating that right-wing campaigners such as Whitehouse aim to ban 'things that are trying to question or change society's view of women and sex' (p. 46). Wallsgrove articulates an anti-pornography argument but is aware that one of the 'dangers of legislating against pornography' is that such legislation will be used to police any representation of sexuality that falls outside the mainstream (p. 46). The risks of co-option by the right has been emphasised by feminist scholars such as Rubin (1984, p. 26), who argues that 'the right wing opposes pornography and has already adopted elements of feminist anti-porn rhetoric'. This suggests that there was a danger that the other differences between right wing anti-pornographers and feminist anti-pornography activists would be underestimated by a seeming alliance between the two groups on the issue of pornography.

This idea has been further explored by Strub (2011, p. 336), who describes the relationship between feminism and conservatives as a 'marriage of convenience' given that the anti-pornography movement had greater resources if feminist and conservative activists could work together on the issue. Whilst Strub (2010) is writing in a US context, Ellis et al. (1990, p. 15) state that this was an issue in the United Kingdom as well. Wallsgrove's reference to Mary Whitehouse shows awareness that this is a possibility since Whitehouse represents conservative attitudes towards representations of female sexuality in the media.

Feminists Against Censorship (1991) led a campaign against what they saw as the censorious aims of anti-pornography feminists. They note that prosecutions for obscenity were associated with homophobia, since it was gay publishers and retailers who bore the brunt of state of state intervention. Wallsgrove (December 1977, p. 46) similarly expresses unease at how expressions of female or LGBT sexuality have been the targets of censorship by the right, using the example of *Spare Rib* being banned in Ireland for being '"frequently indecent or obscene"' for demonstrating to women how to check their breasts for signs of cancer. Wallsgrove ultimately argues that we should 'not agitate for more laws against pornography' (p. 46). The article demonstrates the tension between objecting to pornography because of its representation of women, whilst on the other hand understanding the potential harms of censorship. This suggests that being anti-censorship is not the same as being pro-pornography. Wallsgrove instead argues for an alternative course of action, one where women protest and campaign against newsagents that stock pornography.

However, the advocacy towards protest is juxtaposed against the use of explicit pornographic images in the article itself, including sadomasochistic imagery and pictures of women masturbating. Whilst the argument can be made that the use of such images shows the reality of pornography and does not sanitise the ways that the images objectify women, they seem jarring in the context of *Spare Rib*, especially in an article where the author states that she finds pornography repulsive. Boyle (2000) discusses how pornographic images are used to support anti-pornography arguments, suggesting that such images are taken out of their original context. This is clearly how such images are being used in Wallsgrove's article. However, if pornography is understood as fundamentally exploitative, the article further exploits the women involved in the images through their reproduction. A similar criticism was made about the August 1977 *Ms.* pornography issue where the cover uses an image of a seemingly underage girl in an image that whilst not explicit was at the same time suggestive. Letter writers criticised the double standard to critiquing pornography, and child pornography in particular, whilst at the same time utilising such images (*Ms.* December 1977, pp. 6–7).

Wallsgrove's article demonstrates the tension between viewing pornography as harmful and not wanting to cooperate with censorship efforts that potentially limit representations of women's sexuality. *Spare Rib* was less likely to view pornography and the sex industry as something that needs to be legislated against. Other articles such as Sherri Krynski's 'Sex Objects' (March 1982, p. 6) see the benefits of expressions of female sexuality. In this article Krynski points to the ways in which women-centred sex shops may help a woman in 'claiming power over other parts of her life' through the expression of her sexuality. This can be understood within the context of

Duggan's (2006, p. 56) argument that pornography 'serves some social functions which benefit women' and is contrasted with a feminist position that does not see any benefit to women from pornography and the sex industry. This suggests that *Spare Rib* did not just position itself as anti-pornography but presented a range of views on the issue.

SPARE RIB AND THE DISCUSSION OF PORNOGRAPHY IN THE 1980S

The analysis of 'Pornography: Between the Devil and the True Blue Whitehouse' shows that *Spare Rib* recognised the ambivalence towards pornography and measures taken to control it. By 1982, the sense that pornography was an issue with conflicting opinions had become more prevalent, and this can be seen in the June 1982 article 'What Is Pornography?: Two Opposing Feminist Viewpoints'. The debate format is used, suggesting that there is no definitive right or wrong and both sides are given equal space to make their case. The article was published in 1982, a year after Andrea Dworkin's book *Pornography*, so at a time when pornography was prominent. It begins by acknowledging the 'considerable and often heated discussion throughout the women's liberation movement about the cause, effect and meaning of pornography' (p. 52). The statement that the article will present 'two very different viewpoints' (p. 52) reinforces the sense that this is a highly contentious discussion.

The article shows the awareness of the risks of censorship enabling the right and questions the extent to which pornography needs to be treated any differently than any other cause of women's oppression. Journalist Ros Coward, whilst not necessarily pro-pornography, argues that she doesn't 'think that pornography is in and of itself violence against women' (p. 52). Coward argues that the pornography industry 'thrives on being thought illicit' (p. 52), and this suggests that censorship could have the unintended consequence of making pornography more attractive because it is taboo. Coward questions the extent to which we can even define pornography in the first place. She argues that 'our definition of what is pornographic changes over historical periods', so that what would have been considered pornographic previously is not today (p. 52). However, Coward argues that whilst society's definition of what pornographic is fluid and 'any explicit description and detail of sexual activity', regardless of the context can be viewed as pornographic (p. 52). This means that even well-intentioned education texts such as *Our Bodies Ourselves* (1973) could be viewed as pornography (Hunter, 2006, p. 37). This reinforces the idea that pornography is to some extent in the eye of the beholder and that legislation against pornography risks legislating against representations of female sexuality that celebrate it. This idea is further emphasised by Coward's (June 1982, p. 52) statement:

> Notions of respectability, decency and reasonable display are connected with the form of sexual relations endorsed by our society that is the heterosexually dependent unit, usually the family. What would offend this unit would be considered indecent. *There is no understanding of how one group – women – might be degraded.* (Emphasis in original)

This again reinforces the argument that although pornographic images reinforce patriarchal ideas about women, what is considered pornographic is influenced by the patriarchy. It is likely that what is considered indecent is that which is likely to disrupt heteronormative notions of the nuclear family. As with Wallsgrove's article, the concern that anti-pornography feminism will be co-opted by conservatism can be seen.

The second part of Coward's argument questions the extent to which 'pornography' can be 'in and of itself violence against women' since 'no representations have intrinsic value' (p. 52). Coward argues that pornographic images must be seen within a wider context of harmful representations of women. This can be linked back to the article discussed at the beginning of this chapter 'Aftermath of the Bosom Boom' (July 1972), where pornography was viewed as one harm of many because of the ways it perpetuates narrow beauty standards and not necessarily because it involves images of sex. Coward suggests that it is not pornography as such which feminists find offensive but is instead 'the *form* in which sexuality is shown in pornography' (p. 52). By linking the offensiveness to the content of mainstream pornography, rather than pornography as a form more generally, Coward can consider the opportunity for pornography to exist as a feminist art form. Furthermore, Coward argues that we should 'stop setting up pornography as a separate problem, as self-contained rather than as a manifestation of sexuality in our society' (p. 52). Pornography is seen as symptomatic rather than causative, meaning that pornography is not understood as inherently harmful. It instead reflects harmful views of sexuality because it reinforces the male gaze (Mulvey, 1989) that can be seen in all aspects of the media. A similar argument has been put forth by Duggan (2006, p. 52), who asks the question 'why is sexual explicitness singled out as the cause of women's oppression?'

Coward critiques the legislative agenda of campaigners such as Mary Whitehouse, similarly to Wallsgrove in her 1977 article. Both articles view Whitehouse as 'reactionary' (Coward, June 1982, p. 53) and express concern that feminist principles will not be incorporated into the campaigns influenced by conservatives such as Whitehouse. Coward proposes that 'it might be productive to think about anti-sexist legislation like that proposed by the socialist government in France' (p. 54). This would involve 'clauses prohibiting the use of images or language considered degrading to women'. Coward acknowledges it would be 'difficult' to enforce; she argues that 'it would be a propaganda idea for feminism, rather than letting feminism be swamped with, or by, anti-porn, anti-sex moralism' (p. 54). This supports the argument that feminists who disagreed with the anti-pornography feminist position were not necessarily pro-porn but instead were concerned about the extent to which anti-pornography ideas were being co-opted by the right.

Instead of legislating against pornography, Coward states that 'feminists would have to refine our discussions of what is sexist, what is offensive and what is degrading', whilst arguing that 'we need more open, more explicit discussions of sexuality rather than any premature closing of the issue' (p. 54). The invocation that 'anti-sexist legislation' could reduce the number of degrading images of women leads to the same issues that those who more clearly pro-legislation have, since there is the question of how we are to define degradation. Secondly, the focus on degradation ignores the fact that, as anthologies such as Nancy Friday's *My Secret Garden* (1973) attest to, some women are themselves aroused by the idea of being dominated or degraded, and so degradation is not necessarily seen as offensive to those women.

A key difference between *Spare Rib* and *Ms.* is that in *Ms.* the editorial content was much less likely to acknowledge differences in opinion, although these discussions were debated in the letter's pages. As will be discussed later in the chapter, the emotional conflicts between women who fantasised about submissive sex but identified as feminists can be clearly seen, even if the editorial content did not raise such issues.

ANTI-PORNOGRAPHY ARGUMENTS

Women Against Violence Against Women (WAVAW) provide a counterargument to Coward's. They begin with a quotation from Hugh Hefner, owner of *Playboy*: "'these chicks [feminists] are our natural enemy . . . it is time we do battle with them'" (p. 54). This suggests that even as *Playboy* became somewhat socially acceptable, Hefner was still misogynistic and anti-feminist. The first line of the main body of the article states that 'pornography is about power – men's power over women' (p. 54). This echoes the anti-pornography rhetoric asserted by Brownmiller (2013 [1975]), Dworkin (1981) and MacKinnon (1985), who understood pornography as an assertion of male dominance. Anti-pornography feminists argue that women in pornography are portrayed as 'vulnerable, helpless, open, submissive and longing to be violated' (WAVAW, June 198, p. 54). Women's agency is viewed in this article as impossible since the 'sexual act is described as a power struggle in which the man is always dominant. The penis is described as a weapon and penetration is an act of misery' (WAVAW, June 1982, p. 54). Whereas Coward described pornography's harms within a wider cultural context of women's oppression, pornography is presented here as uniquely harmful towards women.

The problems with pornography are reinforced by the suggestion that 'pornography is not a harmless fantasy indulged by a few limp perverts. It is a multi-billion dollar industry' (WAVAW, June 1982, p. 54). The juxtaposition of the 'limp perverts' who are presented as 'harmless' with the 'million-billion dollar' pornography industry reinforces the idea that stereotypes of the pornography consumer as pitiful and impotent (since in this context, 'limp' suggests literal impotence) belie the fact that the industry is big enough to be a threat to women. WAVAW argue that 'it must not be forgotten that real women are used within it' (p. 54). The verb 'used' suggests that the women involved in pornography are not there of their own volition and are objects rather than agents. Pornography is presented in a similar way in *Ms.*, as demonstrated in a 1977 article from Gloria Steinem that will be discussed later in the chapter.

When discussing what can be done to 'fight pornography' the group again position pornography as being something that has 'directly influenced all the images of women'. Pornography is understood as the cause of other negative images in the media, whereas Coward views pornography as symptomatic of sexism that pervades all of society. WAVAW differ in how they would address the issue, suggesting that one action that can be taken would be to picket 'sex shops which sell not only magazines and films but whips chains and bondage gear' (p. 54). Again, this positions any kind of sexual behaviour that involves dominance and submission as problematic, reinforcing Rubin's (1984) argument that opposition to pornography was linked to a more implicit critique of sadomasochism.

WAVAW suggest that opposition to pornography is broadly supported by women since 'women of all races, class and ages have either joined us on the picket or signed our petitions' (p. 55). This positions the anti-pornography argument as a universal one that transcends race, class and age. This is further emphasised in the footnotes to the article which state that though the group 'do not suggest that [they] are speaking for every woman . . . the response of women we talk to, and women who sign petitions and join pickets against porn indicates that most of us oppose it' (p. 55). The suggestion of wide appeal amongst women positions anti-pornography sentiment as a popular opinion and has the effect of placing women who may not agree with them in the minority. Furthermore, the fact that the WAVAW opinion is written by a collective of women, as opposed to Coward's singular perspective, reinforces the idea that being anti-pornography is the majority opinion.

The use of the debate format is what allows for more than one perspective to be articulated. This highlights the way that format influences the kind of arguments that can be seen in the magazine, and in the case of *Spare Rib* shows how the magazine was more likely to provide space for differing opinions than *Ms.* was.

SEX AND VIOLENCE

Lynne Segal's 'Sex and Violence' (February 1987) is emblematic of the ways *Spare Rib* represented the conflicting feelings around the issue of sex. The article begins with the rhetorical question:

> How can feminists challenge the sexual-power relations between women and men? Through the 'orgasmic equality' of sexual liberation? Or through anger at male violence? (p. 40)

Though the article is not a debate like 'What is Pornography: Two Opposing Feminist Viewpoints' (June 1982), the rhetorical questions that Segal asks sets up an opposition between feminists who see the potential for sexual liberation as empowerment and those who focus on the ways in which discourses of sexuality reinforce male dominance. Segal states that:

> [B]y 1975 some feminists in the women's liberation movement, particularly those connected with Women's Aid and Rape Crisis Centres had increasingly more to say on one aspect of men's sexual behaviour: it's coercive and violent manifestations. (p. 40)

This positions male heterosexuality as dangerous, and this perspective can be seen in anti-pornography arguments by writers such as Dworkin (1981) and Brownmiller (2013 [1975]) who critique the dominance of male sexuality more generally as a form of power over women. However, Segal contrasts it with 'other feminists, especially those who had sexual relations with men [who] felt increasingly less able to talk about their own sexual practices and experiences' (p. 40). This again suggests a tension between acknowledging the ways that patriarchal sexuality negatively impacts women and what the policing of desire means for people who feel that their sexual desires are wrong or politically incorrect.

Segal's article is similar to others from *Spare Rib* in that it discusses the conflict between acknowledging how discussions of sex must bear in mind the fact that women enjoy sex, and sometimes that sex can involve being dominated. This is tempered against the fact that this is potentially harmful to women as a class. This can be seen, according to Segal, in the fact that there was, on the one hand, an increased acknowledgement of the importance of female pleasure, but also an acknowledgement that 'women only formed romantic attachments with men because they had no secure sense of themselves' (p. 41). Segal argues for the developing of an:

> Optimistic feminist vision of women's powerful sexuality with the depressing awareness of men's sexual violence towards women and the misogyny and sexism embedded within the imagery and language of heterosexuality, it was almost inevitable that these opposed preoccupations with the sexual would collapse into the idea of opposed sexual natures. (p. 42)

Although Segal is not specifically addressing pornography, pornography was often interlinked with debates around sadomasochism and the way that this is intertwined with heterosexual desire. Brownmiller (2013 [1975]) suggests that from an early age women are conditioned to understand sexuality as being in submission to men. Furthermore, Brownmiller is 'vehemently hostile to suggestions that some known, popular sex fantasies attributed to women are indeed the product of a woman's mind' (p. 480). If it is the case that heterosexual fantasies are governed by male desire, it can be easy to understand how pornographic representations of sexuality are seen as male fantasy, and that the idea that some women might be aroused by pornography is undermined.

Segal argues that the focus on 'men's sexual domination of women' has 'prevented the emergence of women's self-defined sexuality', and this has 'now been formally accepted as the pivot of women's oppression' (p. 43). However, Segal argues that one of the consequences of the focus on the harms of male domination is that some feminists felt accused of involvement in 'incorrect' sexual and personal relationships' (p. 43). This is in contrast to WAVAW's argument that women generally supported anti-pornography activists. One of the consequences of this assumption is that women whose sexual desires either involved the consumption of pornography or were based on fantasies of male dominance were likely to feel marginalised. Throughout the articles that have been discussed in this chapter so far, there is a clear tension between opposing pornography as a form of male violence and acknowledging that some women's desires utilise some the common narratives of pornography. This challenges the notion that women do not consume pornography actively. Contrary to understanding pornography as a polarising issue, *Spare Rib* presented it as a complex issue that could not be polarised. It is important to note that throughout the articles that are discussed in *Spare Rib* the tension described above is highly visible. This is in sharp contrast to the representation of the issue in *Ms*. Although letters in *Ms*. demonstrate that there was some ambivalence present in the magazine, editorial discussions of pornography were more likely to present an anti-pornography perspective. Glick (2000, p. 22) argues that 'it is well known that the pro-sexuality movement emerged as a response to radical and anti-porn feminists'. However, the discussion of pornography and sex in *Spare Rib* was more ambivalent than this and it is difficult to describe most of the articles that have been analysed as fundamentally 'pro-sex' or 'anti-porn'.

FEMINISM AND CENSORSHIP

This chapter has identified how *Spare Rib* did not take a firm stance in the 'sex wars'. The articles analysed so far acknowledged the problems with pornography and dominant representations of sex, whilst also acknowledging how anti-pornography arguments do not always reflect the ways that women's desires may involve these dominant representations.

By 1992 when 'Feminists Against Censorship: or a Campaign for Pornography' was published, anti-pornography feminists such as Andrea Dworkin and Catharine MacKinnon had campaigned to legislate against pornography in the United States as part of a wider feminist campaign against pornography. The article is from the perspective of anti-pornography feminists and critiques the work of Feminists Against Censorship (FAC). The authors reject the idea that concerns around censorship can be understood as an issue of 'freedom', arguing instead that concerns about censorship instead 'shows a shocking naivety about the reality of the pornography industry' (p. 50). The same rhetoric is being used here as with the article from WAVAW from 1982, where pornography's perniciousness is linked to the fact that it is an industry, suggesting an implicit relationship between pornographic representations of women and capitalism. As the next chapter on politics will demonstrate, this is just one example of the ways the magazine became increasingly explicit in its critique of capitalism.

In contrast to the previous articles analysed in this chapter, this article is much less concerned about censorship and is much more polemical in its position. The article undermines FAC, suggesting that viewing pornography as a free choice is an example of a 'Thatcherite economic argument' (p. 50). Thatcher was consistently positioned in opposition to feminism, both in *Spare Rib* and in wider feminist discourses (Bashevkin, 1998). The invocation of Thatcherism therefore serves to question the feminist credentials of FAC. The use of scare quotes around both 'freedom' and 'freedom of speech' within the article further undermines the argument of FAC since it suggests that their claims are questionable. Furthermore, the use of rhetorical questions such as 'What then if anything, is a problem for FAC?' (p. 50) serves as a persuasive device since it begs the questions but provides no space for FAC to respond.

The authors suggest that the emphasis of FAC on censorship of pornography, as opposed to censorship more generally, undermines their legitimacy, questioning, 'why it was . . . that FAC had chosen to defend pornography as a priority' when 'what we need to address is the continuing racism, the frightening rise of fascism, the violence and sexual abuse of women' rather than 'indulge the privileged few who find it sexy' (p. 50). This suggests that FAC have got their priorities wrong and could focus on more worthwhile issues. A significant difference between this article and the 'What Is Pornography? Two Opposing Feminist Viewpoints' from 1982 is that there is no alternative perspective given. Whilst the article from 1982 actively encouraged readers to join in the discussion no such invitation is given in this article. On the one hand this suggests a sense of coherence within the magazine, whilst on the other hand it perhaps means that the voices of readers are given less space within the magazine.

Throughout this chapter I have argued that for the most part there was a tension in *Spare Rib*'s coverage of pornography and sexual politics between acknowledging the harms of pornography with uneasiness with the censoring of female pleasure. It is not possible to identify a hegemonic position within the magazine. *Spare Rib*, which often articulates a view on the issue that cannot be easily positioned as being staunchly anti-pornography but is instead keenly aware of the problems with both sides of the argument. Although Glick (2000) argues that pro-sex or sex-positive feminism is associated with a rejection of anti-pornography feminism in the 1980s, the only article that is unambiguously anti-pornography in the sample is from 1992, where one might have expected a more 'pro-sex' response to anti-pornography feminism. This suggests that the way that pornography has been historicised is not necessarily reflected in the way that the discourses around pornography changed in *Spare Rib*. In comparison to *Spare Rib*, there was even less discussion of the issue in *Ms.* and it is to *Ms.* that this chapter will now turn.

RHETORIC AROUND PORNOGRAPHY IN *MS.*

There were significantly fewer articles about pornography in *Ms.* than in *Spare Rib*, with only 1.66 percent of the total sample (compared to 7.18 percent in *Spare Rib*) about the issue. This is particularly surprising since the United States was the locus of many key campaigns against pornography, such as the Minneapolis Ordinance. Without interviewing the editorial team, it is difficult to speculate why there was not more discussion of pornography in the magazine; however, the magazine's reliance on advertising revenue and its aim to appeal to the mainstream (Erdman Farrell, 2011) may explain the relative paucity of discussions of such a controversial issue. This highlights the extent to which the way that *Ms.* positioned itself in relation to the mainstream potentially had an impact on the extent to which it could discuss sensitive issues such as pornography. However, it is also possible that the paucity of discussion is because, despite historical readings of the issue, it was not something that was of primary concern to the *Ms.* staff or readers. In this chapter I argue that the magazine's editorial content was explicitly anti-pornography, but that letters to the magazine demonstrate some of the tensions inherent in balancing desire and feminist politics.

Where pornography was explicitly discussed in the magazine it was constructed as inherently harmful. Since there was such little discussion of pornography in the magazine that one of the few discussions was about child pornography is significant. Child pornography is undeniably abusive and unequivocally non-consensual. Gloria Steinem's article 'Pornography: Not Sex but the Obscene Use of Power' (August 1977) positions pornography as a form of control in which men assert dominance over women and girls. This statement can be understood in relation to Dworkin's (1981, p. 9) argument that 'the insult pornography offers, invariably to sex, is accomplished in the active subordination of women'. Steinem's article supports this argument, and this is further emphasised by the comparison of child pornography victims who are described as 'even more powerless and without alternatives than the women who are the subjects of most "adult" pornography' (p. 44). The use of the word 'even' is important here, because as well as affirming that children trafficked into pornography are powerless victims because they are unable to consent, it positions adult women involved in pornography as non-consenting, and therefore victims.

Andrea Dworkin (1981, p. xvi) begins *Pornography* with accounts of women involved in pornography, who she states often feel 'ignorant' and 'may not know the value of her human intellect'. The implication is that if she did 'know the value of her human intellect' she would not 'choose' to be involved in pornography in the first place. Participation in pornography is presented as an uninformed choice, and the argument that women do not choose to be involved in pornography is further emphasised through the reference by Dworkin to Linda Marchiano (aka Linda Lovelace). After starring in *Deep Throat* (1972), a pornographic film which had huge mainstream success, Marchiano wrote an autobiography documenting the abuse she suffered at the hands of her former husband, stating 'every time someone watches that film, they are watching me being raped' (Marchiano, quoted in Dworkin, xvi).

Letters sent to the magazine after Steinem's article generally supported the argument that pornography reinforced ideas of female submissiveness. For example, one reader suggests that in adult pornography 'docile and passive poses and facial expressions reinforce the idea of childlike innocence', whilst suggesting that 'child porn seems to be a logical extension of [a] view of male-female relationships' in which 'males are taught to believe that females are more desirable if they are a few years younger, a few inches shorter, a few pounds lighter, a few degrees less educated, less sexually experienced' (*Ms.*, December 1977, p. 5) This supports the idea that pornography is harmful to women because it reinforces stereotypical gender roles that oppress women.

Since pornography was seldom discussed in *Ms.*, it is significant that when it was featured in the magazine it was presented as wholly negative. This can be contrasted sharply with *Spare Rib*. There was a greater scope for arguments that questioned the extent to which pornography could be understood as a unique harm (Coward, 1982) and an acknowledgement of the ways in which women's desires might be incompatible with their feminist values (Segal, 1987). However, pornography in *Ms.* was understood as unsupportable in the only article from the sample years that discusses pornography in depth.

SEX AND PORNOGRAPHY IN LETTERS TO *MS.*

Letters to *Ms.* were an important para-text for debate that was not seen in the editorial content of the magazine. There was an awareness of the ways in which desires might contradict feminist ideals. In Janice Radway's influential study *Reading the Romance* (1984) she describes how feminist readers of romance novels, a form linked to the reproduction of traditional gender roles, reconcile their interest in romance novels and their feminist ideals. A similar theme can be seen in the letters sent to *Ms.* on the issue of sex.

In response to the article 'A Report on the Sex Crisis' (March 1982) readers used the letter page as a forum to express the ambivalence that they feel about their desires. The letters added the opinions of readers to ongoing debates around sex and pornography. The first letter has been chosen because it demonstrates how readers showed nuanced understandings of the issue. This can be contrasted with more recent historicisations of the period (Mennel, 2010 Duggan and Hunter, 2006) that have presented it as a polarised issue. The letter begins with an anonymous reader lamenting the fact that:

> There isn't some sort of erotica that is non-sexist, non-exploitative and gives equal time and validity to the sexuality of both women and men for the pleasure of both women and men. (September 1982, p. 6)

Strub (2011) describes how attitudes towards sex and pornography changed, so that earlier arguments that assumed the possibility of non-sexist pornography gave way to anti-pornography feminism that did not see this as an option. The assumption that second wave feminism was solely anti-pornography 'obscure[s] several years of diverse thought on the topic' (Strub, 2011,

p. 331). The letter writer's statement assumes there are no women attempting to create non-sexist pornography and assumes that all existing pornography and erotica is sexist.

Throughout the letter, feelings of ambivalence are repeated. For example, the letter writer argues that 'there must be some middle ground' in discussions of pornography and erotica, whilst arguing that women must

> dispel the guilt we feel over our own ambivalence and accept that we are all part 'clitorally centred and potentially insatiable' and part 'wimmin holding hands, taking their shirts off, and dancing in a circle'. (September 1982, p. 6)

One critique of anti-pornography feminism was that it failed to acknowledge how women's sexual desires were not necessarily feminist, and that women risked being judged for expressing sexuality that was perceived as incorrect (Daileader, 1997). Two extreme versions of sexuality are presented, with the highly sexualised image of the 'potentially insatiable women' contrasted with the image of 'wimmin holding hands'. The term 'wimmin' alludes to an earnest feminist, whilst the image of women 'holding hands' and 'dancing in a circle' reinforces the stereotype of feminists as de-sexualised.

The issue of the correctness of certain sexual behaviours can be seen in a series of letters from 1983[1] and included in Mary Thom's anthology *Letters to Ms.* The letters discuss the place of sadomasochism within feminism and whether it is possible to be a feminist who enjoys sadomasochism. The first letter is from a woman who introduces herself by identifying as 'a feminist' who 'holds graduate degrees' (p. 16). The letter writer is presented as educated and therefore the fact that she likes to be spanked by her husband is portrayed as a choice not made out of ignorance. Similarly, the letter writer points out that her husband is 'highly educated' and 'has done a great deal in our community towards advancing the rights of women' (p. 16). By referring to both of their educations, and the fact that he is interested in women's rights, the letter writer suggests that being interested in sadomasochism is not necessarily reflective of their opinions outside of the bedroom, or the power relationship between them. Duggan (2006, p. 137) argues that being tied up or spanked can be consensual and 'not particularly sexist'. However, despite professing to be happy with her sexual relationship, the letter writer does wonder if 'in the far recesses of our minds, have male dominance so imprinted that our intellects to the contrary – we need reassurance to the contrary' (p. 16). This suggests that sadomasochistic behaviour is a reassertion of the 'biological differences' (p. 16) between men and women, so that despite beliefs in gender equality, women essentially need to be submissive in the bedroom. This argument relies on gender essentialist arguments that were common in anti-feminist discourse.

In response to the letter described above, a reader describes the 'flood of relief' that she felt as she too enjoyed being spanked by her partner too. However, despite the relief felt by this recognition, there is still a sense of secrecy as the writer admits that 'she can't bring [herself] to sign this letter' (p. 17) and that she finds sharing her desires with her female friends 'impossible' (p. 17). In the editor's introduction to this section of letters, Mary Thom (1987, p. 16) discusses 'sexual orthodoxy' and it is clear that the letter writer feels some embarrassment, or even anxiety from straying from that orthodoxy. The reader expresses her 'shock [which] came not from righteous indignation but from recognition' (p. 17). This clarification suggests that the assumed response to the original reader's letter would be 'righteous indignation', further reinforcing the idea that the assumed response to admitting that you enjoy sadomasochism is one of disapproval. The sense of shame is further reinforced by the fact that the writer of the letter withholds their name, suggesting an unwillingness to make sexual desires that are seen as incorrect public.

The letters that have been discussed so far have been sympathetic to women who enjoy sadomasochism or have been open to the idea of feminist erotica. Other letters disputed the idea that women should willingly enjoy sadomasochism or reinforce the extent to which pornography is harmful to women. In response to readers who express that they enjoy sadomasochism, one reader states that the idea of women enjoying sadomasochism 'gross [es] [her] out' (p. 17). The reader questions the veracity of letters from women who describe themselves as feminists whilst at the same time enjoy being sexually submissive. She describes such women as suffering from 'internalized oppression' (p. 17). It is useful here to relate this letter to Susan Brownmiller's (2013 [1975], p. 481) work, and her assertion that when women profess to enjoy being dominated this is in response to 'male conditioning'. This means women's fantasies and preferences are not necessarily reflections of natural desires, and instead are evidence of women's oppression. The letter articulates this argument in two ways. Firstly, the writer attributes the desires of the women she is critiquing to being oppressed. Secondly, the allusion that the original letter may not be real and instead could be a 'copy of a *Penthouse* fantasy letter' (p. 17) further reinforces the idea that women cannot have these fantasies. By introducing the letter with the phrase 'gross me out' the letter writer suggests she is physically disgusted by the idea that women might find sadomasochism desirable.

The idea that women who enjoy sadomasochism should not enjoy such activities is seen in another letter from a reader who argues that a woman who enjoys being spanked can call herself a feminist but 'that doesn't make her one' (p. 19). This suggests that personal desires can undermine your political identity as a feminist. Furthermore, the letter writer suggests that the woman 'needs to read Andrea Dworkin's book *Pornography*', gesturing towards the extent to which Dworkin's work was becoming influential. This is contrasted by a letter which suggests that 'being a woman is tough enough without having to worry whether our sexual impulses are "politically correct"' (p. 17). This rejects the idea that women necessarily have much control over their impulses and opens the question as to whether or not stigmatising women who have sexual desires that are not 'politically correct' does in fact cause more harm to women.

Whilst there was relatively little discussion of pornography and the politics on sex within the *Ms.* sample, the letters to the magazine demonstrate that this was an issue that concerned *Ms.* readers. An analysis of the letters to *Ms.* shows the ambivalence inherent in the issue, and this is a microcosm of the wider debates that were circulating within the feminist movement. Although there was little discussion of pornography in *Ms.* the letters show that this was an issue that readers were passionate about. This shows the importance of reading the para-text of the magazine, since the letters show discussions not fully explored in the magazine's articles.

CONCLUSION

Spare Rib and *Ms.* both showed ambivalence towards pornography, but in differing ways. In *Ms.* the editorial content of the magazine was predominantly anti-pornography and there was less room for debates around pornography. Where pornography was discussed the focus was on child pornography which is indisputably harmful and morally repugnant. In contrast, *Spare Rib* was more likely to present conflicting perspectives using the debate format. Furthermore, even in places where an anti-pornography argument was propagated, there was still complexity in the way in which the issue was understood. This is important because it suggests that the issue was more complex than has been recounted in historical accounts, demonstrating the importance of looking at primary materials, and not just relying on historicisations. This is a key argument of this book.

In *Ms.* nuance on the issue was much more likely to be seen in the letters to the editor. This highlights the importance of looking beyond the editorial material in order to understand the discourses that were present in the magazine. Strub (2011) argues that the dominance that anti-pornography feminism has had in defining the feminist position has meant that the extent to which pornography and sex were often issues that were contentious and contradictory has been ignored. However, whilst the only article from *Ms.* which substantially discusses pornography is very clearly against it, there was more ambivalence when discussing the relationship between sadomasochism and feminism. Furthermore, in the case of *Ms.* the letter pages provided a space for women to be open about their sexuality, though the backlash against this from other readers suggests that this was not necessarily a non-judgemental space. This is significant because it demonstrates the ways in which para-textual elements of the magazine such as letters complicate the representation of pornography or sadomasochism and suggests that readers are not necessarily as unequivocal about the issue as the editorial staff.

NOTE

1. Although the content analysis included articles that discussed the sex industry broadly, the chapter will focus on pornography.

Chapter 5

Political Engagement in *Spare Rib* and *Ms.*

The final chapter in the first part of the book explores the relationship between *Spare Rib* and *Ms.* and politics. Although feminism is inherently political, this chapter will explore specifically the way that the magazines engaged with what we might describe as politics with a capital 'P'. The differing political contexts between British and American feminisms need to be considered when establishing how *Spare Rib* and *Ms.* represented the feminist movement, especially since, as has been shown in previous chapters, differing relationships to capitalism impacted the representation of the state as well. In this chapter I will explore exactly how *Spare Rib* and *Ms.* engaged with mainstream politics, and how the differences between the two represent the ideological and geographical differences between the two magazines. *Ms.* was much more likely to engage with mainstream party politics and expect this engagement to lead to change. In contrast, *Spare Rib* was suspicious of politicians and showed less willingness to engage with them.

This chapter begins in the 1970s, before moving on to discuss the impact of Thatcherism and Reaganism on *Spare Rib* and *Ms.* Both magazines rejected right-wing politics, though *Spare Rib* was much more explicit in its rejection of neoliberalism. *Ms.* promoted the more ostensibly apolitical aspects of neoliberalism and post-feminist discourses, with a focus on individual success that meant that rejections of neoliberalism were harder to identify.

The content analysis included articles that discussed the following:

1. Engagements and critiques of state politics (e.g. discussion of parliament or congress, laws) (table 5.1).
2. Discussions of the Backlash, Neoliberalism and Post-feminism (table 5.2).

Table 5.1.   Discussions of Politics in *Spare Rib* and *Ms.*

Year	1972	1977	1982	1987	1992	Total number of articles in the sample
Total number of articles *Spare Rib*	54	75	79	89	90	387
Number of articles discussing politics in *Spare Rib*	10	18	11	16	17	72
% of total	**18.52**	**24**	**13.92**	**17.98**	**18.89**	**18.60**
Total number of articles *Ms.*	68	121	82	134	15	420
Number of articles discussing politics in *Ms.*	7	10	13	6	0	36
% of total	**10.29**	**8.26**	**15.85**	**4.48**	**0**	**8.57**

Table 5.2.   Discussions of the Backlash in *Spare Rib* and *Ms.*

Year	1972	1977	1982	1987	1992	Total number of articles in the sample
Total number of articles *Spare Rib*	54	75	79	89	90	387
Number of articles discussing the backlash in *Spare Rib*	0	0	1	3	2	6
% of total	**0**	**0**	**1.27**	**3.37**	**2.22**	**1.55**
Total number of articles *Ms.*	68	121	82	134	15	420
Number of articles discussing the backlash in *Ms.*	1	1	1	1	0	5
% of total	**1.45**	**0.83**	**1.21**	**0.75**	**0**	**0.95**

Although there was discussion of politics throughout the sample, it is useful to point out times where there was an increase in discussions. In 1982, for example, there was an increase in discussion of politics in *Ms.* and this was also the year of the deadline for ratification of the ERA. This chapter will analyse how *Ms.* campaigned for the ERA. The ERA was passed by congress in 1972 and then sent to be ratified by stage legislators. This chapter will explore the role *Ms.* played in lobbying for the ERA. *Ms.* provided a space for feminists to express their feelings and latterly their regrets when it was clear the amendment was not going to pass.[1] The coverage of the ERA is emblematic of how the magazine engaged with mainstream politics and exemplified liberal values of working within current systems rather than attempting to overthrown them.

In contrast, *Spare Rib* had a more hostile attitude towards politicians and government. The magazine included more political coverage than *Ms.* and this coverage was more likely to critique mainstream politics from an 'outsider' perspective. This intensified in the Thatcher years. A sharp contrast can be seen between *Ms.*'s fundamental faith in the political system and *Spare Rib*'s resistance to it; this reflects a difference in how British and American feminists understood their relationship to the state and this is linked to how each country's feminists organised themselves. American feminism coalesced around large and influential organisations such as the National Organization for Women (NOW); British feminists were much more likely to eschew organised groups (Gelb, 1989).

In the latter part of the chapter, I discuss how *Spare Rib* and *Ms.* approached the backlash against feminism in the 1980s. Though there were relatively few articles about the backlash in either *Spare Rib* or *Ms.*, the ones that were included were rich in quality. They help to identify why the backlash can be understood as highly ideological. The rise of neo-conservatism in the United States and organisations such as Phyllis Schlafly's Eagle forum were understood as a threat to feminism by *Ms.*, as the analysis of articles in this chapter will demonstrate. However, despite being highly critical of how feminism was being presented within the mass media as irrelevant, the magazine was amenable to some aspects of post-feminism, particularly the focus on individual success. The key tension in *Ms.* was between the desire, on the one hand to remain relevant to advertisers and readers, whilst also carrying a strong feminist message. *Spare Rib*'s reaction to Thatcherism and the rise of the right in the United Kingdom was different. The magazine became more explicit in its rejection of capitalism and as the magazine's staff became more diverse, the magazine moved towards a post-colonialist feminism that questioned the dominance of Western political institutions. Since this was happening at a time when post-feminist ideas were assumed to be prevalent this is significant since it counters the idea that feminism had wholesale become increasingly amenable to post-feminist ideas.

THEORISING THE STATE: THE STATE AND FEMINISM IN THE UNITED STATES AND THE UNITED KINGDOM

In order to contextualise the representation of the state in *Spare Rib* and *Ms.* it is important to outline the ways that feminists have theorised the state. There has been ambivalence about the relationship feminists should have with state institutions. Waylen (2012, p. 4) describes that state as 'empowering for women' but others have theorised it as a means of control (Rowbotham, 1989). MacKinnon (1989, p. 157) questions the extent to which feminists have engaged with the state at all, arguing that 'feminism has no theory of the state'. In the introduction to *The New Women's Movement*, Drude Dahlerup (1986, p. 15) suggests:

In some countries, notably the USA, the movement directly addresses political decisions makers. In most other countries, its influence on the political system has been exercised indirectly by 'the strength of being outside'.

Gelb (1986, p. 105) points to the fact that whilst in the United States lobbying can be a successful way to effect change, in the United Kingdom 'grass roots lobbying . . . has little impact in a system so centralized'. As this chapter will show, although the ERA was ultimately unsuccessful, it mobilised feminists in a way that no British campaign did. Furthermore Gelb (1986, p. 109) argues that there was an 'ambivalence about lobbying in Britain, and that the 'major locus of activity is the small local group'. In contrast to the United Kingdom's small group approach, Sapiro (1986, p. 221) states that organisations such as the National Organization for Women were 'particularly active in pursuing legal changes in the status of women' through lobbying. Furthermore, she states that 'feminist organizations have become increasingly active in electoral campaigns' (Sapiro, 1986, p. 221). This focus on mainstream politics as locus of change can be seen in *Ms.* and is correspondently lacking in *Spare Rib*.

THE EQUAL RIGHTS AMENDMENT

Ms. featured a number of articles that campaigned for the ratification of the ERA, including 'A Mormon Connection?: The Defeat of the ERA in Nevada' (July 1977), 'Alice Paul: Mother of the ERA' (October 1977) and 'Is God for the ERA?' (May 1982), as well as the articles that will be analysed in this chapter. The ERA was first proposed by Alice Paul, founder of the National Women's Party in 1923 (Adams and Keene, 2007). It states:

1. Equality of rights under the law should not be denied or abridged by the United States or by any state on the account of sex. (*ERA*, n.d).

The legislation was first proposed in 1923 but it was not ratified. It was not debated again a legislative context until the 1970s, leading Freeman (1975, p. 64) to describe it as 'the best kept government secret of the century' since it had fell off the radar of political discussion when it was not ratified first time round. In 1972 the ERA was reintroduced and passed by congress. It then needed to be approved by 38 states (75 percent of states) to be ratified (*ERA*, n.d). The battle for ratification became a key concern for the women's movement in the United States and political discussion in *Ms.* often focused on the ERA.

MS. AND THE ERA

Ms.'s first issue was in 1972, the same year that the ERA was sent out to be ratified. The ERA featured heavily in *Ms.* in the next ten years and there were a number of articles that informed readers of what they could do to ensure that their state ratified the ERA and informed them of what was happening nationwide. As it became clearer that the ERA was not going to be ratified, the magazine provided space to discuss what had happened and what would happen next.

In 1972 there was only one article on the ERA. This is perhaps surprising given that the amendment was being debated in Congress. There were articles about politics, but these focused on the upcoming presidential election between Democrat George McGovern and Republican Richard Nixon ('Women Voters Can't Be Trusted', July 1972; 'Memo for Election Day, November 1972). Ann Scott's 'Equal Rights Amendment: What's in It for You?' (July 1972) asked what the ERA would do for women and there is an implicit assumption that the ERA would be ratified. This is reinforced in the article where Scott describes the amendment as 'something – an enormous something – that women in this country did for themselves, with little help' (p. 82). The optimistic tone of the article and the emphasis on what has already been achieved assumes that congressional passage was the biggest barrier. This is reinforced by the statement that 'ratification by mid-1973 looks probable, but not easy' (p. 82). Although Scott acknowledges the potential difficulty in ratification, it is assumed that it will not take even half of the amount of time given, suggesting a level of confidence and optimism that was to be undermined in future years.

Scott argues that 'all of us, men and women, must lobby for it' (p. 82). However, the ERA was not just opposed in the early stages by those on the right but by other feminists as well. In 1970, before the amendment was ratified, Robin Morgan (1970, p. 92) urged readers to:

> refuse to support an Equal Rights Amendment which would have (1) thrown away any protective labor legislation (2) made it more difficult for women to get alimony (i.e. reparations for unpaid labor) (3) made eligible for the draft.

Ms.'s coverage of the ERA is, by contrast, universally supportive and there is no discussion of the potential disadvantages of the legislation, ignoring the criticism of the ERA that was being circulated within the mainstream press (Mendes, 2011). If *Ms.* is to be understood as the paper of record for American second wave feminism (Erdman Farrell, 1998), it would be more difficult for feminist criticisms of the ERA to circulate because it is only ever viewed in positive terms.

As it became clear that the ERA was going to take longer to be ratified than had been anticipated, *Ms.* approached the topic differently. In 1972 the focus was on why women should support the ERA, with an underlying assumption that it would be ratified, but by 1977 the focus had changed to reflect doubts about the likelihood of it passing. 'Equal Rights Amendment: Back to Basics for This Year's Fight' (Peratis and Ross, January 1977) reflects this change. The ERA is now presented as a battle that needs to be won and ratification is not viewed as a foregone conclusion; by 1977 the original deadline for ratification was approaching and the ERA had still not been ratified by the required number of states.

Another tactic that can be seen in 1977 but was missing from 1972 coverage was the use of celebrity endorsement to encourage campaigning. The use of celebrity in broadening feminism's appeal will be discussed later in this book in a contemporary context' however, its use in 1977 suggests that this is not a new phenomenon. 'Guess Who's For the ERA? Mary Kay Place and Bruce Solomon' demonstrates this (Wheeler, 1977). The halting progress of the ERA signified the increased danger from the right. Although neo-conservatism has been historicised as a threat to feminism in the 1980s (Faludi, 1991), by 1977 *Ms.* had begun to understand how anti-feminist discourse was being used to undermine feminist gains. In 'Guess Who Is for the ERA' the ERA is presented as a populist common sense cause. The use of actors Bruce Solomon and Mary Kay Place from the television show *Mary Hartman, Mary Hartman* draws upon the influence of celebrity to suggest that the ERA should have a similar mass appeal. Solomon states that 'as a child, I had always assumed that women were equal' (p. 78). Women's equality is presented as an obvious belief. This is particularly importance since many anti-ERA arguments focused on the idea that he ERA would subvert "natural" gender roles that assumed female submissiveness and domesticity (Foss, 1979). The common-sense necessity of the ERA is further reinforced by Place's statement that she supports the ERA because 'she believes in equality for all' (p. 79).

Supporting the ERA is presented as reasonable, and the common sense position to take. However, by addressing the campaign at a national, rather than local level, *Ms.* ignores how local level activism was being used to defeat the amendment at state level. This speaks to the difficulty for a national magazine such as *Ms* to address local issues. It had to address a national audience that comprised of states where the ERA had been ratified, and places where the ERA was either very unlikely to be ratified in the first place, or where ratification could not be guaranteed. Although *Ms.* attempted to appeal to a general audience, Critchlow and Stachecki (2008, p. 159) argue the problem was that 'ERA proponents failed to organize their supporters at the grass roots level' and this was something that *Ms.* would find difficult since it was a national magazine. Given that the audience of the magazine covers several grass roots constituencies across the United States, it is difficult to see how the magazine could mobilise in the same way that campaigns at the local level did. In addition to this, the failure of the ERA in spite of the mobilisation of celebrity suggests that this is a strategy that has limited success. The debate around the usefulness of celebrity in presenting a mainstream feminism will be elaborated on further in later chapters.

MS. AND THE RIGHT

The strong opposition to the ERA from the right marked the beginning of an increased backlash against feminism. Faludi (1991, p. 12) describes an 'attempt to retract the handful of small and hard-won victories that the women's movement did win for women'. This was alongside neoliberal conservatism that gained traction in the 1980s. Harvey (2007, p. 2) describes neoliberalism as:

> A theory of political economic practices that proposes that human wellbeing can best be advanced by liberating individual entrepreneurial freedoms and skills within an institutional framework characterized by strong private property rights, free markets and free trade.

Harvey (2007, p. 49) argues that the Republicans, alongside adopting neo-liberalism in the 1980s also 'sought an alliance with the Christian right' to increase its base, leading to focus on the individual, combined with what Gilheany (1998, p. 60) describes as an attempt to 'roll back the gains of feminism' by the American Right. *Ms.* engaged with the rise of the right, partly through taking a more individualistic approach to feminism, but also through challenging the right. This contrasts with Faludi's (1991, p. 134) argument that *Ms.* 'retreat[ed]' in response to the backlash. This is a simplistic reading that ignores the negotiations that the magazine made between remaining relevant in a new cultural landscape and challenging the rightward turn of US politics.

Throughout the 1980s the magazine made several attempts to challenge the stranglehold that the right had on American politics and society by specifically addressing how the New Right was curtailing women's rights. However, alongside this, articles also emphasised liberal feminist values such as an emphasis on female empowerment and women in high profile roles (for example January 1987 included profiles of prominent female figures including Dolly Parton and Margaret Atwood). This suggests an individualised understanding of success which fits neatly into a neoliberal framework.

The increased focus on entrepreneurship and business success is evident in articles such as 'Entrepreneurs: Making a Healthy Business of Fitness' (April 1987) and 'Careers: Executive Assistants: Is There Power Behind the Throne?' (October 1987). The magazine critiqued neoliberalism whilst also being enmeshed in it, as the analysis in this chapter will demonstrate.

MS. AND NEOLIBERAL FEMINISM

The September 1972 'Women and Power' issue is a good example of how *Ms.* presented a neoliberal feminism that emphasised female empowerment within capitalism. The front cover features Loretta Swit, a white television actress and the subject of the issue's feature interview. The issue features interviews with '12 high-power women' (p. 41). Celebrity is used differently in this case than in 'Guess Who's for the ERA' (April 1977). Whereas in that article celebrities were presented as relatable, in contrast Swit is presented as an example of female power that is not achievable for most women. On the cover image, Swit is holding a large electric switch with the word 'Power' lit up behind her. This alludes to the idea of having your name up in lights, further reinforcing the link between power and celebrity. Swit is wearing a suit, locating power within the business world and the private sphere. As a composite image, the front cover presents power as measured by personal success in a prestigious and exclusive industry. Since Swit is the only person on the cover, power is further constructed as an individual phenomenon. This can be linked to the de-politicisation of feminism. Dean (2010, p. 391) argues that domesticated feminism is the 'explicit or implicit affirmation of a safe, unthreatening form of feminism via a disavowal of a more radical feminism position'. In the *Ms.* Power issue, power is framed as an individual endeavour and not something systemic.

Dean (2010, p. 398) describes how feminism has been de-politicised through the:

> Tendency to seek to broaden the appeal of feminism by discursively linking it to relatively uncontroversial notions such as individual agency and a critique of 'stereotypes'.

The emphasis on individual power is reinforced in the articles throughout the 'Women in Power Issue'. The issue includes a quiz similar to those in popular women's magazines such as *Cosmopolitan*. In the quiz 'What's Your PQ' Carrol Tarvis (December 1982, p. 49) suggests that readers can find out what their own 'power quotient' is, locating power as an individual phenomenon. Power is described as a 'shifty commodity' suggesting that it is tangible; gained or lost within the capitalist system (p. 49). There is no acknowledgement either in the introduction to the quiz or in the quiz itself of how systemic power structures influence access to power. The questions asked to assume that access to power is available to all women, ignoring the differing ways that women are oppressed due to intersecting oppressions that some women, such as poorer women, disabled women, transgender, lesbian and bisexual women and women of colour, face (Crenshaw, 1989).

The first question in the quiz asks, 'How do you get your own way – or make your way known?' and the responses to this question are:

a. I whine, cry pout or sulk
b. I manipulate, sneak around behind my targets back, inveigle or make what
   I want seem like someone else's idea
c. I shout, yell, threaten or demand
d. I reason calmly, argue my points, inform or insist (p. 49)

The quiz is marked so that the reader is given 'three points for every d answer, two points for every c answer, one point for every b answer and no points for every a answer' (p. 49). The quiz assumes that a woman can change the way she is perceived by others through her own actions. To some extent this may be the case, however this ignores how class, race and sexuality impact on how a woman is perceived. The reader may feel that she is arguing calmly but persistent stereotypes of women as emotional may mean that the listener interprets her actions as 'whiny' and this questionnaire reinforces the idea that typically 'feminine' actions such as showing emotion are negative. This ignores the existence of power relationships between women which mean that, for example, the actions of a white woman will be interpreted differently than if a Black woman is doing the same thing.

Erdman Farrell (2011, p. 398) argues that the emphasis on the ways in which the individual can change their situation through their own actions is linked to 'focus on the transformation of the person' that occurred in *Ms.* in the 1980s. Dean (2010) argues the mainstreaming of feminism is done in part to make feminism more palatable to a mainstream audience. This, according to Dean (2010), can be understood in relation to McRobbie's (2009) argument that feminism is on the one hand part of mainstream discourses, whilst on the other hand this is used as an excuse to decry feminism's redundancy. As Erdman Farrell (2011) explains, for *Ms.* in the 1980s it was important to maintain the balance of mass appeal with a feminist message. A focus on relatively inoffensive ideas such as more individual power helped to ensure that the magazine still had a feminist message but that its content was unlikely to be perceived as overly 'extreme'.

The emphasis on individual success is linked to the need for an affluent audience that would bring in advertising revenue. Erdman Farrell (2011, p. 399) argues that 'the staff emphasised the editorial copy that would simultaneously attract those readers and assure the advertisers that these were the readers they were trying to attract'. However, the consequence of this was that:

> articles that would speak to and about poor women, women in jail, uneducated women and women of colour, all articles the editor had no problem including in the pages – needed to be jettisoned or at least hidden. (p. 399)

The 'Women in Power' issue demonstrates the use of less controversial articles. This is significant because this less controversial, liberal feminism was less likely to challenge capitalism and was therefore limited in the change it could affect. Erdman Farrell (2011, p. 401) argues:

> The editors of *Ms.* walked a narrow tightrope . . . designing a magazine that highlighted the individualistic monied feminism on the front cover while hiding the diverse range of feminist perspectives and well researched studies on the inside.

It is tempting to interpret this as a willing capitulation to capitalism. Faludi (1991, p. 135) criticises *Ms.*', for 'pacifying' advertisers. However, this does not adequately consider the constraints *Ms.* faced. Seeing *Ms.* as capitulating to neoliberalism because of a disavowal of its feminist values fits neatly into a backlash narrative. However, this ignores the complex negotiations that the magazine made to survive within a competitive capitalist market. It is to those complex negotiations that this chapter will now turn.

THE HOSTILE POLITICAL CONTEXT

There was evidence from within the magazine that *Ms.* was aware of the wider hostile political context it was operating within. A 'No Comment' feature for the tenth anniversary issue (July/August 1982, p. 265) illustrates this self-awareness. The 'No Comment' section was a regular feature where readers wrote in with examples of sexist advertising and news coverage. For the tenth anniversary, the section focused on how the women's liberation movement had been derided and declared passé by the mainstream media. Headlines such as 'Requiem for the Women's Movement' (1973), 'Women's Lib Is Dead' (1973) and 'Is Feminism Finished?' suggest that feminism has always been judged in this way, with a continued emphasis on the 'pastness of feminism' (Tasker and Negra, 2007, p. 1) by those who want to discredit it.

The inclusion of these examples in the tenth anniversary issue is a defiant answer to the question of whether feminism is 'finished', since the continued existence of the magazine suggests its ongoing relevance. Using examples from as early as the 1970s reinforces the fact that discussions of feminism's supposed demise are not new, even if 1982 was, as Mendes (2011) argues, the year that the news media started to declare the feminist movement 'dead'. Indeed, throughout *Ms.'* history there was evidence that the magazine was aware of the backlashes against feminism. The review by Barbara Harrison of Midge Decter's *Bible of the Backlash* in 1972 suggests that the term pre-dates its popular usage in the 1980s and 1990s. This is particularly significant since 1972 can be understood as a year of feminist achievements; *Ms.* was successfully launched, the ERA gained congressional passage and Roe vs. Wade was debated by the Supreme Court (and anti-abortion laws would be struck down as unconstitutional in January 1973). Harrison critiques Decter's argument that 'women's liberation has accused [women] of failure' whilst accusing Decter of trivialising the women's liberation movement and suggests that 'Angry voices are being raised against feminism now because it is a social force to be contended with' (p. 32). This provides further evidence that the backlash indeed began before the 1980s, refuting notions it was caused by complacency by feminists, or abeyance.

BURNOUT, NEGATIVE FEMINIST AFFECT IN THE 1980S

Whilst backlash against feminism was not necessarily a new phenomenon, in the 1980s there was an increased focus on the practical and emotional impact of anti-feminist attacks on feminist gains. The regular 'Watch on the Right' feature is evidence of this and tracked threats from the right on women's rights. In a similar vein, 'Burn Out: What Happens when the World won't Change' (May 1982) provides a personal perspective on the disappointment that feminists felt when it became clear that change was not going to be as rapid as expected. The subtitle of the article positions this feeling of burn out because of the world not changing in response to feminist activism. This is an important distinction since it acknowledges continued feminist activism.

The main body of the article does, however, reinforce the idea of a vibrant women's movement in the 1970s, compared to a worn-out feminist movement in the 1980s. Dean (2010, p. 34) argues that the narrative that assumes feminism's demise is predicated on the assumption of a 'genuine radicalism [that] is situated in an imagined "seventies" past and as such has now declined, fragmented and become institutionalised or disappeared altogether'. This means that contemporary feminisms are understood as less politically engaged and less radical since institutionalisation is linked to political conformity. In the article Van Gelder (May 1982, p. 60) describes how at a march in the 1970s she:

> saw a sea of women, *thousands* rather than dozens of us. The effect was electrifying. For the first time in my life I felt like part of a force infinitely larger than myself.

The use of the word 'electrifying' suggests a charge, and that women had power. Van Gelder states that she felt that 'we could change the world' but that 'today I am not so sure'. The optimism of the 1970s has not been carried over to the next decade; this reflects the idea that some feminists became less engaged in the 1980s. However, rather than being presented as something caused by complacency or a post-feminist belief that equality has already been achieved, this demonstrates how emotion impacts of feminists' ability to continue fighting.

Hemmings (2011, p. 22) in her account of the way that feminism has been historicised, describes how the 'past [is] marked by a politicized unity and the present by apolitical individualism'. In Van Gelder's article, the unity of marches is juxtaposed with the individualised affect of the 1980s. Van Gelder describes not being able to 'hack it' and states that 'Reaganomics' make her 'want to quit the human race and become a dolphin' (p. 60). Pessimistic in tone, Van Gelder states that 'these are hard times for feminists' and 'if we lose the Equal Rights Amendment (there I said it) they will get harder' (p. 60). The use of the parentheses around 'there I said it' suggests that Van Gelder has been attempting to remain positive but cannot continue to do so. This is further emphasised by the fear that in voicing concerns she will be '"playing into the hands of the Right as I write this"' (Van Gelder, May 1982, p. 60). This demonstrates the difficulty of acknowledging problems within the women's movement without providing political ammunition for anti-feminists who are likely to use this acknowledgement as evidence that feminism is in decline.

Van Gelder (May 1982, p. 60) states that 'for those of us who see feminism as an *identity* as well as an ideology, the problem is as much psychological as political' (Italics in original). This is not as easily conveyed in a backlash narrative that assumes feminism had a less broad base because it has become more individualised (Faludi, 1991). Feminism is presented as at an impasse, since 'too many of us got too accustomed to equating feminism with the majority will' and Van Gelder argues that 'we have to re-evaluate our context and our self-images honestly, even if it hurts' (p. 60). This suggests that the methods previously used by feminists, and the expectations of feminists need to change. However, the pessimism Van Gelder articulates is not post-feminism and does not assume women's equality has already been achieved. This is further emphasised by Van Gelder's (May 1982, p. 62) suggestion that she would like to 'draw a line between fighting back and giving up' whilst recognizing the risk of 'winding up in a body bag stamped "Demoralized by the Moral Majority"' (Van Gelder, 1982, p. 62). There is a tension evident between understanding the emotional impact of navigating a changing political climate and maintaining a defiant stance.

The article also notes the different responses women had to the rise of the right, suggesting that for some it 'galvanized them into renewed action'. This shows that it is too simplistic to view feminist activism in the 1980s as in abeyance. However, the statement that 'the rest of us are finding a variety of ways to pick ourselves up off the floor' suggests the extent to which feminists were being aggressively challenged by the right through legislation such as 'the Family Protection Act', the Human Life Amendment and the teaching of creationism in the public schools' (Van Gelder, 1982, p. 62).

Ms. often found itself in the difficult position of on the one hand attempting to challenge neoliberalism, whilst on the other hand having to showcase less political aspects of feminism to maintain a mainstream appeal and attract advertisers; rather than unquestionably reinforcing neoliberal ideas, *Ms.* was keenly aware of the contradictions involved in being a feminist in the 1980s. This chapter will now move on to look at the way *Spare Rib* discussed politics and challenged the rise of the right in the 1980s. *Spare Rib* did not have the same commercial concerns as *Ms.* and was, therefore, more outspoken in its criticisms of neoliberalism. Indeed, as the following analysis will show, *Spare Rib* became more radical in its approach to criticising capitalism.

SPARE RIB AND BRITISH POLITICS IN THE 1970S

Spare Rib was much more cynical towards the state than *Ms.* and only became more cynical over time. In earlier issues, there is some evidence of support towards mainstream politics. However, by the late 1980s, the magazine was much more hostile to politicians. In 1972 *Spare Rib* shared many more similarities with popular women's magazines than it did in later years (Hollows, 2012). The magazine was also more accepting of mainstream politicians and featured their writing in the magazine. This can be seen in 'Patience Is a Vice' from October 1972, written by Labour MP Will Hamling. The article was part of the 'Man's World Column', which featured columns written by men in 1972. The article discusses the Equal Pay Act, which was passed in 1970 and was due to come into effect in 1975. The column begins by introducing Hamling as a 'lecturer, a member of the Fabian society and campaigner for women's rights' (p. 7). The inclusion of Hamling's credentials at the beginning of the article presents him as authoritative so that his words carry merit. The fact that he campaigns for women's rights is used as justification for his inclusion in *Spare Rib*. The article takes an educational tone and includes facts such as 'new minimum wage rates are laid down of £25 a week for craftsmen, £20 for labourers and £18 a week for women' (p. 7). This shows that wage inequality is something that can be quantified. However, Hamling argues that 'you cannot easily legislate against public opinion' (p. 7). This suggests that despite evidence of unequal pay, legislation to combat this is unlikely to be enacted if popular opinion does not change. Hamling argues that it was not only men who were prejudiced against women:

> Most middle class people involved in the movement to rid the world of this absurd prejudice against women, don't meet the deep rooted anger of a great many working class women at the thought that some women, and particularly a single woman, should take home the same pay as her man. (p. 7)

It is significant that middle-class women are presented as fighting for equal pay, whilst working-class women oppose it. Middle- and working-class women are positioned in opposition to each other, ignoring the extent to which working-class women were also campaigning for equal pay (for example in the Dagenham machinist strike in 1968) and would benefit from the legislation as workers as well. Hamling educating the reader on what working-class women think suggests that *Spare Rib* is aimed at a middle-class reader that needs educating. This further supports the argument made throughout this book that that readership of *Spare Rib* was originally a white and middle-class one, since it is assumed that the reader will not understand what it is like to be working class from personal experience.

'Patience Is a Vice' is a rare example of a mainstream politician being given space in the magazine. It is one of the few articles from the whole sample where the voice of any politician from one of the three main parties (Conservative, Labour and the Liberals/SDP/Liberal Democrats) has their voice privileged. The inclusion of a mainstream politician in the magazine shows that *Spare Rib* was more inclined to engage with mainstream politics than can be seen in later years, perhaps indicative of a willingness to engage with mainstream culture more generally (Hollows, 2012). This willingness was replaced by a sense of cynicism towards politicians and the thesis will now move on to discuss this cynicism.

POLITICAL CYNICISM

The changing relationship with mainstream politicians can be seen in 'Mice in Manchester' (Stephens and Ades, July 1977). The article is critical of the government's attempts to legislate against inequality. It criticises those who are leading the Equal Opportunities Commission[2] as 'mice', suggesting that they are timid and cowardly (p. 10). The illustration for the article shows three mice – one covering its eyes, and one its mouth, whilst a sleeping mouse lies between them. The government is presented as wilfully ignorant and ineffectual. This is reinforced by the statement that 'while not expecting revolutionary action from a government body and accepting its own definition of itself as a "middle aged Establishment pressure group" we did expect to see some results after a year and a half' (p. 10). The government is presented as incapable of making changes, whilst the description of commission as 'middle aged' and 'Establishment' further reinforces this, since the establishment is associated with maintaining the status quo.

The ineffectiveness of the EOC is compared to women's liberation groups who have less power and do not have 'easy access to government and power to amend legislation' (p. 10). Despite this power, Stephens and Ades suggest that the EOC has 'made very little impact', whilst a feminist is quoted as describing how the EOC 'crept off like mice to Manchester and we've hardly heard a squeak out of them since' (p. 10). The ineffectiveness of the EOC is also argued in other articles from 1977 and described as a way to 'divert women's militancy' (Gharial, April 1977, p. 22). This suggests that the EOC discouraged grass roots feminist activism.

This mistrust of authority is further highlighted in the way that the chair of the EOC is introduced as 'The Chairman (she insists on this title)' (p. 10). The use of the parentheses undermines the chair Betty Lockwood by questioning her use of the term, signifying the writers of the article distance themselves ideologically from her. This suggests that the EOC is being chaired by a woman who does not share the values of feminists because she insists on using a sexist title. The article criticises the vice-chair 'Lady Howe', who is implicated in the political establishment because she is 'married to the Shadow Chancellor'. This is seen in an article about the Conservative Party Conference where Anny Bracx critiques Vice Chair Lady Howe as not 'a feminist' because Howe's concept of feminism is related to 'not being an extremist and being a member of the Conservative Party' (Bracx, July 1977, p. 39). Being a member of the Conservative Party is presented as the antithesis of feminism.

In 1972 involvement in mainstream politics was seen as a claim to authority; in this article it is viewed with mistrust. Articles that mentioned Parliament in 1977 often focused on protests ('Women Talk About Why They Marched', January 1977; 'Secret Deal', December 1977). Ades and Stephens were critical of cross-party cooperation with regard to women's equality. They question the usefulness of the 'political balancing act' of having a 'Labour Chairwoman and Tory Vice Chairwoman' and suggest that 'it is a factor in the Commission's obvious difficulties in reaching decisions, taking actions and making swift public statements of relevant issues' (p. 10). This further reinforces the idea commission is toothless and the article provides a 'brief guide through the red tape' further critiquing the commission as overly bureaucratic (p. 10).

Alongside the critiques in the piece, the photographs used to illustrate the article further ridicule Lockwood and Howe (p. 11). In the photograph of Lockwood, the word 'chairman' is placed in scare quotes to indicate that Ades and Stephens do not approve of the use of the term. On the photograph a speech bubble is superimposed, and Lockwood is made to say, 'two strategic rolls and a cuppa', implying that Lockwood is more concerned with being comfortable and taking advantage of the hospitality offered than doing anything to change anything for women. The use of bubble quotes creates a mocking or satirical effect.

By 1977 there was a more critical approach that questioned the extent in which the state could enact social, cultural or economic change for women. In 1972 MPs were viewed as authority figures and their views were legitimised by the magazine, but by 1977 politics was viewed as bureaucratic and unable to enact meaningful changes for women. The chapter will now move in to look at how Thatcherism further intensified *Spare Rib*'s distrust and antagonism towards British politics.

SPARE RIB AND THATCHERISM

'Mice in Manchester' is emblematic of the ways that the magazine critiqued the government's role in enabling equal opportunities for women. The Thatcher government in the 1980s represents a further shift in the magazine's relationship with the state. The magazine became increasingly hostile towards the government, and many articles focused on the damaging effect that Thatcher's government was having on women's lives, including: 'Falklands "Brides and Sweethearts" Bite Back' (August 1982), 'Who Pays for Pregnancy' (January 1987), 'What's in a Vote' (May 1987) and 'State of the Economy' (August–September 1992). Segal (1999, p. 208) argues that Thatcher's politics 'in alliance with Reagan and the American Right' aimed to 'overturn all traces of the post-war Keynesian economic orthodoxy with its support for spending on welfare'. In this section I am going to use 'Surviving the Recession', an article from April 1982 as a case study. This article has been chosen because it explicitly refers to the effect of the Thatcher government on women.

'SURVIVING THE RECESSION'

The article describes the impact of the recession and Thatcher's policies in working-class areas, with a focus on South Wales, an area particularly affected by Thatcher's policies,[3] stating, 'In February 1982, 174,878 people in Wales (16.1 percent) were officially unemployed' (p. 6). The use of statistics highlights the extent to which the recession impacted a large number of people, but the article itself focuses on personal stories of individual women living in South Wales. Vaughan describes South Wales as 'culturally and economically destroyed' (p. 6). This situates the recession as not only something that means that people have less money but as something that affects communities' ways of life since the risk of pit closures has led to an 'effect on the morale of the people' (p. 8). The article focuses repeatedly on the emotional impact of the recession, with anger being a common emotion. Vaughan describes how one of her interviewee's 'anger exploded' as they recounted their lack of money (p. 7). The sense that this is an emotional experience for the women interviewed is further highlighted by the comment from one of the interviewees, Mary. In response to the news that Margaret Thatcher's son Mark had got lost in the desert whilst taking part in the Dakar Rally in 1982 she states:

> I've never been vindictive, but when that come on the news about Margaret Thatcher's son getting lost in the desert, I said, I'm glad, I hope she's suffering. (p. 7)

For women who have been impacted by Thatcher's policies there was a visceral hatred that went beyond political disagreement. The expression of contempt for Thatcher in this article illustrates the hostile relationship that the women's movement had with her and vice versa. Vinen (2010, p. 42) states that 'Thatcher was emphatic that she was not a "feminist" and she often spoke of what she described as "women's lib" with some disdain'. Furthermore, as Leung (1997, p. 38) argues, 'it is not women as a community that Thatcher aligns herself with, but instead powerful, individual women'. Although she was the first female prime minister, many of her policies such as cuts to social security were anti-women. *Ms.* often featured politicians in a positive manner and viewed further participation of women in both Republican and Democratic politics as a sign of progress. (See: 'The secretary of commerce on the future for working women' (March 1977); 'Feminist Notes: Women in Power, An Agenda for the '80s' (May 1982); 'Barbara Mikulski: US Senator' (January 1987).) In contrast, *Spare Rib* consistently viewed the Conservative Party as a political enemy and was not sympathetic to the Labour Party either. The lack of sympathy and support for mainstream politics can be further seen in Vaughan's article with interviewee Mary, who is described as 'obviously cynical about the Tories and about the Labour Party – having heard one too many stories about corruption' (p. 8). British politics is perceived as mistrusted and therefore not somewhere change is achievable.

The sense that Thatcherism is the enemy to women is further seen in articles such as '5 More Years of Desolation' (Whitlock, July 1987), which was published three months after Thatcher's third electoral victory. It focuses on the impact that Thatcher's first two terms have had on society. Whitlock suggests that it is 'chilling to reflect on the cruelty already inflicted on the most vulnerable in our society by the government in the past 8 years' (p. 15). The use of 'cruelty' and 'inflicted' suggests that the impact of Thatcherism on vulnerable members of society was the intention of the government, rather than a side effect. This can be contrasted to the way *Spare Rib* viewed politicians in 'Mice in Manchester'. Whilst the article was critical of politicians, their actions were viewed as apathetic rather than malicious. In contrast, Whitlock (July 1987, p. 15) states that 'to anticipate what is in store now for the old, sick and the unemployed is truly depressing', further highlighting the sense of hopelessness that Thatcher and her government elicited.

'MERRY CHRISTMAS BRITAIN'

The discourse that Thatcherism was having a disastrous impact on British society was seen throughout the 1980s. The December 1987 issue presents a bleak version of Britain that attests to this. The December issue had in early years of the magazine been used to provide a roundup for the year and included seasonal articles such as gift ideas (White, December 1972). In contrast, the December 1987 suggests that Christmas is not a time for celebration. The cover title for the issue is 'Merry Christmas Britain?' and is laid over a black-and-white image of two children looking through a hole in a fence, out onto an industrial landscape. The question mark is significant as it suggests that a time of year that is traditionally associated with joy cannot be taken for granted. The photograph looks like it is from the 1940s or 1950s, evoking a sense that Britain is moving backwards. It is important to note that the welfare state had just been established around this time (Fraser, 2009) and so the picture alludes to the danger that Britain is moving back to a time when the welfare state could not be relied on.

Although the magazine presented a pessimistic view of Britain's state of affairs, this pessimism counters that which states that neoliberalism will lead to greater prosperity (Kosofsky Sedgwick and Frank, 2003, p. 70). *Spare Rib*'s pessimism can be read as bringing to light the human impact of Thatcherism. In the United States, *Ms.* aimed to create a feminist magazine that could be successful within the existing capitalist system; in contrast, *Spare Rib* did not see capitalism as something it could cooperate with. The result of this was that *Spare Rib* was much more likely to present an anti-capitalist perspective. The feature article from the issue, 'Thatcher's Britain', juxtaposes the situation for the rich and the poor, suggesting that 'it is a time when millions, living on or below the poverty line look on while the affluent amongst us indulge in the seasonal orgy of consumption' (p. 6). The word 'orgy' suggests that consumption is obscene, whilst the use of the plural pronoun 'us' implicates both the reader and the writer.

In contrast, in *Ms.* the prolific use of advertising alongside articles which appealed to readers' aspirations to succeed meant that there was limited critique of what success looks like within capitalism. The threat of the New Right in *Ms.* was predominantly linked to the restriction of women's individual freedom and rights, such as access to abortion and reproductive services (Cronin-Wohl, February 1982; Connie Paige, February 1987). This can be linked to the way that liberal feminism in the United States was to a large extent predicated on the idea that women's freedom can be increased through entrance into the male public sphere, as seen from the influence of Friedan's *The Feminine Mystique* (1963), which argued for women's increased participation in public life.

SPARE RIB AND THE BACKLASH

The term 'backlash' is first identified in this sample in *Spare Rib* in September 1982, the year that feminism has been widely understood as 'over' (Mendes, 2011). The magazine's response to the backlash can be seen in a number of articles from the 1980s, beginning with Linda Bellos' September 1982 article where she argues that 'the pretence that men and women, and Black and white, are already equal became obvious and blatant of late' (p. 16). In 1987, three articles discussed the backlash, an increase from previous years. The July 1987 editorial is most explicit in its rejection of post-feminism and neoliberalism. The editorial states that 'feminism is the belief that a woman ought to be free to decide how she would like to conduct her life' (p. 5). *Spare Rib* was much less likely to include discourses that encouraged individualism, so it is interesting that the editorial begins with an individualistic statement. There is a suggestion of a choice-based feminism that is often found in post-feminist discourses (Ferguson, 2010, p. 247). However, this individualism is countered by the statement that 'feminism is the belief that women together could change the patriarchal ways of life that permeate our society' (p. 5). This reinforces the idea that feminism is collectivist. The editorial reminds the reader that feminism has demands such as 'equal pay for equal work' and 'free abortion and contraception on demand' (July 1987, p. 5). There is a tension evident between the idea of feminism and collective and a rhetoric around individualism.

The article acknowledges that 'the 80s have been very hostile years for any liberation movement' and that Thatcherism has led to the perpetuating of 'two dimensional stereotypes' of feminists as man hating and strident. In contrast, the editorial suggests that 'every woman who has ever fought or is still fighting for her right to work, her right to equal opportunity and equal pay is a feminist' (p. 5). However, this suggests that participation in the labour market is equivalent to a feminist identity. McRobbie (2009, p. 78) argues that the figure of the working woman is 'integral to the post-feminist masquerade' because perceived equality in the workplace leads to the assumption of equality where it does not exist. Instead, she argues that the focus on work leading to empowerment 'creates a thriving and re-energised consumer culture directed towards women' (p. 82). As Margaret Thatcher's rise to power illustrates, women who are successful should not automatically be considered feminist (Bashevkin, 1998, p. 170). The article rejects post-feminism's belief that feminism is over, stating 'Post feminism? We don't think so. What we need now is some positive criticism of our movement and some fresh organisation to fight the backlash' (p. 5). However, the editorial does aim to make feminism more palatable by distancing itself from radicalism through the suggestion that feminism is about equality within the public sphere (Dean, 2010) rather than restructuring society.

Other articles from 1987 were more vociferous in their rejection of popular feminism, as seen in articles such as 'Blood Sister's (October 1987) and 'Where We've Been' (July 1987). Taking a closer look at one article in particular, 'From Liberation to Confirmation' (McManus, August 1987), we can see how feminism is positioned in opposition to the 'vicious criminal conservatism' of Thatcher. Furthermore, McManus critiques the 'flowing rightward tide' of feminism, suggesting that its 'critical radical spirit [has been] diluted beyond recognition' and has become more conformist and therefore more conservative' (p. 7). She goes on to question the 'popular feminism which unabashedly celebrates anything female' and laments that there was 'no radical feminist agenda during the 1987 General Election campaign; critiques of men and the relentlessly vampirish nuclear family were cynically dropped to avoid offending conventional wisdom' (p. 7). McManus pints to a de-radicalisation of feminism in response to the rise of the right. However, it is important also to note that *Spare Rib* rejected this, suggesting that it aimed to provide an alternative.

This can also be seen in McManus' rhetorical question: 'Why not then invite Thatcher to bask in the sweetness and light and torrential caring of this sisterhood solidarity? If we continue to rush from reason, it's only a matter of time' (p. 7). This can be linked to the arguments of feminist scholars such as McRobbie (2009) Tasker and Negra (2007) and Fraser (2013), who argue that the emphasis on empowerment is used to neutralise feminism's more radical potential. The sense that feminism has become de-radicalised can be seen through McManus' critiques of the ways in which some second wave feminists such as Germaine Greer and Betty Friedan, who 'inspired women to reject domestic confinement', have now 'come full circle back to motherhood and the family'. Faludi (1991, p. 352) suggests that one of the features of the backlash was the recantation of second wave feminism, suggesting, 'A handful of authors whose bestselling books helped popularize the women's movement in the 1970s were busy issuing retractions'. Similarly, McManus (August 1987, p. 7) points to Judith Stacey, who states that 'aging in the right wing and "postfeminist" climate of the 1980s, has been a traumatic experience for Second Wave feminists' leading to the 'strident and unmodulated quality of recantation in the new pro-family feminism'.

There was a clear awareness of the extent to which feminism needed to be guarded from populist influence, an idea that did not gain as much traction in *Ms.*, in part because *Ms.* was more amenable to the capitalist ideas that underpinned populist understandings of feminism (Erdman Farrell, 2011).

SPARE RIB AND LIBERATION POLITICS

Another key way that *Spare Rib* rejected the rise of post-feminist discourse was through its increased discussion of liberation politics and global feminist issues. Mann and Huffman (2005, p. 57) describe how in the 'third wave' period there was a:

> More profound development; the rise of a new discourse or paradigm for framing and understanding gender relations that grew out of a critique of the inadequacies of the second wave.

Mann and Huffman argue that this can be most clearly seen through the increased focus on the different experiences that women have, and by 1992, *Spare Rib*'s content and style was much more likely to take this into account. Whilst there was always an anti-capitalist undercurrent within *Spare Rib* (Winship, 1987), by 1992 this had become increasingly overt alongside an increasingly explicit critique of neoliberalism. Hazel Smith's 'Capitalism Isn't Working' (February 1992) is an example of this and suggests that the magazine did not alter its content to suit an increasingly post-feminist political climate, but instead strongly critiqued the environment that led to neoliberalism. Smith states that 'the system which dominates the international economy – free-market profit led capitalism – is anarchic' (p. 38). This is a stronger critique of capitalism than any of the articles that have been discussed in this chapter, and certainly more so than any article that has been analysed from *Ms.* Furthermore, this was not anomalous, and throughout

1992 there was an increase in articles which challenged Western politics and capitalism. For example, in August there was 'State of the Economy' and in October 'A Major Crisis: The British Economy Goes into Freefall'.

The critique of Western democracy is illustrated in 'Election Special (April 1992), published prior to the 1992 election. The article is critical of the 'ugly tradition of the Parliament of Westminster' whilst stating that 'for 500 years, successive British governments have murdered and raped people all over the planet' (p. 10). Although articles from 1982 and 1987 were critical of the governments of the day, the focus was on the effect that the government had on Britain and the criticism of the government was temporal, focusing on the impact of the government in contemporary Britain. In contrast, 'Election Special' implicates parliamentary democracy with colonial rule and does not present an alternative within the current political system. All politicians from all political parties are viewed as complicit. This is further emphasised by the statement that democracy is 'simply a myth' and that 'the thing about voting Labour or Tory is that it doesn't really matter, both are driving the same system' (p. 10). This is a much more extreme position regarding British politics than has been seen in any previous *Spare Rib* articles analysed in this chapter. This discussion of politics must be read in relation to an increased anti-colonial perspective regarding race, as discussed in the chapter on race in this book. John Major and Margaret Thatcher are described as 'dictators' (p. 10), whilst Colonel Gadhafi is viewed in positive terms. The article quotes Gadhafi:

> After the successful establishment of the era of the republics, and the beginning of the era of the masses, it is unreasonable that democracy should mean the electing of only a few representatives to act on behalf of great masses. This is an obsolete theory and an outdated experience. The whole authority must be the peoples. (p. 10)

The approving use of Gadhafi's words to critique Western democracy suggests a radical and contrarian view of politics. This demonstrates a feeling of disenfranchisement with British politics. What is clear is that this is a much more radical discussion of politics than was seen in previous years, which whilst critiquing the government of the time, did not go as far as critiquing the concept of a Western government.

CONCLUSION

As this chapter illustrated, *Spare Rib* and *Ms.* provide vastly different perspectives on the utility and value of engaging with mainstream politics and the state. In the United States the magazine supported the ways the wider women's movement engaged with state politics, as reflected in its supportive coverage of the ERA. *Spare Rib* on the other hand was much less likely to engage with state politics and this was reflected in both the content and tone of political discussions.

Using the ERA as a case study, this chapter argued that the ways in which *Ms.* engaged with the fight for the ERA demonstrates both the ways it assumed that change could come through engagement with mainstream politics and the challenge that was faced by American feminists from an increasingly hostile political environment. *Ms.* did demonstrate that it was more amenable to individualist feminism that suited a neoliberal culture but there was also evidence of *Ms.*' challenging neoliberalism. In comparison, there was a noticeable shift in *Spare Rib*'s willingness to engage with the state and politicians in particular. While politicians were invited to write for the magazine in 1972, *Spare Rib* became increasingly distrustful of politicians. As Margaret Thatcher took power in 1979 the magazine's stance was fiercely critical. Interestingly, while individual politicians such as Thatcher were critiqued, the discourse analysis reveals the ways that systems such as neoliberalism became a target of criticism, particularly in the early 1990s.

In the final part of the chapter, I argued that to some extent *Spare Rib* at times reproduced post-feminist ideas such as the emphasis on freedom and choice. However, for the most part the magazine rejected post-feminism, both the idea that we are 'post' feminism and the post-feminist sensibility that focused on individualism. Indeed, the chapter has demonstrated the ways in which the magazine's radicalism increased towards the 1990s, to point in which not only the current government was critiqued but the concept of Western democracy as a system. This is significant because it demonstrates the ways in which *Spare Rib* provides a counter narrative to one which argues that feminism was less likely to engage with radical politics during and after the 1980s (Hemmings, 2011).

In the first part of this book I have identified the ways in which *Spare Rib* and *Ms.* engaged with capitalism and how this impacted both the assumed reader and the content of the magazines. Using both a content and textual analysis has been vital for illuminating the impact that existing within a capitalist publishing industry has had for *Spare Rib* and *Ms.* In the next part of the book, I shift focus and look at the ways in which feminists in the 1990s engaged with zine making as a form of resistance, but also how the encroachment of capitalism impacted their ability to do so. I begin this next part with an overview of Riot grrrl, before moving on to look at *Bitch* and *Bust* as my case studies.

NOTES

1. Interestingly, despite the deadline for ratification having passed, states are still approving the ERA, with Virginia being the latest in early 2020 (Williams, 2020).

2. The Equal Opportunities Commission (EOC) was an independent non-departmental public body (NDPB) in the United Kingdom, which tackled sex discrimination and promoted gender equality. It was replaced by the Equality and Human Rights Commission' (http://www.eoc.org.uk/).

3. This includes the closure of coal mines which were integral to many communities in South Wales.

Part III

BEYOND THE 'SECOND WAVE'

Chapter 6

Riot grrrl and Feminist Media in the 1990s

Riot grrrl was a music and social movement that came out of the punk and hardcore scenes in the United States, and in Olympia, Washington and Washington, D.C. in particular (Marcus, 2010). Although most strongly associated with the music of bands such as *Bikini Kill, Heavens to Betsy* and *Bratmobile*, zine publishing was also a central feature of Riot grrrl. In this chapter I argue that Riot grrrl provides a valuable link between second wave feminist media activism and digital feminist media activism today. Piepmeier and Zeisler (2009, p. 25) note the genealogy of feminist media, arguing that zines 'also have predecessors in the informal publications, documents and artefacts produced by women during the first and second waves of feminism'. Viewing Riot grrrl in the context of both what came before it and what came after it helps us to understand the role of feminist media across history, identifying key continuities and differences between past and present.

Second wave feminist activists and Riot grrrl zinesters both needed to negotiate their relationship with the mainstream. This chapter will begin by providing an overview of Riot grrrl, before moving on to discuss how the movement interacted with the mainstream and how it developed a wider audience. The primary aim of the chapter is to compare and contrast how feminist media activists engaged with the mainstream in the 1990s, with how they did this in *Spare Rib* and *Ms*. The chapter will also identify how zines and associated Riot grrrl media represented feminist issues. The chapter begins by discussing Kathleen Hanna's zine *Bikini Kill*, one of the most well-known zines. After this it will explore how Riot grrrl zine makers engaged with mainstream publishing, using *Bitch* and *Bust* as case studies.

The chapter will then explore the ways that 1990s feminism can be read in relation to the second wave but will also show how we can draw the link between the feminism of the 1990s and the present day.

A BRIEF HISTORY OF RIOT GRRRL

Riot grrrl was born out of the punk scenes in Olympia, Washington and Washington, D.C. There were similarities with the second wave feminist movement through the emphasis on the personal as political and the recognition of the importance of feminists making their own media. The movement can be historicised as beginning in 1989, and its heyday being in the early 1990s (Marcus, 2010). Gillis and Munford (2004, p. 171) suggest:

> The Riot Grrrls forged a unique feminist space for young women (usually aged between fourteen and twenty-five) that was not structurally dissimilar to that sustained by the second wave consciousness-raising groups and resistance.

Riot grrrl chapters met regularly in a way that was comparable to the consciousness-raising groups of the second wave and provided an important space for younger women to share their experiences of sexism. Riot grrrl also utilised zines in a way that can be compared to second wave feminist media production. A key thread that runs throughout this book is the importance of feminist spaces for women to share their experiences, and feminist media has historically provided this space.

Riot grrrls utilised technology such as the photocopier and later the internet to produce zines, something they could do completely independently (Monem, 2007, p. 103). Zines also served as a network: writers and readers wrote to each other, met at shows and corresponded through letters' pages. As with the second wave period, correspondence was important (Erdman Farrell, 1998; Jolly, 2008). This suggests continuity in the way that feminists fostered networks that is unacknowledged in histories of feminism that emphasise the differences between the second and third wave.

DEFINING ZINE CULTURE

Zines have long been an important form of expression, especially for those involved in subcultures that are not represented in the mainstream media. Duncombe (2008, p. 8) describes how 'zines are speaking to and for an underground culture', whilst Poletti (2005, p. 184) suggests that 'zine culture is a productive community' which critiques the 'commercialization of youth cultures'. Zines were popularised as part of the punk movement in the 1970s, and Atton (2002, p. 1) suggests that 'the rise of the fanzine as an integral part of the punk subculture of the late 1970s was instrumental in generating a second wave of underground-like publications'. Zines are often created by one person, who acts as designer, writer and editor. Atton (2002a, p. 55) states: 'the fanzine is the quintessence of amateur self-published journalism. It is typified for the most part by a single editor and a small pool of writers, though just as often entire issues are written by the editor'. However, as this chapter will demonstrate, *Bust* and *Bitch* aim to attract a wider audience and are run as businesses. Writers are able to write about what they want free from the restrictions that writing for mainstream publications may incur. The zine writer does not need editorial approval and can therefore publish what they want. The idea of autonomy is further emphasised by Sutton (1999, p. 166), who argues that 'zines and web-based journals are fast becoming outlets for the voices of many who would otherwise remain silenced'. This is further emphasised by Poletti, who suggests that alternative media is 'one of the few instances of young people exerting cultural and political power' (p. 186). This suggests that zines play an important role in giving those who traditionally do not have the opportunity to speak a place to do so.

Triggs (2010, p. 7) suggests that zine producers focus on 'communicating a particular subject to a community of like-minded individuals' and therefore they are less concerned with issues such as 'copyright, grammar, spelling, punctuation or the protocols of page layout'. This sense of community is aided by the way in which zines are circulated, usually relying on zine producers contacting each other, rather than by picking up a copy in a newsagent. Atton (2002a, p. 55) argues that 'at the heart of zine culture is not the study of the "other" (celebrity, cultural object or activity') but the study of self, of personal expression, sociality and the building of community'. This is especially important because it questions traditional distinctions between readers and writers (Poletti, 2005). As zines can be written by anyone, the writer does not hold a privileged position (as anyone can be a writer). As a result, dialogue between readers and writers is opened up because there is less of a power imbalance (Atton, 2002a).

RIOT GRRRL AND ZINE PRODUCTION

Riot grrrls tended to be young women in high school or university and as a result they did not have access to the means to produce mainstream media. As a result, they created their own media. Schilit (2003b, p. 79) argues that 'by making a zine, girls learn that if they do not like the cultural products offered to them, they can produce their own'. Zines are a way for young women to reject attempts to mould their tastes by the mainstream media. They also provided a supportive space to share experiences such as sexual abuse (Schilit, 2003b). Zines have a diary-like purpose, reinforced by Mann and Huffman's (2005, p. 71) suggestion that 'many of their zines are personal – much like journals written to vent anger and frustration'. Harris (2003, p. 38) argues that zines 'create a community for young women within which they can participate in debates about the meaning of girlhood under late modernity'. Zines provide a place for young women to understand themselves and their place within society. This is supported by Duncombe's (2008, p. 73) statement that Riot grrrl zines provided the 'forum to talk back to the demands of the media and men about how a woman ought to look or how a woman ought to be'.

Zines were also a way for young women to engage with feminist ideas outside of the classroom. Piepmeier (2009, p. 9) suggests that 'girl zines are often the mechanism that third wave feminists use to articulate theory and create community'. The emphasis on zines as providing spaces for learning is also suggested by Thomas Flannery (2005, p. 25), who notes that zines provided an 'informal network that constituted the women's university-without-walls'. Zines, therefore, share common goals with second wave feminist media production which aimed to put theory into practice (Travis, 2008) and had a heavy emphasis on democratising the media (Thomas Flannery, 2005).

ZINES AND THE MAINSTREAM

Much of the literature that has been identified so far has pointed to the extent to which Riot grrrl is both a DIY movement and one that has a straightforward history; Radway complicates this. She suggests that histories of Riot grrrl 'organize a messy, distinctly wild range of social practices into the "thing-ness of a movement"' (2016, p. 4). Although this chapter will primarily utilise 'Riot grrrl' as a general term, it is also important to consider the extent to which, just like the wave metaphor, these unifying terms also obscure complexity. More specifically, Radway (2016, p. 6) points to the:

> intersections, tensions and quarrels that were generated as youth sought to cope with the effects of the neoliberal high-consumerist social formation then being consolidated all around them.

It is important not to homogenise Riot grrrl or zine culture more widely. However, access to zines, an ephemeral media makes it difficult to access and assess the full range of zine culture. Furthermore, the aim of this chapter is to explore the engagement that Riot grrrl media had with capitalist culture. Therefore, this chapter focuses largely on more accessible texts. Although I am well aware of the problems of this, focusing on the most visible media outputs of Riot grrrl is useful since it is the most visible forms of feminist media that are analysed in other chapters. It is also these visible forms that are most likely to intersect with the mainstream. Radway (2016, p. 9) describes how Riot grrrl was covered in the mainstream in a way that 'expanded the audiences for Riot grrrl associated bands', whilst noting that this also produced 'dissention'. Indeed, as Jacques (2001, p. 48) argues, although there was a media blackout that aimed to prevent problematic representations of Riot grrrl by the mainstream press, ultimately there was 'no monolithic RG resistance to co-option'. As with the *Ms.* in the 1970s and 1980s, and *Teen Vogue* more recently (as will be discussed in the next chapter), there is a tension between visibility and popularity and maintaining principles and authenticity (Banet-Weiser, 2018).

Piepmeier and Zeisler (2009) note that the structurally innovative form of Riot grrrl zines makes them difficult to compare to mainstream publications. Furthermore, they note that 'zine creators widely acknowledge that zines cost money rather than making money' (p. 74). This can be understood in direct opposition to the commercial imperative that assumes that a publication exists to make money. The use of bartering systems where one zine is swapped with another further reinforces this distinctiveness from capitalism, since money is not the primary currency.

However, there are also questions about the sustainability of a model that is based on volunteerism and non-profit. Whilst zines may be 'distributed in ways distinct from the consumer culture industry' (Piepmeier and Zeisler, 2009, p. 74), zine makers themselves exist within a capitalist culture where financial means will have an impact on who has the leisure time and the financial resources to make zines. The integration between zines and the mainstream will be explored in relation to *Bitch* and *Bust*. A similarity can be drawn with second wave feminist media and the tensions between feminist ideals and the wider capitalist publishing industry. This book has looked at the impact of capitalism on feminist media, and more specifically, the extent to which it impacts on both the kind of content that is created by feminist media and who can create this content. The importance of individual financial and mental capacity is also noted by Downes (2010, p. 443), who found in her research on contemporary Riot grrrl that 'participants find themselves stretched and capable of different levels of commitments, leaving structural inequalities between participants unexamined'. It is important to recognise this when discussing any feminist media, since access to resources, whether intentionally or not, means that not all people have equal access or ability to participate. The paradox of feminist media is that it is likely to be the most accessible way for feminists to reach a wider audience, whilst at the same time it is also not itself representative of all women or feminists. It is still entangled in the class and race oppressions of the wider world. Fundamentally, this highlights the importance of acknowledging the extent to which feminist media exists within capitalism and is therefore working with or against capitalism.

Downes (2010, p. 245–246) also argues that often feminist organisations themselves are structured in a way that suggests a 'white middle-class normative framework'. Again, obvious parallels can be drawn with the experiences of women working for both *Ms.* and *Spare Rib*, in terms of the extent to which a middle-class assumption was made that meant that the financial practicalities of working for a feminist magazine were under-appreciated.

In the case of Riot grrrl this is complicated further by the clear intersections between it and wider popular culture. Radway (2016, p. 15) points to the various career destination of women interested in Riot grrrl as writing for 'outlets like the *LA Weekly* and the *Chicago Reader*, for *Sassy* and *Seventeen*, and some worked in publishing houses trying to reach what was thought of then as the *MTV* generation'. The question to be begged is whether such a movement was more likely to make those publications more feminist and more political, or whether it was more likely to dilute the message.

RIOT GRRRL AND RACE

Another important way that Riot grrrl can be understood both in relation to second wave feminism and more contemporary feminist movements is through a discussion of the way that women of colour have been underrepresented. This book has already discussed the extent to which *Spare Rib* and *Ms.* were unable or unwilling to adequately represent women of colour in a way that did not lead to tokenistic approaches in the case of *Ms.*, or excessive complaints from white women about hurt feelings in the case of *Spare Rib*.

This can also be seen in Riot grrrl; Zobl (2009, p. 3) argues that 'zines lacked a reflection on white privilege'. Furthermore, Mimi Thi Nguyen (2012), a zine maker and now academic, has cogently argued that the focus on whiteness has not been adequately dealt with. She explicitly links the 'subculture of intimacy' that can be seen within Riot grrrl movement to consciousness raising, suggesting that there was belief in the notion that 'radical knowledge stemmed from their specific social position' (p. 179). However, Nyugen (2012) also questions 'how could experience yield revolutionary knowledge about race, when the dominant experience was whiteness?' This is a question that mainstream feminist media has and continues to be confronted with. Furthermore, Nyugen (2012, p. 181) argues that the emphasis on intimacy meant that racism was not understood as a structural problem but was instead positioned as 'ignorance, and ignorance as the absence of intimacy'.

What is also striking are the similarities between white women's responses to being asked to confront their own complicity with white supremacist ideology in *Spare Rib* and Riot grrrl. Nguyen (2012, p. 179) refers to a workshop at the 'first Riot grrrl convention' that was 'troubled by the young white women's clear discomforture with the prospect of their complicity'. Clear parallels can be drawn here with the way that race was discussed by some white women, specifically in *Spare Rib*. In the examples from the conference on race and class in 1982, and the Women's Liberation Conference in 1977, white women were clearly uncomfortable with confronting their complicity in ways that went beyond lip service and required them to give up some of their privilege. Furthermore, Nguyen's (2012, p. 184) reference to Sara Ahmed's argument that 'anti-racism becomes a matter of generating a positive white identity' is useful for understanding how the performance of anti-racism was often a useful tool in allowing white feminists to excuse themselves from their own racism. Piepmeier and Zeisler (2009, p. 31) note that there was a tendency to espouse a 'sisterhood that flattens difference, or more insidiously, functions to mask racial hierarchies'. It is therefore important to consider how this may be evident in feminist publication from the period, as well as considering what these continued re-occurrences of white feminism say about the ability for feminism to be truly intersectional.

So far, in this chapter I have noted the ways that Riot grrrl neglected discussions of race in order to draw a through line with historical, second wave discussions of race, but also with the more contemporary discussions of white feminism. Alongside the impact that this had on these feminisms at the time, it is also important to consider the continued impact that the privileging of whiteness has had on the way that these feminist histories are told, since 'certain stories are easier to tell then others' (Nguyen, 2012, p. 188). This has been a continued theme throughout this book, suggesting that this is a problem that feminism continues to grapple with. Now that I have provided an overview of some of the similarities with Riot grrrl and second wave feminist media, this chapter will now move on to analyse Riot grrrl media, beginning with *Bikini Kill*.

ZINES AND ACCESSIBILITY

As has been previously stated in this book, Riot grrrl was explicit in its feminism, and this can be seen in *Bikini Kill* (1991) by Kathleen Hanna, who was also a member of the band *Bikini Kill* and is perhaps the most well-known riot grrrl. In addition to this, some issues of *Bikini Kill* are available online (*Artzines* website). This demonstrates the importance of archiving in helping to preserve ephemeral media such as zines. The article discussed in this chapter is from *Bikini Kill #2* and was accessed via the Nottingham Contemporary Art Gallery (Nottingham, UK) during their 'Still I Rise' exhibition in 2018. The ephemeral nature of zines, often produced in small print runs and distributed at gigs, means that they are relatively difficult to catalogue and access. I am focusing on *Bikini Kill*, though I acknowledge that there are zines that have received less attention because they are more difficult to access. However, given that a central aim of the project is to look at feminism's relationship with the mainstream, it seems fitting to discuss a well-known zine. In the article from *Bikini Kill* that this section will explore, Hanna identifies some of the arguments that have been made to her against feminism. This can be read intertextually with more recent articulations of young feminism, and *Teen Vogue* (Keller, 2015), as well as with second wave ideas.

The article takes a list form, with the first item on the list dealing with the accusation that 'You Take Things Too Seriously. You Are Paranoid'. Written in the personal, diary style that is common of Riot grrrl work, the article is still highly political. Nguyen (2012, p. 277) warns of assuming that the personal style of Riot grrrl writing means that the magazine was not written for an audience, since 'zines often enacted a sly awareness of mediation, simultaneously refused and also acknowledged'. Nguyen (2012, p. 177) suggests that this was part of an attempt to fashion 'an authentic self'. However, as with much of the media that has been discussed in this book, there is a tension between this construction of an authentic self and the demands of both the audience and capitalism, especially if the aim is to reach a wider audience.

Hanna's discussion of paranoia echoes the use of the phrase 'gaslighting' by Lauren Duca in her article for *Teen Vogue*, 'Donald Trump Is Gaslighting America' (December 2016), and makes explicit the extent to which young girls are not imagining their subjugation by referring to 'anti-female propaganda' and the 'exclusion' that women feel. Duca's article will be discussed in detail in the next chapter. This differs from some of the articulations of popular feminism that we will discuss later in this book which focus heavily on the extent to which women need to 'lean in' (Sandberg, 2013) in order to succeed. Instead, the focus is on calling out the way that women are actively excluded. The Riot grrrl ethos of 'girls to the front' suggests that the way to challenge this exclusion is to force men to take a back seat, meant literally in the case of gigs. This highlights an uncomfortable truth that is often missing from discourses around increasing women's participation in traditionally male realms: men may need to give up space in order for women to claim theirs. The second item in the list is equally as radical, challenging the accusation that 'you are exclusionary and alienating to men'. Again, it is useful to compare Hanna's attitude towards this and the way that men are increasingly being invited into feminism (Obama, 2016; Emma Watson's *He for She*). Hanna sarcastically notes:

> I guess its [*sic*] for people who have been continually fucking excluded from everything to make their main priority BEING ACCESSIBLE to the very people who perpetuate and profit from their exclusion.

It is striking here, in comparison to some of the examples that we will look at in the next chapter, that men are being identified explicitly as a problem. It is also telling that *Bikini Kill* is a zine that was not created explicitly to reach a large audience (Mann and Huffman, 2005) and is DIY in its aesthetic. This is perhaps indicative of the extent to which the introduction of market forces has had an impact on the extent to which feminists could be radical.

Hanna further lacerates post-feminist arguments in the article by critiquing the 'humanist' argument that has become increasingly prevalent, especially when celebrities want to equivocate about their relationship with feminism. (Numerous celebrities such as Meryl Streep and Sarah Jessica Parker have distanced themselves from feminism; see *Huffington Post* (2013) for an overview.) Hanna makes the argument that such statements are a way to distance yourself from other woman, something which, she argues, means that amounts to turning 'our backs on the girls/women who don't feel "transcendence" as a viable option in our own lives' before urging the reader to 'make girl love real, okay???'. In another counter to the emphasis on 'individualistic striving' (McRobbie, 2015), Hanna reinforces the need for women to act collectively, and to recognise the extent to which women and girls need to eschew individualism.

The next item in the list reinforces the need for a 'pluralistic' feminism. Hanna is answering critics who suggest that she is 'not a real feminist because [she] used to be a stripper' by suggesting that 'Well, motherfucker, this world doesn't make any sense but I *do* exist. Deal with it. Deal with my existence'. Furthermore, she questions the usefulness of the binary of 'Right/Wrong, Male/Female, Feminist/Homemaker', suggesting 'This is the 90's, give it up'. The aim to destabilise dichotomies is also yoked to the need to challenge power hierarchies. Hanna notes that the discussion of who is or is not really a feminist is linked with 'white straight patriarchalllogicRules or ideas of LinearPowerControl'. As with the previous item on the list, there is an understanding of the extent to which power is integral to oppression. Again, this is missing from much of the discussion of feminism in popular outlets. Furthermore, the focus on challenge hierarchies can be understood within the context of a third wave feminism that is post-structuralist in its aims (Mann and Huffman, 2005) since it doesn't see gaining power in a traditionally hierarchical sense beneficial.

The article also shows an understanding of the extent to which popular culture contributes to the way that women are oppressed. Hanna takes the view that popular culture such as 'Mainstream movies' are 'propaganda', which is a position that shares similarities with second wave critiques of popular culture. As Radway (2016) argues, the genealogy of Riot grrrl often emphasises the similarity with second wave feminism. Though Radway is critical of how this history is constructed, there are clear similarities between

Riot grrrl and their second wave foremothers, most clearly seen through the attitude towards popular culture and the use of the manifesto. The mainstream movie that Hanna is critiquing is *Fatal Attraction*, which she suggests ignores that 'so like, 99.9% of all abusers/harrassers [*sic*] in heterosexual relationships are male and then this movie comes out where this woman is running around totally scaring this man'. Susan Faludi (1991) uses *Fatal Attraction* as one example of the way that the backlash against feminism was articulated within popular culture, suggesting that this was significant in shaping the public's understanding of women. Hanna's critique of the film demonstrates an understanding of how feminism has been undermined by popular culture, and how it perpetuates negative representations of women.

The focus on sexual violence and its relationship to power also shares similarities with second wave feminist concerns. Hanna argues that rape needs to be understood within the concept of male authority, suggesting that women may be less likely to report who raped them since:

> It might be safer to say a stranger did it (the courts understand rape as an aberration where a big scary evil guy comes limping from the darkness to 'take' a damsel, okay?) then to tell the truth that was DAD or uncle henry or joe bob captain of the football team, or the whole football team including the coach or the rich doctor who everyone loves and respects and no one can imagine doing such a thing.

This understanding of sexual violence as an abuse of power can be linked to previous articles that we have discussed here, for example in *Ms.*'s representation of pornography, and in landmark texts such as Susan Brownmiller's *Against Our Will* 2003 [1975]. This is important to point out because it provides a counter-narrative to that which assumes a post-feminist move in the 1990s and shows the continuations within feminism. Similarly, the suggestion that women are 'HUMILATED [*sic*] BY THE COURT SYSTEM OR SCARY MUSTACHE COPES WHO WANNA MAKE US FEEL LIKE HELPLESS LITTLE VIRGIN GIRLS OR DESERVING WHORES' precursors the Slut Walk movement that was a response to the suggestion that women could prevent being sexually assaulted by moderating the way they dressed (Mendes, 2015).

The item 'YOU ARE JUST TRYING TO BE POLITICAL' reinforces the extent to which *Bikini Kill* is a politicised text, arguing that 'EVERYTHING IS POLITICAL' and recognising that apathy, the alternative to action, is itself a political choice. The final items refute the idea that oppression is a points-based system, suggesting that 'people think of oppression as a test you can either pass or fail'. Hanna affirms her right to be upset, suggesting that all women are oppressed. Hanna's article demonstrates the through lines that can be drawn not only between second wave feminism and Riot grrrl but also between Riot grrrl and more recent articulations of feminism. This chapter will now move on to look at two texts, *Bust* and *Bitch*, that help us further bridge the gap between the texts studied in the first part of this book, and the internet feminisms that will be discussed in the last part of the book.

BITCH AND *BUST*

The importance of Bust and Bitch has been highlighted by Helmbrecht and Love (2009), who argue that they write about 'issues important to other women' (p. 152). These magazines have been chosen for this book because of their relative visibility in comparison with zines that had a smaller distribution, and therefore are analogous to an extent with *Spare Rib* and *Ms.* Helmbrecht and Love (2009, p. 155) note that at the time that they wrote their article, *Bitch* was reaching 47,000 readers and *Bust* was reaching 93,000. In addition, both magazines have produced books based on their content for established publishers. *The Bust Guide to the New Girl Order*, edited by Marcelle Karp and Debbie Stoller, was published by Penguin books in 1999, whilst *BITCHfest: Ten Years of Cultural Criticism from the Pages of Bitch Magazine*, edited by Lisa Jervis and Andi Zeisler, was published by Farrar, Straus and Giroux in 2006. That mass market books based on the magazine could be published suggests that there was enough of an audience for them, further gesturing towards their popularity and accessibility. This is a point that is suggested by Helmbrecht and Love (2009, p. 155), who describe how 'these zines can be purchased at major chain bookstores such as Barnes and Noble, making them accessible to a wider reading public'. There are clearly benefits to this; however, it is also important to consider how this visibility within popular culture impacts on the kind of feminisms that can be presented within the magazines.

Since it is through the two books that the magazines potentially had the widest audience, this chapter will focus on how they represented feminism. This will include an analysis of the content that was included within the books, as well as what was excluded or missing. This chapter will now move on to consider the histories of *Bust* and *Bitch* in turn.

Bust

Bust began in 1992, and in *The Bust Guide to the New Girl Order* (1999, loc 6377), the magazine's founders Marcelle Karp and Debbie Stoller describe themselves as 'a couple of overeducated, underpaid, late-twenty-something cubicle slaves, working side by side at a Giant Media Conglomerate'.

Although they paint a bleak picture, it is important to note the extent to which this is in itself a privilege. Zarnow (2010) describes the differing professional histories of the *Bust* founders and *Ms.*'s founders, who were by and large already professional journalists within the industry. In comparison, *Bust* at the beginning is described as 'more of a weekend hobby than a business venture' (Zarnow, 2010, p. 282). However, we must consider the extent to which such hobbies tend to be the privilege of those who work in a job that allows leisure time to indulge in them, as well as providing the financial resources to do so. Similarly, Zarnow (2010, p. 282) notes that the founders had postgraduate degrees in gender and there is an additional privilege evident here too.

Originally, the magazine 'sought to create an egalitarian working environment' and 'chose not to take job titles' (Zarnow, 2010, p. 282). However, this did not last and 'as *Bust* moved closer to the commercial magazine mould, Stoller opted out of feminist egalitarian business models'. As with *Ms.* there was a potential disconnect between the feminist aims of the magazine's content, with the maintenance of clear hierarchies in status. There is an underlying concern within feminist media, and therefore within this book, about the extent to which the feminist ethos of feminist magazines is borne out in the working practices of the magazine. As the chapter on *Ms.* demonstrated, this was not always the case, and led to a hierarchical structure that ultimately benefited white middle-class women and disadvantaged women of colour in particular.

Bitch

Bitch began in 1995 and was originally a 'black-and-white, stapled together zine' (Zeisler, 2016, p. 1). In the introduction to her 2016 book on the 'commodification of feminism' (p. 1) *Bitch* founder Andi Zeisler states that she 'always believed that the realm of media and popular culture was where feminism would truly change hearts and minds' (p. 1). Zeisler argues that the magazine was called:

> *Bitch* because we hoped to reclaim the word, and to make its verb form into something that could effect change just by speaking up and end encouraging others to do the same. (p. 1)

The aim to 'speak' and 'effect change' suggests that the magazine had an activist aim from the beginning and this is reinforced by Zeisler's description of the magazine as an 'activist project'. Laing and Sutton (1999) point to the extent to which feminist magazines 'are fast becoming outlets for the voices of many who would have otherwise remained silent'. Similarly, Helmbrecht and Love (2009, p. 160) note that '*Bitch* frequently calls for readers to take action'. However, it is also worth going beyond simply stating that the magazine is an act of speaking up, and to look also at the perspectives that are being articulated within the magazine. The book *BITCHfest* is particularly useful here, since it highlights what was considered the most interesting or the most important aspects of the magazine, and the features that were deemed as able to appeal to a wide audience.

There are similarities that can be drawn between how second wave feminist magazines *Ms.* and *Spare Rib* negotiated their position within the market and how *Bitch* and *Bust* did. Although it has been noted the magazine can be bought in major bookstores, suggesting a wider audience (Love and Helmbrecht, 2009), it is important to recognise that *Bitch* did not straightforwardly embrace, or was embraced by, the mainstream. Bailey (2003, p. 1) notes that although the magazine was included on newsstands it was relegated to the 'back racks' and this 'has consequences for the circulation of its feminist discourses'. Furthermore, she notes that the lack of visibility that the magazine has 'restrict[s] its circulation to those who might be predisposed to hunt it down'. Although the inclusion of the magazine in bookstores is a marker of accessibility, the placing in the bookstore also needs to be considered. Of course, much has changed since Bailey first wrote her article in 2003, not least the fact that the growing popularity of Amazon and declining magazine sales means that placement in a book store has less impact. However, it is also worth noting that *Bitch* being relegated to the back racks can be understood as a metaphor for the ways in which a lack of visibility means that feminist media is more difficult to access.

Bailey (2003, p. 1) also notes that the 'practice of privileging local bookstores over major chains shapes its geographical accessibility'. This can be linked to criticisms of *Ms.*, as discussed in chapter 2, that pointed to its relative expensiveness and the impact that this had on the ability for poorer readers to access it. This points to one of the paradoxes of feminist magazine publishing: in making the decision to step away from the mainstream you lose a lot of the privileges that come from this: most notably the capital and advertising revenue needed to produce a publication that is cheap enough to reach a wide audience.

Parallels can also be drawn between *Bitch* and *Ms.* in terms of the way that the magazines framed their readers as viable consumers for advertisers. Thom's (1997) book on the history of *Ms.* notes that the magazine promoted its readers as valuable consumers to advertisers. I have previously noted in this book that one of the consequences of this was that a white and middle-class reader was privileged. Bailey (2003, p. 2) describes advertising in *Bitch* as a 'cultural commodity', whilst suggesting that the data that the magazine presents to potential advertisers are of a readership that is 'young, upwardly mobile, tech savvy consumers, which is perhaps not that different from the vision sold to advertisers by *Cosmo* and *Marie Claire*'.

This can certainly be seen in the magazine's sponsorship kit from 2017. The kit's front cover suggests that 'our sponsors are our partners'. The magazine obscures the potential financial transaction taking place by framing it as a 'partnership', suggesting a more intimate relationship than would have otherwise been assumed. The interrelation between genuine community and commercial promise can further be seen in the blurb to the media kit. The magazine claims that '*Bitch* readers are too smart to listen to just anyone, but when our community cares, the connections we make are powerful'. As Bailey (2003) notes, the magazine is actively utilising the intelligence of its readership as a potential selling point. However, more than that, the magazine is utilising the political commitments of the its readers to suggest that this makes them more proactive consumers who are likely to buy a product that is advertised to them from the magazine. They are described as 'steadfastly committed', which again conflates commitment to social justice with the commitment that a consumer might have for their products. Here, *Bitch* readers are re-worked not only as politically committed readers but as valuable consumers. Commodity feminism has been noted through the increased market for feminist goods (Banet-Weiser, 2018). However, the *Bitch* media kit shows how this goes beyond simply the buying of feminist branding, but instead can also be seen through the qualities associated with committed feminist being exploited for commercial gain. *Bitch*'s reader's 'engagement' is reinforced throughout the media kit. Even if *Bitch*'s origins and aims are radically different from those magazines, they still need to appeal to the same advertisers. Furthermore, this leads to a privileging of middle-class educated women from metropolitan areas that are the target of these advertisements, meaning that 'the feminist subversion performed in *Bitch* is not universal, but partial, contradictory and contingent' (Bailey, 2003, p. 2). It is also worth noting that as a magazine that currently costs $7.50 (*Bitch*, 2020) it is not necessarily going to be accessible to poorer women. This chapter will analyse whether this privilege is evident in the range of articles that can be seen in *BITCHfest*.

The tensions between appealing to a wide audience and maintaining feminist values have been noted by Zarnow (2010), who links *Ms.*, *Bust* and *Bitch*, suggesting that a lineage can be drawn between the magazines. She argues that they have 'all grappled with a central dilemma facing creators of popular feminist magazines – how far feminism can be mainstreamed before selling out'. Zarnow (2010, p. 289) points to the relatively low-fi production of *Bitch* in comparison to *Bust*, noting that the magazine began with 'start-up capital of $350 for three hundred zines' from the grandfather of founder Lisa Jervis. However, the reliance on family support is evidence of the privilege that is needed to set up a feminist magazine in a capitalist culture. Similarly, Zarnow (2010, p. 291) notes that for the first two years of the magazine, contributors were 'largely Jervis's and Zeisler's friends'. There is a question here about the extent to which a magazine can be inclusive if the contributors come from the narrow social circle of the magazine's editors. Having a more professionalised setup means that you can reach both a wider audience of readers and potential writers and can also pay those writers. However, as this book has argued throughout, there is also a compromise made if you work with the market.

THE BUST GUIDE TO THE NEW WORLD ORDER AND BITCHFEST

This section of this chapter will provide a thematic analysis on *The BUST Guide to the New World Order* and *BITCHfest*. Thematic analysis has been chosen as it is the most suitable method for 'identifying, analysing, and reporting patterns (themes) within data (Braun and Clarke, 2006, p. 6). It has also been chosen as a method in order to be consistent with the analysis that was carried out in the first part of the book. As with Part I, content analysis will be used to identify what key themes are discussed in the books. This will be followed by a textual analysis that will analyse how the books discussed the feminist issues that were most prevalent in the thematic analysis.

THE BUST GUIDE TO THE NEW WORLD ORDER

The Bust Guide to the New World Order is split into eight sections (table 6.1).

Most of the chapters have around eight articles in them. Interestingly, given that this is a book of articles from a feminist magazine, the section on men has the most articles, followed by the chapter on sex. The inclusion of men in the book (alongside discussions of men in this chapter; there are additional

Table 6.1. Bust

Name of Chapter	Number of articles in chapter
Our Womenly Ways	8
Feminist Fatale: Busting the Beauty Myth	6
Sex and the Single Girl	10
Men are from Uranus	11
Growing up Girl	6
Yo' Mama, Yo' Self	8
Media Whores	8
Herstory: Girls on Girls Feminism	8

articles written by or about men in the rest of the book) means that the book differs dramatically in the extent to which men were discussed in *Spare Rib* or even *Ms*. The book presents a version of feminism that is pro-sex, pro-popular culture and pro-consumer culture. For example, in the article 'The Rise and Fall of My Boobs', Ophelia Lipps declares: 'I love being a woman and I love having breasts. I love the attention they can get and the way that they can turn on a lover' (p. 11). Here expressions of femininity are not understood as reinforcing gender stereotypes, but instead as potentially empowering. Similarly, in the introduction to 'Femme Fatale: Busting the Beauty Myth', Debbie Stoller rejects the views of second wave feminists by arguing that 'thirty years later, it seems we gals have rummaged through that trash can and recycled just about everything in it' (p. 42). The use of the informal term 'gal' rather than 'woman' is repeated throughout the anthology and suggests an ironic playfulness that also arguably serves to distance *Bust* from the second wave. Similarly, Esther Gyn implores the reader to 'remember my adage: a little bright red lipstick will always brighten your day' (p. 56).

Alongside an attitude that celebrates make-up and fashion, there is also a very sex-positive tone in the anthology. Articles about sex are the second most prevalent within the magazine. Although the introduction to the chapter on sex acknowledges that the impact of feminism has been less 'apparent' in the 'bedroom' (p. 75), the chapter generally views sex positively. For example, in the article on the Magic Wand vibrator, Betty Boob suggests that she was 'trying to feel empowered, sex positive and daring' (p. 85). Other articles in the chapter discuss giving blow jobs, and 'how to be as horny as a guy' (p. 101). This can be contrasted with the ambivalent and often hostile ways that the sex industry was viewed in *Spare Rib* and *Ms*. However, this is not to say that the presentation of sex in *Bust* is necessarily more progressive. Glick (2000, p. 19) critiques 'those contemporary pro-sex and queer theories that encourage us, as feminists and sexual minorities, to fuck our way to freedom'. Similarly, Gillis et al. (2004, p. 169) quote Heywood and Drake, who argue that third-wave feminists 'often take cultural production and sexual politics as key sites of struggle, seeking to use desire and pleasure as well as anger to fuel struggles for justice'. The frequent linking of sex with empowerment in *Bust* is arguably an example of this. It is also important to note that for the most part, there is less discussion of queer sex. This suggests that even if the magazine is sex positive, this is still viewed within a heteronormative framework.

Another significant chapter focuses on the relationship between feminism and popular culture. In the introduction to the chapter, Debbie Stoller argues that 'most of us '90s-type gals like to immerse ourselves in the current pop culture like it's a warm scented bath'. Whilst the chapter is critical of some pop cultural products, for the most part, popular culture is not viewed as 'unavoidably antagonistic' as the relationship between second wave feminism and popular culture has been characterised (Gillis, 2004, p. 169). This is reinforced by the inclusion of pieces by Courtney Love, and an interview with Iggy Pop as part of the section on history, as well as an interview with Sonic Youth's Thurston Moore. This again reinforces the extent to which popular culture was viewed as a potential pleasure, with less focus on the potential problems with it.

A key difference between *Bust* and *Spare Rib* and *Ms.* is that there is very little discussion of politics. Although there is some discussion of racism and sexism, this is viewed as a personalised issue, as seen through the use of first-person narrative. Similarly, the use of pseudonym throughout reinforces this sense of personalisation since pseudonyms were often comical nicknames such as 'Betty Boob' or 'Scarlett Fever' that further reinforce the playful tone of the magazine. The personal nature of most of the articles arguably makes it difficult to view these issues on a structural level. This is noted by Nyugen (2012, 178), who argues that the focus on the personal means that 'intimate cultures sought to build a company of persons whose hopes for authentic self-knowledge and communion somehow become the foundation of a more just world'. The extent to which this can lead to change is debatable. Whilst it is unfair to expect a zine, a media that is personal, almost by definition, to do this, it is important to acknowledge the extent to which feminist media represent the wider movement and help to shape priorities. Therefore, if these priorities are generally focused on personal empowerment, this will mean that this is the message that will be transmitted.

BITCHfest

BITCHfest was published in 2006 and differs significantly in tone to the *Bust Guide to the New World Order*. Whilst the *Bust* book has a personal tone and the contributors are often writing about their own experiences, *BITCHfest* takes a much more formal tone. This can be seen in the subtitle of the book: 'Ten Years of Cultural Criticism from the Pages of *Bitch* Magazine'. This suggests that the aim of the collection is to highlight the contributions that *Bitch* made to criticism, rather than focus on women's personal experiences. The book is split into eight sections (table 6.2).

As table 6.2 demonstrates, there is a fairly even spread across all of the topics, though some articles are represented more than others. There are also features that are included in *BITCHfest* that were not included in the *Bust Guide to the New Girl Order*. *BITCHfest* includes a resource list at the end of the book, which aims to be an 'all-too-brief guide to some of our favorite writers, thinkers, organizations' (p. 353). This suggests that the book aims to be a starting point for a wider feminist learning. In this respect, the book

Table 6.2.   *BITCHfest*

Name of chapter	Number of articles in chapter
Hitting Puberty	7
Ladies and Gentlemen: Femininity, Masculinity and Identity	9
The *F* Word	7
Desire: Love, Sex and Marketing	8
Domestic Arrangements	5
Beauty Myths and Beauty Projects	6
Confronting the Mainstream	7
Talking Back: Activism and Pop Culture	5

shares similarities with feminist magazines *Spare Rib* and *Ms.* in that they aim to provide a way for women to find out more about feminism (Erdman Farrell, 1998; Laing and Sutton, 1999).

Throughout *BITCHfest* there is constant critique of the way that feminism has been commodified. Whilst *Bust* makes some concessions to consumer culture, this is not evident in *Bitch*. For example, in 'Teen Mean Fighting Machine' Gabrielle Moss (2005, p. 45) describes girl power as 'less a movement than a marketing pitch', suggesting an awareness of the commodification of feminism. Similarly, in the introduction to the chapter of articles on 'The *F* Word', *Bitch editor* Lisa Jervis points to 'the distinction between feminism's vibrancy, nuance and commitment to social justice and the superficial appropriation of its catchphrases'. This is something that has a continuing relevance, since feminism has become increasingly ripe for commodification (Banet-Weiser, 2018). *Bitch* differs from *Bust* in the extent to which it critiques this commodification. The differing attitudes of *Bust* and *Bitch* is important to consider. As with *Spare Rib* and *Ms.*, analysis of *Bust* and *Bitch* alongside each other helps us to identify the multiple perspectives within feminism. This is especially important in helping us to consider feminism as a plural, rather than singular movement.

The critique of the commodification of feminism can also be seen in an article from Fall 1998. The range of articles that discuss this issue suggests that this was an ongoing issue for *Bitch*. Hao (1998, p. 111) argues that we cannot take for granted the 'apparently unquestioning acceptance of women and feminism'. The use of 'apparently' suggests doubt in this acceptance. Again, it is interesting to note that this is an issue that has continually been discussed by feminists, since it is something that was argued by writers in *Spare Rib* and is also something that will be explored in the chapter on digital feminism. This suggests that the relationship between feminism and capitalism continues to be one that feminist media returns to. On the one hand, this counters the notion that feminism has become completely neoliberal. On the other hand, the fact that this is an issue that feminist media is coming back to again and again suggests an entanglement that is difficult to escape from.

The tension between the recognition of the nefarious impact of capitalism can be seen when reading Hao's article intertextually with the advertising material analysed earlier in this chapter. Hao is clear that her position as a 'twenty-five-year-old woman working a corporate day job' means that she represents a 'cash cow' (p. 112). Similarly, she also acknowledges that corporations have 'learned that the best way to sell to women is to make them feel as if they're important. As if they matter. In short, to speak to them as feminists' (p. 112). However, as this book has already attested to, *Bitch* themselves are aware of the extent to which their readers as feminists are clearly valuable consumers, in the same way that *Ms.* positioned their readers as valuable consumers in the 1980s (Thom, 1997).

However, whilst there are contradictions between the rhetoric that is seen by *Bitch* in their corporate materials and Hao's essay, it is interesting to see that the extent to which feminism has become individualised is called out. Hao (1998, p. 114) notes that advertisements 'put forth a vision of feminism that is increasingly devoid of any sense of community or vitality', whilst also noting that 'capitalism isn't about welcoming women into the fold or using our newfound economic clout to make changes in the way the system works. It's about making money'. Although *Bitch* is ultimately concerned with popular culture, as Hao's essay shows us, this does not mean that it consumes this popular culture without interrogation. It is particularly interesting that the way that feminism has become individualised is remarked upon here. As the discussion of *Teen Vogue* and *xoJane* in the next chapter will demonstrate, feminist media was much more likely to use this personalised address and as a result a much more individualistic feminism can be seen. Similarly, Nyugen (2012) critiques the emphasis on personal subjectivity by some riot grrrls. However, Hao's essay suggests some awareness of the ways in which individualised feminism can have an impact on the extent to which feminism can engage with capitalism.

Since celebrity culture is itself a lucrative industry, it is also an issue that needs to be discussed in relation to capitalism. 'Celebrity Jeopardy: The Perils of Feminist Fame' (2003) engages with the concept of the feminist leader, a concept that we will also discuss in the next chapter. Fudge (2003) suggests that the figure of the celebrity feminist is in part constructed since 'one is not born but rather made a famous feminist' (p. 126). However, rather than view the feminist leader as a wholly negative aspect of feminism, she warns feminists against 'vilifying leadership and fame' since this this 'results only in our icons being chosen for us – not by us' (p. 126). This suggests that the feminist leader can be positive because she provides a way for feminism to present itself in the press in an independent way, not one that is dictated to by the mass media.

However, Fudge goes on to quote Baumgardner and Richards, who note that '"[People] have begun conflating celebrity with expertise. She who gets the most attention is presumed to be the "leader" regardless of the content of her message or her character' (Baumgardner and Richards, qtd, in Fudge, 2003, p. 132). This is an important point to consider, since visibility favours some women over other. For example, in discussing the concept of feminist visibility, Banet-Weiser (2018) suggests that feminisms that are more amenable to capitalism are more likely to be more visible. Interestingly, whilst Fudge (2003, p. 133) suggests that 'we shoot ourselves in the foot when we punish or ostracize leaders'; she also notes, 'Feminists have to let go of the notion that to be a public figure is to seek personal glory and personal glory alone'. Arguably, this is a pragmatic approach that acknowledges both the need to work collectively whilst also acknowledging the fact that we exist within a patriarchal and capitalist society.

The concept of choice within capitalism can also be seen in Andi Zeisler's article on plastic surgery. Whilst *Bust* was at times quite permissive about the beauty industry, as seen in some of the articles that have been mentioned previously in this chapter, *Bitch* is much more nuanced. The concept of choice is invoked by Zeisler (1998, p. 259), who acknowledges:

> Feminism these days is about defining our own terms, being able to adapt former definitions and shift them around to suit us. This is why we not only no longer have to shun lipstick but can actually turn the act of wearing it into a feminist statement.

In spite of this, there is an understanding that these choices need to be framed within their context. McRobbie (2009) notes that post-feminism relies on appropriating concepts of empowerment and choice from feminism. Zeisler suggests to the reader that we should not judge women for their choices, which on the face of it supports a post-feminist idea that choice is all that matters when judging whether an action is feminist. However, Zeisler goes onto acknowledge the way that society has a 'cultural ideal' that affects the choices that women make (p. 259). This shows that *Bitch* understood the tensions between, on the one hand, acknowledging the pleasures of consumer culture, whilst on the other acknowledging the extent to which this culture also has a potentially coercive influence. The discussion of the relationship between *Bitch* and the mainstream is detailed in a whole chapter of *BITCH-fest*. The title of the chapter, 'Confronting the Mainstream' (Zeisler, 2006, p. 281) points to the extent to which the mainstream is adversarial. However, the aim of *Bitch* is to interrogate popular culture, often leading to a tension between enjoyment and oppression. Zeisler (2006, p. 282), suggests that:

loving pop culture comes at a price, and for many women that price is most often a deep sense of betrayal at being told the lives that we're shown onscreen, in books, and in advertising are accurate, important and charmingly quirky reflections of our own.

Furthermore, Zeisler suggests that 'fictional women have been asked to symbolise their generation'. This highlights the important of interrogating popular culture, since it is so important in shaping how women are seen in the world.

The final chapter of this book will analyse *xoJane*, which was founded by former *Sassy* editor Jane Pratt. It is particularly significant, then, that *BITCH-fest* has such a blistering attack on *xoJane* precursor *Jane*. As has already been alluded to in this book, Jane Pratt edited *Sassy* and then *xoJane*. Groeneveld (2016, p. 26) notes that both Lisa Jervis and Andi Zeisler did internships at *Sassy*, and Jervis and Zeisler are complimentary of *Sassy*, describing it as 'the sharp, celebrated teen mag that was staunchly unwilling to pull its readers into the spiral of insecurity and product consumption' (p. 285). However, the article then goes on to critique successor *Jane* at some length. The aim of analysing this article in this book is to demonstrate how even texts which might be considered feminist were open to critique by other feminists. It helps us to resist the urge to see feminist media as monolithic, in the same way that earlier chapters of this book.

Zeisler and Jervis (2006) describe *Jane* as 'fake and sanctimonious' (p. 286). Furthermore, they argue that 'the fact that every page of the magazine has been injected with irrelevant personal titbits is precisely what's supposed to make *Jane* more accessible than women's glossies like *Elle* or *Glamour*. This is interesting, because it suggests that this accessibility is actually a way of maintaining power since 'their in-jokes and self-congratulatory tone aren't so much about reaching out to their audience in an effort to make them feel comfortable and understanding as about holding themselves above said audience'. This suggests that the personal address is not in service of maintaining a feminist community but is instead a way to maintain dominance.

Another interesting point is the extent to which Zeisler and Jervis critique the workplace politics of *Bitch*, noting that in one issue 'Jane Pratt lashes out at an intern who thought that it might not be such a hot idea to put Pamela Anderson on the cover' (p. 288). One of the critiques of the magazine is that it is an inequitable workplace. Furthermore, they note that 'anything run by a major media conglomerate can hardly buck the ad-driven culture of women's magazines that literally depends on the product plug for its revenue stream' (p. 289). This suggests that it is important to consider the economic environment that magazines are produced within, something that has been continually discussed in this book. The tensions between the corporate mainstream and *Jane*'s political ideals, as well as the working practices within the magazine has been discussed here, because it provides a pre-cursor to remarkably similar discussions on the topic a couple of decades later in *xoJane*, which will be discussed in detail in the next chapter.

CONCLUSION

This chapter has identified the ways in which feminist media production in the 1990s need to be read in relation to second wave feminist media, in order to understand feminist media history as a continuum. As has been demonstrated in this chapter, there were clear parallels in the way that feminists in the 1990s used the media in order to create spaces in which to explore their experiences. This highlights the continued importance of feminist media.

However, as the second part of this chapter demonstrates, feminist media in the 1990s did not exist in a vacuum. As feminist magazines with some commercial success, *Bitch* and *Bust* provide useful case studies for helping us to understand the relationship between the magazines and capitalism. In *Bitch*'s case, the analysis of corporate material for advertisers highlights the way that their readership was presented as attractive to advertisers, and how feminism was used as a potential selling point.

The content analysis that was presented in this chapter shows how for *Bust* in particular there was a much greater focus on the individual and a narrative of empowerment and choice. This was not seen in *Bitch*, which had a much more ambivalent attitude towards popular culture. The differences between these two magazines highlight the need to provide comparative analyses that do not assume a homologous feminist media landscape.

In the next and final chapter of this book, I move on to look at the ways that contemporary feminist and women's blogs engage with feminist ideas within a capitalist digital publishing industry in the twenty-first century.

Chapter 7

Digital Feminist Media

In this chapter, I explore how feminists are using the internet to produce feminist media today. The aim of this chapter is not to overemphasise the differences between 'fourth wave' feminists and their predecessors. Instead, I chart the ways that contemporary feminists are engaging in debates about the relationship between feminism and capitalism, in ways that show a continuity between feminism past and present. I begin by outlining the existing research on digital feminism, before moving on to discuss four case studies. The case studies for this chapter are *xo Jane*, *Teen Vogue* and *gal-dem*. These have been chosen because of the differing ways each site represented feminism and engaged with capitalism in order to operate as media organisations.

FEMINISM ON THE INTERNET

As with the historical examples described in this book, feminism on the internet provides an opportunity for feminists to communicate with each other and mobilise around key feminist issues (Everett, 2004). Researchers have recognised the importance of new technologies for feminists. Kahn and Kellner (2007, p. 621) note that 'scores of feminist organizations deploy internet politics and increasing numbers of women are active in blogging and other cutting edge cyberculture'. In the years since Kahn and Kellner made this statement, the internet has become increasingly important.

Blogs have key features that are distinct from offline media, both for the reader and for the researcher, most notably in the level of interactivity that can be seen as well as the quicker turnover of posts. Key features of blogs include 'links to sources of the story in question as well as other commentaries and analysis', whilst the comment section invites contributions from readers (Doueihi,

2011, p. 59). Commenting is encouraged as a way for the author and readers to communicate with each other, in both positive and negative ways. The ability to provide links to other sources within blogs distinguishes them from media formats, whilst Lovink (2008, p. 2) notes that blogs allow for sharing of posts and creating of communities. The sharing of posts across the internet is also aided by social media platforms such as Twitter, Instagram and Facebook.

Schuster (2013, p. 16) describes feminist blogs as a 'popular way of raising awareness and sharing information'. This is supported by Keller (2011, p. 4), who highlights the importance of feminist blogs as sites where young women have 'political agency' when this might not be afforded to them in the wider culture. It is the creation of this alternative space that links blogging to earlier forms of feminist media activism. Feminist blogging, especially amongst young women can be compared to the media production of Riot grrrls and feminist magazines in the 1970s and 1980s. They are opportunities for young women to circumvent mainstream media outlets and satisfy a 'need to act as cultural producers at a time when they feel overwhelmingly interpellated as consumers' (Harris, 2008, p. 486).

The extent to which online feminism has become an important tool is also argued in the *#Femfuture* report (2013), which analyses how online feminism is becoming an increasingly potent force. The report writers Courtney E. Martin and Vanessa Valenti argue that:

> the explosion of feminist blogs, online organizing (including online petitions) and social media campaigns has transformed the ways in which the movement's most scrappy entrepreneurs, thought leaders and grass roots activists think about feminism. (p. 3)

Similarly, they argue that 'online feminists have served as powerful allies for feminist organizations'. This has also been argued by Retallack et al. (2016, p. 86), who note that the internet is an 'unprecedented platform for participatory engagement with feminism' and argue that this has led to feminism's increased visibility. Given that this is the case, it is important to analyse the ways in which online feminist media represents feminism, both at the smaller grassroots and in larger organisations.

CRITICISMS AND LIMITATIONS OF FEMINIST BLOGS

There has been debate about the impact feminist blogging has in comparison to previous forms of activism. Schuster (2013, p. 10) points to the way in which feminist blogging has been derided by some as '"slactivism", which has little impact on political decisions and potentially distracts from more effective forms of participation'. Whilst feminist blogging provides a community for feminists, there are questions about its efficacy in enacting change. Schuster (2013, p. 9) suggests that older feminists are not always aware of the digital activism of their younger counterparts, so that 'the use of online tools contributes to making young feminists "invisible" not only to the wider public but also to their political peers of older generations'. In Schuster's research, such narratives place modern feminists as apathetic in contrast to predecessors who took part in concrete and tangible action on the streets.

Now that I have provided an overview of how feminist media operates in the present day, I will be exploring this in relation to the concept of the mainstream. This chapter will move on to explore feminism's current and historical relationship with the mainstream to provide context to discussion of feminism and *The Feminist Times*, *Teen Vogue* and *xoJane*.

CELEBRITY FEMINISM

The relationship between feminism and the mainstream has been discussed throughout this book. However, the concept of the feminist leader provides a link between the feminist media of the past and present. As with Gloria Steinem and *Ms.*, the relationship between feminism and mainstream can be identified in *Teen Vogue*, through the visibility of their former columnist Lauren Duca. Feminist media production has always to some extent been engaged with mainstream media cultures. Murray (2004) notes, for example, that despite her criticism of women's magazines, extracts from Betty Freidan's *The Feminine Mystique* (1963) were still included in popular women's magazines such as *McCall's* and *Ladies Home Journal*. Even though Freidan was critical of the magazine publishing industry, this did not stop the inclusion of her work within those same magazines. It is important to consider these relationships, not least because it suggests a continuum between historical feminist media production and the present, as the analysis of *Teen Vogue* will demonstrate.

Another key figure who has both strong feminist credentials and a mainstream appeal is Gloria Steinem, the founder of *Ms.*, which has been discussed substantially in earlier chapters. Steinem has cultivated an image of a famous feminist, seen through interviews with Jennifer Aniston for the *Makers* conference (Makers.com. 2014), and a guest appearance on female-led legal drama *The Good Wife* (2014). Later in this chapter I will explore the similarities that can be drawn between Steinem and *Teen Vogue's* Lauren Duca. One key indication of how Steinem has been represented as a leader can be seen through how she is described on her *Wikipedia* page as:

an American feminist, journalist and social and political activist who become nationally recognized as a leader of, and spokeswoman for, the feminist movement.

Although one must of course take whatever is said on *Wikipedia* with a pinch of salt, it is used as a source for many who are researching topics they are unfamiliar with. It is therefore telling that Steinem is positioned as so significant. It is also significant that 'the women's movement' is presented as a monolithic entity since, as Barbara Arneil (1999, p. 3) argues that 'no definition of feminism is satisfactory because the term is amorphous and ever changing and because there are so many schools of thought'. By positioning Steinem as the leader of a movement that is so multifaceted, a liberal version of feminism is prioritised, since this is the feminism Steinem is so clearly related to. As David Bouchier (1987, p. 45) argues, the goal of liberal feminism is to 'reform the social system in line with American liberal values'. This is the version of feminism that has continually been reinforced in the popular imagination. Alice Echols (1989) has noted that radical feminists often rejected this view of feminism, representing the heterogeneous nature of feminism. I will explore in this chapter the extent to which these contradictions can still be seen today.

The recent rise in popular feminism has coincided with the rise of celebrity. The concern about the extent to which popular feminism is understood within an individualistic discourse also has a historical precedent. Susan Brownmiller (2000) notes that there was often conflict within the women's movement over the extent to which an individual could use their position to develop a profile within the wider culture. The model of the high-profile feminist is one that has endured and has been intensified by the current emphasis on celebrity feminism. Recent high-profile declarations of feminism by celebrities such as Emma Watson, Taylor Swift, Jennifer Lawrence, Beyoncé and Lena Dunham (Keller and Ringrose, 2015) have demonstrated the continued need to affix social and political value onto specific people, who then become representative of a much wider movement. This individualistic feminism can be understood within the context of a post-feminism that focuses on individual choice and empowerment (McRobbie, 2009; Gill, 2011, 2017). On the one hand, the prominence of female celebrity feminists is beneficial, as it widens access to feminism. On the other hand, focus on the individual ignores the effectiveness of collective action. The tension between the individual and the collective will be explored throughout this chapter.

WOMEN'S MAGAZINES AND ENGAGEMENT WITH FEMINISM IN THE TWENTY-FIRST CENTURY

As this book has already argued, there has been a rich history of criticism of women's magazines by a number of scholars (Friedan, 1963; Tuchman, 1978;

White, 1970). However, it is also important to recognise the extent to which women's magazines did begin to integrate feminist themes, and therefore need to be understood as sites of feminist discussion, even if they did not present themselves as feminist. This is especially important when discussing a magazine like *Teen Vogue* and the way in which it discusses feminist issues.

Anna Gough-Yates (2012, p. 376) refers to the work of Charlotte Brunsdon, who 'observed that to be a feminist in the 1970s and enjoy popular culture was sometimes seen to be akin to "collaborating" with the enemy'. One consequence of this was that there was a lack of engagement with the ways that women's magazines often began to integrate feminist topics into their magazines. Gough-Yates (2012, p. 381) notes that popular magazines such as *Cosmopolitan* 'attempted to introduce broader ranges of social issues to their editorial mixes but were careful to avoid any political edge for fear of antagonizing readers'. This points to the extent to which women's magazines operate within a marketplace that impacts their ability to be overtly political. However, as this chapter will suggest *Teen Vogue* differs in that it has not only become overtly political, it has still done this within a framework that supports capitalist aims of profit generation. Furthermore, *Teen Vogue* differs from older teen magazines that 'touched on feminist ideas without calling them "feminist"' (Gough-Yates, 2012, p. 394).

As I will argue in this chapter, this is reflective of the ways that feminism has become increasingly popular and acceptable. However, as I will also argue, alongside this popularisation we can also see a move towards a commercialised feminism that exists within capitalist frameworks. Whilst this is not wholly a negative thing, I will explore the extent to which this can be understood within what Dean (2010) calls the domestication of feminism, a move that removes feminism from its more radical elements. This is also a move that has been radically critiqued by Nancy Fraser (2013), who argues that feminism has been instrumentalised by neoliberalism in a way that ultimately removes the possibility of a critique of capitalism more broadly.

It is at the intersection of this debate that *Teen Vogue* and other women's magazines and blogs can be seen. Although blogs have a democratising function, in that they can be produced by anyone, they also exist within a capitalist framework, and as with earlier feminist media, the distinction between margin and mainstream needs to be considered (Sutton, 1999). This can be seen most clearly in *xoJane* and *Teen Vogue*. Although *xoJane*'s roots were in independent women's media, it was brought out by a large multinational (*Adweek*, 2015). Conversely, *Teen Vogue* could never be described as 'alternative', yet it has become a key site of resistance since Donald Trump's presidential election win in 2016, due to his racist and sexist policies.

XOJANE: FEMINISM, CAPITALISM AND
THE PERSONAL ESSAY

Although now defunct, *xoJane* is an excellent example of the entanglement between feminism and capitalism. The women's site was founded by former *Sassy* and *Jane* editor Jane Pratt. As with the feminist media that has been discussed throughout this book, there was a strong emphasis on the personal as political. However, as this chapter will argue, emotion was capitalised on within *xoJane* in order to further the visibility of the site. The emphasis on the personal can be seen in an interview with Pratt for *The Guardian*. Pratt suggests that 'the more personal and vulnerable a writer is, the better' the interviewer; Kira Cochrane describes xoJane as 'one of the most notable examples of the galloping trend for confessional writing' that 'can attract enormous audience and doesn't require extensive reporting' (Cochrane, 2013). This, coupled with the fact that 'freelance contributors are generally paid just $50 a post', means that the emphasis on confessional writing is financially beneficial to the site. It is, therefore, important to view *xoJane* as both a site where feminism is articulated and a site that aims to make money, especially given that in 2013 the site reached '2.6 million readers' (Cochrane, 2013).

The website presents an individualistic version of feminism 'where women go when they are being selfish, and where their selfishness is applauded' (*xoJane*, 2016). Feminism is presented as being about individual empowerment and 'not about changing yourself to fit into any mould of what others think you should be. It is about celebrating who you are'. The continual use of the second-person pronoun further reinforces the magazine's sense of individualism, whilst the focus on the site being 'a place to indulge in what makes you feel good' further emphasises pleasure as imperative. Although the website was originally founded by Pratt in conjunction with Say Media, it was acquired by *Time* in 2015 (Trachtenberg, 2015). Being owned by a conglomerate means that the feminism that is presented is done so through a capitalist lens. The site closed in 2016, and in the aftermath was accused by former writer Mandy Stadtmiller (2016) of 'monetiz[ing] oversharing'. The analysis in this chapter will focus specifically on the way that the confessional narrative was prioritised in *xoJane* and how this affected the presentation of feminist issues on the site.

However, it is also important to note that as Tressie McMillan Cottom (2019) argues, the personal essay is also a way that Black women were afforded a voice in a media industry that systemically marginalises them. McMillan Cottom (2019) discusses the tension between on the one hand understanding how the personal essay exploits Black women, whilst on the other acknowledging that it provides a space for complex analysis that is not available anywhere else.

XOJANE ANALYSIS

When *xoJane* ceased operation in 2016, an archive of articles was not maintained and the Wayback machine was used to access articles and therefore features such as the search engine were disabled. I analysed 300 articles from the 'issues' section of the website, fifty articles each from 2011 to 2016. These articles were selected randomly and therefore reflect a broad range of topics on the site (table 7.1).

As table 7.1 demonstrates, there was a range of topics that were discussed in *xoJane*. The most prevalent topics were politics, personal stories and stories about sexual harassment, domestic violence or abuse. It is also worth noting that as an issue the focus on individual disclosures of experiences with gender-based violence can be linked to wider emphasis on personal narratives, as this chapter will go on to demonstrate. There was also a focus on politics, with a definite uptick in discussions of politics in 2016. There were presidential elections in two of the sample years (2012 and 2016). However, there was much less focus on politics in 2012. This is perhaps unsurprising since the re-election of Barack Obama in 2012 presented fewer problems for feminists than the election of Donald Trump in 2016, and therefore it was less likely that there would be a need to discuss the election beyond congratulatory posts.

Table 7.1.   Issues Discussed in *xoJane*

Topic	2011	2012	2013	2014	2015	2016	Total number of articles	% of total
Reproductive Rights	2	1	4	0	1	3	11	**3.67**
Fashion	0	1	1	2	0	0	4	**1.33**
Entertainment	0	0	0	3	0	0	3	**1**
Audience input	0	0	1	0	1	1	3	**1**
Education	0	0	0	0	3	0	3	**1**
Religion	0	0	0	0	0	1	1	**0.33**
Health and disability	4	2	3	8	6	7	30	**10**
Politics	6	4	1	6	6	16	39	**13**
Body image	7	5	1	3	5	2	23	**7.67**
Protest	2	0	0	3	0	1	6	**2**
Careers and business	3	4	4	0	2	2	15	**5**
Parenting	1	4	1	2	4	1	13	**4.33**
Race	5	2	8	10	1	7	33	**11**
Sexual harassment/ harassment/ abuse	9	10	7	5	6	9	46	**15.3**
Personal stories	9	10	16	6	12	0	53	**17.7**
Sex and relationships	2	6	2	2	3	0	15	**5**
Environment	0	1	1	0	0	0	2	**0.67**

This chapter will now move on to focus more specifically on the way that articles in *xoJane* often focused on the personal narrative. Before doing this, I will outline how changes within the journalism industry have led to a move towards the personal. This is important to consider, since it acknowledges the extent to which the move towards the personal in *xoJane* can be understood within a wider industry context.

INTIMACY AND ONLINE JOURNALISM

There is an emerging literature on the relationship between journalism and intimacy. Beckett and Deuze (2016, p. 2) note that the media has 'become more intimate' and as such we have become 'deeply attached to our medi- ated activities'. Further to this, they argue that 'as journalism and society change, emotion is becoming a much more important dynamic in how news is produced and consumed' (p. 2). This suggests that there is an expectation that both journalists and readers have much more personal relationship with the journalism they either write or consume. There is an argument that for feminist media, this is nothing new, and that the wider industry is moving towards a mode of journalism that has historically been used within feminist discourse and women-focused journalism more generally (Steenson, 2016). However, the rise of social media has had an impact on the way that journal- ists engage with their audience within women's and feminist spaces as well, as this chapter will demonstrate.

Steenson (2016, p. 2) argues that 'the changing boundaries between private and public communication imply that journalism is becoming dominated by a discourse of intimacy'. In *xoJane* there is an increased focus on the personal, with the use of personal address as well as articles about the minutiae of everyday life. Examples of this include 'I'm not nearly as cool with having Christmassses as I thought' (Glenn, December 31, 2015); 'I had an absurd period accident in front of a high school softball team' (Higgins, Novem- ber 25, 2015). This can be linked to Steensen's argument that 'the more jour- nalism moves to social media, the more dependent on the personality of its practitioners and hence a discourse of intimacy' (Steenson, 2016, p. 26–27). This chapter will now move on to identify the way that this discourse of inti- macy is presented in *xoJane*.

CENTRING THE SELF

It is important to read the articles in *xoJane* in relation to the social and politi- cal contexts in which the articles were written within. The articles published in 2016 must, therefore, be read within the context of the US presidential election in 2016 where Donald Trump unexpectedly won. Twenty-one of the total articles from 2016 are about the election, mirroring the increase in discussions of politics around specific political events in other texts analysed in this book.

However, where *xoJane* differs from earlier texts such as *Ms.* is that alongside this political discussion there is a heavy focus on the individual. Of the fifty articles in 2016, thirty-two used a first-person pronoun or possessive pronoun such as 'I' or 'my'. In some cases, this was in reference to very personal experiences, such as sexual violence ('I thought yoga, meditation and Instagram could save me from PTSD after I was raped' (Loomes, October 21, 2016); 'I had a Halloween experience so scary that I got sober' (Hovitz, October 28, 2016)). However, in other cases, the discussion was being narrated as a personal story, even if the topic being discussed had wider political implications. For example, one S. E. Smith describes how 'when [they] voted [they] issued the country an ultimatum: it's them or me' (November 7, 2016). Similarly, Alfre Woodward's article 'I'm Alfre Woodard in This Is #whyI'mwithher' (November 2, 2016) makes the identity of the author part of the headline, suggesting that it is especially important that we know who wrote the article, not only what the article is about.

In some respects, this focus on personal narratives can be linked to much older discussions about the personal as political; for example, Thi Nyguen (2012) notes the use of the personal in the feminist media of the 1990s. However, on the other hand, this move towards personal narrative can be linked to what McRobbie (2002) describes as an increasingly personalised and individualistic narrative that is directed towards women. *xoJane* also shares its DNA with *Sassy* due to the editorship of Jane Pratt. Groeneveld (2016, p. 24) argues that 'Pratt encouraged her staff writers to develop their own individual personae through their writing', leading to writers receiving 'individualized letters from readers who identified with them particularly'. It is important to consider the extent to which collective feminist activism can take place or is even recognised when the narratives that are being emphasised focus on the individual.

THE CONFESSIONAL ESSAY

The use of the first-person narrative can be understood within the context of a boom in confessional writing in the 2010s. Felski (1998, p. 83) describes confessional writing as a 'distinctive subgenre of autobiography' and suggests that its 'importance in the context of feminism is clearly related to

the exemplary model of consciousness raising'. This is something that has
already been discussed in this book in relation to Riot grrrl and feminist
media production in the 1990s and is something that continues in the present
day. Furthermore, Felski (1998, p. 83) draws upon the similarities between
consciousness raising and the confessional essay by suggesting that 'the confessional text makes public that which has been private, typically claiming
to avoid filtering mechanisms of objectivity and detachment in its pursuit
of the truth of subjective experience'. However, in the last decade or so, the
confessional essay has also become increasingly prevalent because of the
economics of the digital media industry. The rise of the confessional essay
monetises personal experience, meaning its feminist potential is ambiguous.
Jia Tolentino (2017) argues that the personal essay came about as the rise
in social media and blogging platforms 'trained people to write about their
personal lives at length and in public'. However, alongside acknowledging
how the confessional essay partly rose as a result of changes in technology,
Tolentino (2017) quotes Sarah Hepola, 'who worked as Salon's personal-
essay editor', who suggests, '"The boom in personal essays – at Salon, at
least, but I suspect other places – was in part a response to an online climate
where more content was needed at the exact moment budgets were being
slashed"'. This highlights the need to understand the cultural economy of
feminist websites. Tolentino (2017) notes that the need to maximise 'page
views quickly and cheaply creates uncomfortable incentives for writers, editors and readers alike' since 'attention flows naturally to the outrageous'.
Furthermore, it is important to acknowledge the contradictions between being
a women's site and potentially a feminist space, in contrast with the potentially exploitative economic models that the blogging industry is based on.
The risk of exploitation is perhaps even more stark when discussing personal
and potentially painful topics since 'many women wrote about the most difficult things that had ever happened to them and received not much in return'
(Tolentino, 2017).

Similar reservations about the extent to which the ethos and financial
model could lead to problematic assumptions being made about what is progressive is also noted by Alana Massey, described in an article about the magazine's demise by fellow former staffer Mandy Stadtmiller (2016). Massey
suggests that the tagline '"where women go when they are being selfish, and
where that selfishness is applauded"' is a 'fundamentally bad premise' since
it led to a 'permissiveness about selfishness'. Although Stadtmiller's article
focuses heavily on a particularly infamous article 'My Former Friend's Death
Was a Blessing', the criticism can be applied to many articles on the site.
Furthermore, the need to stand out within a crowded marketplace means that
more controversial opinions or outrageous stories were more likely to be
prioritised. The 'It Happened to Me' feature and 'Unpopular Opinion' feature

on the site both of which emphasise individual opinion and experiences as a form of capital.

Furthermore, as with the discussion of *Ms.*'s workplace practices, we can look at the discrepancy between the idealism of a nurturing and supportive place for women with the reality of existing within a capitalist workplace that often reinforces hierarchies. Stadtmiller (2016) quotes a source who refers to the contrast between the 'radical transparency' that was supposed to be part of the magazine and the 'nurturing loving and compassionate mission of the site' with the 'façade' that hid 'secrets and a lack of authenticity'. There are also issues about how the site treats their writers, as seen in an article by a former writer for the site (Ani, 2016). Ani notes that instead of being given the '$40 or $45 per piece' that was originally quoted, the price she was given was '$35 (and then later $30). She states that she needed the money and therefore the '$250' that would be paid for eight pieces 'would really make a difference'. Arguably, the low pay given to Ani is indicative of the contradiction between seemingly feminist publications and the reality of their employment practices. A good comparison can be made here with both *Spare Rib* and *Ms.*, especially in relation to how the magazines failed to create the same kind of inclusive environment that reflected the magazines' ethos.

It is also interesting that Stadtmiller (2016) refers to site founder Jane Pratt as a 'star' and to how 'certain staffers were reminded that they were "stars" or told they simply were not'. Throughout this book, there has been a continual reference to the concept of the star. The concept of the celebrity feminist star has already been discussed in this book, but it is worth acknowledging the extent to which this concept has been reinforced throughout feminist media history. In particular, the emphasis on the 'star' furthermore highlights the extent to which feminism is understood through an individualistic lens. Taylor (2017, p. 1) notes that 'feminism has always had is celebrities, a situation that has historically caused much anxiety'. In the case of *xoJane*, the idea of the star seemingly contributed to a dysfunctional working environment. Furthermore, Taylor (2016, p. 2) argues that star feminists 'are all women who have actively worked to shape our understandings of Western feminism'. By describing Pratt as a 'star' Stadtmiller not only reinforces Pratt's influence but also reinforces the extent to which feminist media is viewed through the work of individual women in a way that makes collective work difficult, and the emphasis on the individual is also seen in *Teen Vogue*, which this chapter will now move on to.

TEEN VOGUE AND POPULAR FEMINISM

Teen Vogue is an instructive example of a women's website/magazine that has responded to the Trump presidency and provided a form of resistance that might not have been expected. *Teen Vogue*'s response to the 2016 presidential election and Lauren Duca's 'Thigh High Politics' column in particular is an articulation of what Sarah Banet-Weiser (2018) has described as 'popular feminism'. However, alongside the more progressive representations of feminism within *Teen Vogue*, the magazine is a capitalist venture, meaning that we need to acknowledge both its feminist credentials and also its limitations.

Teen Vogue is a spin-off magazine of *Vogue*,[1] the high fashion magazine. It was launched in 2003 and aimed to compete with other US magazines aimed at the teenage market such as *Cosmogirl, Seventeen* and *YT*. The first editor of *Teen Vogue*, Amy Astley, described the content of the magazine as 'fashion beauty and style' (Carr, 2003). The magazine's original aims were certainly not to discuss political issues or to educate young women on them. The first issue had over '80 pages of advertising', which is very much in keeping with the business model of women's magazines (Carr, 2003). Banet-Weiser (2018, loc 2124) notes that the introduction of new editor Elaine Welteroth led to the magazine 'publishing more overtly political and often feminist articles'. This chapter will focus on the way that this popular feminism exists alongside representations of capitalism.

The election in 2016 of Donald Trump as president of the United States heralded an increase in women's activism, and arguably a move towards popular feminism. The Women's March in Washington, planned for the day after the inauguration, is a good example of the ways that grassroots mobilisation on social media was combined with celebrity visibility and popularisation. Though Nicolini and Steffes Hansen (2018) note that the march began as a grassroots effort, it increasingly became the focus for celebrity activism as well. Hamad and Taylor (2015) describe the:

> figure of the self-professed feminist celebrity [that] was a recurring feature of Anglophone celebrity culture in 2014, snowballing over the course of the year to become a sustained and ongoing flashpoint of the cross-media celebrity landscape.

This is something that has only intensified in the past five years. Key examples of this celebrification of feminism include Emma Watson's *He for She* campaign and Beyoncé's performing with a lit-up feminist sign behind her at the 2014 *VMA* awards, and the £170 Christian Dior 'We should all be feminists' T-Shirt. This move towards 'popular' feminism can be linked to how, according to Banet-Weiser (2018, loc 236), feminism is:

> circulated in popular and commercial media, such as digital spaces like blogs, Instagram and Twitter, as well as broadcast media. As such these discourses have an accessibility that is not confined to academic enclaves or niche groups.

Teen Vogue is a good example of this; both through how its more political work is often shared online through social media and through the ways that it is used to make feminism more accessible.

The move towards a more politicised *Teen Vogue* can be seen in its current mission statement: '*Teen Vogue* is the young person's guide to saving the world' (Condé Nast website, 2019). Rather than being focused on fashion and beauty, the magazine aims to 'empower' young women. This focus on inclusivity and telling untold stories demonstrates *Teen Vogue*'s recognition of the importance of understanding the intersections of race, gender and class and how that means that some young women are less likely to be listened to than others. Jessalynn Keller (2015) argues that feminist blogs can be powerful tools for young women. Although *Teen Vogue* cannot be simplistically read as a feminist blog, and does not have the same grassroots ethos, it still presents itself as a space for young women to become more informed about politics, outside of the 'academic enclaves' that Benet-Weiser (2018, loc 241) refers to. This can be seen alongside a wider emphasis on social justice in online spaces used by young people, in spaces such as *Tumblr*, which have a relatively young demographic (Bell, 2013; Renninger, 2015).

Teen Vogue's shift in focus is indicative of the extent to which concepts such as empowerment have become central to contemporary women's media. Gill (2017, p. 624) argues that 'empowerment' and 'choice' are often utilised with a 'post-feminist' landscape that supports feminist discourses, whilst at the same time reiterating post-feminist notions of individual choice. This is a point also noted by McRobbie (2013, p. 121), who argues that 'there is something of a feminist endorsement in the political air'. Furthermore, she notes the extent to which women's magazines have now moved from including a 'ritualistic denunciation' of feminism in any articles that discuss feminist issues to an approach that 'feels able to make a claim of sorts, to a feminism of sorts'. This provides an important context for discussions of *Teen Vogue*, since the industry as a whole seems to be more amenable to feminist messaging.

However, alongside these positive representations of feminism, it is also important to note, as Banet-Weiser (2018, loc 2142) does, the extent to which *Teen Vogue* is a magazine that targets young women, and this means that it is also delegitimised since society reinforces the idea that 'teenage girls are not supposed to be interested in politics, but only in makeup and boy bands'. It is then, perhaps even more confounding, that the expressions of feminism in *Teen Vogue* sit alongside fashion, celebrity and beauty, since this destabilises the boundary between popular culture and politics.

ANALYSING *TEEN VOGUE*

Teen Vogue's homepage includes articles from a number of categories, including shopping, news and politics and fashion. Political issues sit alongside popular culture and fashion, so it is assumed that a reader is as likely to be interested in an article about immigration as they are about how to best dress for a party. This encapsulates the extent to which feminism can now be understood as popular (Banet-Weiser, 2018) and is integrated into young women's popular media.

THIGH HIGH POLITICS

In order to analyse the extent to which *Teen Vogue* represented feminism and politics, a content analysis was carried out. Due to the large number of articles on the *Teen Vogue* site, the decision was made to focus on the writing of one high-profile writer, Lauren Duca. Duca's work was chosen because she is the most visible writer for the site due to her article 'Donald Trump Is Gaslighting America' (which will be discussed later in this chapter), as well as an interview on Fox News with Tucker Carlson (Johnson, 2018). Duca is best known for 'Thigh High Politics', which demonstrates a new focus on young women's political participation within a wider context of popular culture. The title of the column 'Thigh High Politics' suggests a link to fashion (thigh high boots), and Duca is a young writer in a similar age demographic to the intended readers of *Teen Vogue*.

There were 816 articles by Duca, and 389 are included in this analysis, from a period between July 17, 2016, and August 2018. This covers the final months of the 2016 presidential election campaign, as well as the first twenty months of the Trump administration. Articles were categorised, as table 7.2 shows.

As table 7.2 shows, there is not an equal number of articles published across 2016, 2017 and 2018. However, the per cent changes in the number of articles demonstrate the shift in focus in Duca's work, and arguably in *Teen Vogue* more generally. There is a substantial increase in the coverage given to politics, and much less coverage of other topics.

In 2016, Duca was also writing a significant number of articles about fashion, beauty and celebrity culture, suggesting that her focus was not solely on politics and social justice. The juxtaposition of features of mainstream magazines with feminism can be understood in the context of McRobbie's (1997, p. 200) argument that women's magazines have become more receptive to feminism since the 1990s, though she did argue at that time that 'the place of feminism in the magazines is debateable'. It is also important to consider

Table 7.2.   Thigh High Politics

Topic	2016	% of total 2016	2017	% of total 2017	2018	% of total 2018
Politics	61	**18**	38	**75**	7	**70**
Feminism and sexual politics	14	**4**	6	**12**	3	**30**
LGBT	5	**1**	1	**2**	0	
Fashion	32	**9**	1	**2**	0	
Climate change	1	**0.3**	3	**6**	0	
Celebrity	118	**34**	3	**6**	0	
World news	5	**1**	1	**2**	0	
Beauty	37	**11**	0	**0**	0	
Food	1	**0.3**	0	**0**	0	
Other	40	**12**	0	**0**	0	
Film and TV	17	**5**	0	**0**	0	
Sport	16*	**5**	0	**0**	0	
Total	347	**100.6****	51	**105**	10	**100**

* The majority of the sport stories are regarding the 2016 Summer Olympics in Rio.

** This is a rounded figure.

the current political context in which young people engage with concepts of social justice, which might mean that the juxtaposition of celebrity gossip and feminism is in keeping with an increasingly socially aware demographic that also remains interested in popular culture. Rivers (2017, p. 48) quotes Halls (2006), who argues that "'[m]illenials are a generation defined by words like 'check your privilege', 'feminist', 'consent'". Furthermore, Rivers (2017, p. 48) notes that though maligned by the right, these qualities 'can and also do hold positive connotations'. This gestures towards the extent to which young people have a lexicon for discussing social justice issues that were perhaps not available or as popular to previous generations. Again, the impact of the internet is important to consider, since

> the apparent 'newness' attributed to the fourth wave is associated with developing forms of media and technology such as *Facebook* and *Twitter*, which have led to the emergence of so-called 'hashtag feminism' (Dixon, 2014). (Rivers, 2017, p. 107)

Teen Vogue, Politics and the Trump Era

Lauren Duca's viral article 'Donald Trump Is Gaslighting America' was published online in December 2016. This was around the time that the last print issue of *Teen Vogue* was published (*Teen Vogue*, 2016). The online nature of the article is significant as the article was shared widely and outside of the intended audience. Bruns and Highfield (2012) point to how Twitter in particular is used to increase the network for who sees a piece of work. The article is described in the stand-first as a 'scorched-earth op-ed', indicative of the extent to which Duca pulls no punches and is explicit in her anger. Duca describes how:

> a foreign government's interference in our election is a threat to our freedom, and the President-elect's attempt to undermine the American people's access to that information undermines the very foundation upon which this country was built.

The article assumes a certain level of knowledge from a reader, seen through references to terminology such as the 'electoral college' without explaining what this means to the reader. This is significant because it assumes that the teen-intended audience is already savvy enough to know about it, which alludes to the magazine's mission statement of having a well-informed young female audience. Gaslighting is defined by Duca as to 'psychologically manipulate a person to the point where they question their own sanity'. Gaslighting as a term originates from the 1938 play *Gaslight* where the female protagonist is manipulated by her husband into thinking she is psychologically disturbed (*BBC News*, 2017). It has become a prominent term in recent years to describe the way women are undermined. To suggest that the whole country has been gaslit gestures towards the extent to which Trump has lied consistently, and Duca specifically critiques his lies about immigration, Iraq and unemployment.

However, the use of the metaphor of gaslighting also obscures the extent to which many Americans voted for Trump willingly and assumes a liberal audience that cannot understand the reasons that someone might vote for him. Duca provides practical advice on what to do, including asking readers to 'empower' themselves with information. Duca's analysis is intersectional, as can be seen through the statement:

> When defending each of the identities in danger of being further marginalized, we must remember the thing that binds this pig-headed hydra together.

'Donald Trump Is Gaslighting America' marked the beginning of a series of articles by Duca that discussed the incoming Trump presidency, alongside other political issues such as Black Lives Matter and the Dakota pipeline. As well as articles that were heavily critical of Trump, there were also articles that promoted Hillary Clinton and her campaign, for example, 'Hillary Clinton Encourages Hope and Determination Among Supporters in the New Year' (December 31, 2016). The broadly favourable coverage of Clinton is indicative of how Clinton was endorsed by popular feminism (Banet-Weiser, 2018).

Banet-Weiser (2018, loc 3467) suggests that 'Clinton was a very good representative for popular feminism' due to her amenability to capitalism and the extent to which she was a 'stellar example of an entrepreneurial woman' (loc 3467). Furthermore, Banet-Weiser notes how 'Clinton's femaleness stood in for feminism' (loc 3459). This can be seen in the range of articles about Clinton by Duca, where Clinton is positioned as an ideal feminist figure, especially for young women. It is notable that Clinton's media appearances in the run-up to the 2016 presidential election also included guest appearances on *Broad City*, a show about two young women that has been marketed as feminist (*Comedy Central*, 2017).

However, Banet-Weiser (2018) argues that the positioning of Clinton as the idealised popular feminist figure is problematic because it ignores aspects of her political career that supported capitalism and reduced access to welfare. Although *Teen Vogue* does include more political coverage than previously was the case, it still frames it within the context of established politics, and there is little room to discuss the problems with Clinton and her politics. Comparisons can be drawn here between *Teen Vogue* and *Ms.* As discussed in the chapter that looked at the representation of politics in *Ms.*, *Ms.* tended to take a liberal feminist approach that was amenable to mainstream politics and less likely to critique the existing political system. It is useful to note that both publications aimed to appeal to a broad audience. This shows some of the limitations with popular feminism in that it is not as able to show the alternatives to perspectives within the existing political system.

LAUREN DUCA AND THE FEMINIST BRAND

Duca's positioning as a brandable feminist must also be considered when discussing her work for *Teen Vogue*. Pruchniewska's work (2018) on the way that freelance feminist writers online construct their feminist brand is helpful in analysing Duca's work for *Teen Vogue*. She draws upon the work of Rosalind Gill (2010), Angela McRobbie (2009) and Gina Neff (2012) to argue that 'those who produce cultural content online are working in an increasingly precarious neoliberal environment' (p. 811). It is important to note then that Duca states in her Twitter profile that she is freelance. It is the freelance nature of the work which may explain the diversity of topics that she wrote on, especially before the 2016 election. This suggests that it was the visibility of Duca's work in the wake of the 2016 election that allowed for a shift in focus away from celebrity and fashion as her work became increasingly visible.

It is also significant that Duca has become the most well-known writer for *Teen Vogue* and that a majority of the coverage is about Duca's articles. This can be linked to Pruchniewska's (2018, p. 811) argument that:

the practices of personal branding, promotion and audience interaction in the pursuance of career advancement embrace the rhetoric of individualism emblematic of neoliberalism. Those who write feminist content online must adhere to this.

This can certainly be seen in the case of Duca's work in *Teen Vogue* scans better. Although some of Duca's articles ('We Have to Stop Pretending We Can't Do Anything About Gun Violence (October 2, 2017); 'Harvey Must Be a Turning Point in the Way We Respond to Climate Change (August 30, 2017)) gesture towards a sense of collectivism by addressing an imagined 'we', others emphasise Duca's persona strongly ('Lauren Duca Sounds Off on Why Pop Culture and Politics Are So Intertwined' (May 23, 2017); 'To Trolls, With Love' (January 10, 2017)). The focus on the individual can be linked to the extent to which the 'collectivist goals of feminism' (Pruchniewska, 2018, p. 814) are undermined by a focus on individuals. Pruchniewska's (2018, p. 814) research question: 'How can post-feminist authorship in a digital neoliberal environment be reconciled with feminist values?' is useful to consider in relation to Duca's work in *Teen Vogue*. Whilst on the one hand, Duca's political writing provided a useful primer for young women to understand contemporary politics and feminism, this cannot be divorced from the extent to which Duca is positioned as a central figure in *Teen Vogue*'s coverage, becoming synonymous with *Teen Vogue*'s recent move towards progressive politics.

TEEN VOGUE, COMMODITY FEMINISM AND ENGAGEMENT WITH CAPITALISM

The extent to which *Teen Vogue* can present more radical ideas than might be expected can also be seen in Kim Kelly's (2018) article 'What "Capitalism" Is and How It Affects People', which provides an overview of capitalism, as well as acknowledging the recent move towards socialism for younger people. Although ostensibly a primer on the benefits and disadvantages of capitalism, there are signs within that Kelly takes a critical approach to it, and so it is not unbiased. She describes the 'authoritarian creep of the ultra-capitalist, anti-socialist Trump regime'. This explicitly links capitalism to authoritarianism and government oppression. The juxtaposition of 'ultra-capitalist' and 'anti-socialist' and 'the authoritarian creep' positions being a capitalist as the same as being anti-democratic, and conversely rhetorically links socialism to democracy. An anti-capitalist position can further be seen in the tweet that *Teen Vogue* posted to promote the article. The tweet states that you 'can't #endpoverty without ending capitalism'. This presents a socialist feminist perspective which historically has been less common within a US context

(Humm, 1992). In fact, when compared to Ms., this is particularly radical. However, as this chapter will now go on to show, this anti-capitalist rhetoric sits alongside advertising and the consumerist mission of Condé Nast.

In spite of its political content, *Teen Vogue* is still a commercial site that features fashion, beauty and advertising. This is noted by Banet-Weiser (2018, p. 7), who notes that 'the architecture of many of these popular media platforms is capitalist and corporate'. Similarly, when discussing *Ms.* Erdman Farrell (2011) notes that the magazine was a profit-making venture and therefore relied upon advertising and had an impact on the extent to which it could be a radical proposition. All this speaks to a broader issue with how to use popular platforms to disseminate alternative and at times radical messages, whilst at the same time placing them within an architecture that is by its very nature capitalist. The comparison between *Teen Vogue* and *Ms.* that can be made also demonstrates the extent to which this is an ongoing issue, and one that has a historical precedent. As feminism becomes increasingly popular within mainstream culture, this issue will continue.

A critique of *Teen Vogue*'s relationship with capitalism needs to be understood in relation to the concept of neoliberal feminism. Although Rottenberg (2017, p. 329) argues that we are 'witnessing a historic moment' in terms of feminism's visibility, she also warns that we must understand this within the context of what Angela McRobbie describes as '"accommodating feminism"' (Rottenberg, 2017, p. 330). Rottenberg (2014, p. 419) is critical of the extent to which neoliberal feminism can challenge neoliberalism, arguing that it 'offers no critique'. Furthermore, she argues that the focus on neoliberalism reinforces an individualistic discourse.

Although Kelly's (2018) article 'What "Capitalism" Is and How It Affects People' directly engages with the problems of capitalism, the reliance on the capitalistic publishing industry for this to be possible problematises its potency. Martin and Valenti (2013, p. 3) note that for many independent feminist bloggers there is a significant risk of burnout since 'they are in direct competition with one another for the scraps that come from third-party ad companies'. This points to the extent to which the online feminist media space is not egalitarian, since it is implicated with capitalism. It is also important to note that the current blogging economy, with its focus on freelance work and free labour, also means that those with less economic capital are less likely to be able to participate (Martin and Valenti, 2013). Such critiques are not new. As previously discussed in this book, feminist media has often relied upon a model that assumes women are willing and able to work for little, if no pay (Murray, 2004).

It is also useful to understand *Teen Vogue*'s move towards feminism in relation towards what Banet-Weiser (2012, p. 47) describes as the 'compromise of cultural capitalism'. In the case of *Teen Vogue*, we can see the combination of feminist activism and capitalism. Furthermore, the way that Lauren Duca's column in particular has been branded, and the way that Duca herself has become a highly visible figure, suggests that 'the social activist' in its current manifestation is managed, organised and exchanged not simply as a commodity but as a brand. This can be seen in the way that Duca's column is packaged with 'thigh high politics', an illusion to fashion, and by her recent fame due to columns such as 'Donald Trump Is Gaslighting America'. Furthermore, as I have outlined earlier in this chapter, the branding of high-profile feminists has a historical precedent. This suggests the importance of understanding the continuing importance of looking at the relationship between feminism and capitalism.

THE ALTERNATIVE: COLLECTIVE FEMINIST BLOGGING VS. MEDIA CONGLOMERATES

It is worth noting that there is a plethora of feminist blogs. *xoJane* and *Teen Vogue* were chosen for analysis not necessarily because they are the most popular or prolific but because they clearly represent the entanglements between feminism and capitalism that have been a key theme for this book. However, it would be problematic to present this as the whole story. *Bust* and *Bitch*, which have both been analysed in this book, have websites, as does *Ms*. However, given that they are primarily known as magazines, I will not discuss them here. Similarly, whilst *Jezebel* is one of the best-known women's sites, with a specific focus on gender and popular culture, it is owned by Gizmodo and is part of a wider network of sites (*Jezebel*, 2018). Similarly, *Bustle* is part of a larger digital group that also owns '*Romper, Elite Daily and The Zoe Report*' (Bustle, 2018). This suggests that there are few feminist sites with a large traffic that are independent.

The lack of independent feminist sites is critiqued in an article on the *Bitch* website (Lesniak, 2017). Lesniak focuses on *Bustle* and notes that it is owned by man with the aim to 'build "a billion-dollar company"'. This contrasts with the feminist magazines that I have analysed, where the aim of the magazines was never to make huge profits. Lesniak notes that 'the goal of Bustle was never to move feminism forward by publishing nuanced, witty, helpful feminist perspectives. It was to make money'. She contrasts this with *Bitch*, which needs to rely on readers and subscribers rather than advertising. As with *Spare Rib*, advertising is viewed here as something that should be treated with caution. In contrast to *Bustle*, Lesniak focuses on the concept of *Bitch* as a 'community' and suggests that the aim of the company is to make 'independent, truly feminist media'. However, it is important to note that this comparison is there essentially to encourage readers to donate to an

'$85,000 goal' that needs to be met by 'December 31st'. This further hints to the uneven playing field between independent organisations and those which aim to make a profit as their main priority.

GAL-DEM: WOMEN OF COLOUR AND THE FEMINIST INTERNET

So far, the focus in this chapter has primarily been on mainstream feminist media products, which not only have been created by but have arguably catered for a white audience. In some respects, this mirrors the situation historically, as can be seen in the discussion of *Spare Rib* and *Ms*. Although blogs theoretically provide unlimited space for self-expression, this is not always the case in reality. Schulte (2011, p. 728) notes that 'utopian-dystopian binary driven research' has 'focused on "the virtual" and "the physical" as separate spheres'. It is important when discussing the feminist internet to consider the ways in which some women (white, middle class) and certain kinds of feminism (white feminism) are privileged, just as they are in the 'real world'. It is also important to consider the ways that sites such as *gal-dem* are challenging this privilege, whilst also utilising some of the visibility of the mainstream. In this section, I will begin by providing some background on the relationship between race, white feminism and the feminist internet. I will then move on to discuss *gal-dem* in particular.

Daniels (2013, p. 696) in her work on the way race has been considered in work on the internet quotes Sinclair (2004, p. 1), who states, '"The history of race in America has been written as if technologies scarcely existed, and the history of technology as if it were utterly innocent of racial significance"'. It is, therefore, important to consider how the feminist internet reflects and reinforces oppressive racial hierarchies. One of the case studies that Daniels uses to demonstrate the white feminism of the feminist internet is the 2013 'Future of Online Feminism' report. Daniels (2015, p. 24) notes that the 2013 'Future of Online Feminism' report by Courtney Martin and Vanessa Valenti 'illustrates some of the trouble with white feminism', due to the lack of consideration of the impact of race in the way that feminist blogs can operate. One particular aspect of this criticism that I would like to focus on is the disproportionate resources that some feminist blogs have over others. This will be used as a jumping off point for discussion of *gal-dem* in particular.

Daniels (2015, p. 24) notes that there is a 'wide-range of tactics and strategies to make feminist blogging economically lucrative and more emotionally satisfying'. However, these focus largely on engagement with corporations, suggesting a capitalist feminist framework is being used in order to support these initiatives. As chapters on *Spare Rib* and *Ms*. earlier in this book have demonstrated, engagement with capitalism by feminist media makers often led to the reinforcement of a white feminist privilege in content. The fact that such engagement with capitalism often reinforces white feminist privilege can be seen in Daniels' comparison of two blogging conferences: *Blogher* and *Blogalicious*. Daniels (2015, p. 25) describes *Blogher* as an opportunity for

> thousands of predominantly (though not exclusively) white women come together looking for emotional support and for ways to 'monetize' – make money from – their blogs.

However, whilst this may seem like a positive way for women to get together, a comparison with the *Blogalicious* conference which was 'developed and attended by African American women' shows the way white women bloggers are more likely to be embraced by corporate America. Furthermore, Daniels (2015, p. 26) argues that the relative lack of sponsorship for *Blogalicious* is indicative of

> the racialized political economy in which white women earn more than African American, Native American and Latina women; this includes money earned from doing work online, like blogging for feminist causes.

As Daniels argues, the emphasis on 'corporate-sponsored feminism' is likely to reproduce racial inequalities that exist within capitalism. This is important to acknowledge when analysing mainstream feminist and women's magazines, since they are the ones most likely to be given the capital to maintain their visibility, in comparison to sites that are aimed at women of colour. However, as this chapter will now go on to show, sites like *gal-dem* are disrupting the whiteness that has been seen within the feminist blogging landscape.

gal-dem (2019) describe themselves as:

> a new media publication run entirely by women and non-binary people of colour. With our online and print magazine, we're addressing inequality and misrepresentation in the industry through platforming the creative and editorial work of young women and non-binary people of colour across essays, opinion, news, arts, music, politics and lifestyle content.

The use of the word 'platforming' in the description of the aim of the site highlights the extent to which the representation of underrepresented voices is a key aim of the site. This is reinforced through the citing of figures that show that 'the journalism industry is 94% white and 55% male'. This shows an awareness of the ways that the industry is both patriarchal and also racist. The use of language such as 'taking control' and 'disrupting tired stereotypes' further reinforces the idea that *gal-dem* is providing an alternative.

The *gal-dem* website is split into seven main thematic sections: first person, news, culture, life, music, politics and horoscopes. The inclusion of a section for 'first person' suggests a similar move towards subjectivity that can be seen in *Teen Vogue* and *xoJane*. Furthermore, this move could also be read in relation to the site's aim to provide spaces for women of colour that are not seen within the mainstream. The first-person section provides a space for the site's writers to express their opinions about issues to do with popular culture, race and society. As an indicative example, the first page of articles in the first-person section on April 21, 2019, includes a discussion of blackface on British television, racism at school, disability, campus sexual assaults and historic racist abuse of mixed-race children in Belgium. This suggests that there is a broad range of topics that are discussed. Although these stories are diverse in what they discuss, they all focus on race to some extent. This is important to contrast to the other sites that we have looked at in this chapter, and indeed to *Spare Rib* and *Ms*. As with *Spare Rib* in the 1980s and 1990s, race in *gal-dem* is not a peripheral or token issue but is instead discussed in depth.

This extends for discussions of feminism on the site. A keyword search for feminism brings up three articles that focus on 'white feminism' on the first page. As Aziz (1997) has argued, white feminism centres whiteness in its articulation of feminism. By highlighting that this is the case, *gal-dem* counters the assumed norm that feminism should privilege white women. Of the other articles that are selected as top results, there are two that explicitly mention intersectionality, two that are about Muslim feminism and another article that critiques 'mainstream feminism'. This suggests that *gal-dem* is providing a space for women of colour to reject the oppressions of mainstream feminism.

gal-dem provides an important contrast to some of the texts that we have looked at in this chapter, and in this book more generally. Another important point to make about *gal-dem* is that in contrast to mainstream sites such as *Teen Vogue* is that there are no advertisements on *gal-dem*. As we have already seen in this book, advertisements often served to both dictate the kind of content that is included within feminist media (Erdman Farrell, 2011) and also often contradict with editorial content. The lack of advertising is one way to mitigate this. However, the print issue of *gal-dem* is £12, which is relatively expensive for a women's magazine. Although advertising may be beneficial in allowing a greater amount of editorial freedom, on the other hand, it leads to a more expensive product which may potentially exclude those who do not have the financial means to afford a £12 magazine. Although the lack of advertising in *gal-dem* gestures towards its editorial independence, that is not to say that *gal-dem* has not engaged with the mainstream. The final part of this chapter will analyse the collaboration between *gal-dem* and *The Guardian*.

GAL-DEM AND THE GUARDIAN

In August 2018, *gal-dem* edited a 'takeover' of the *Guardian Weekend*, the paper's Saturday lifestyle and entertainment supplement. This is significant because it suggests an engagement between *gal-dem* and the mainstream. However, it is interesting to note that the site worked with the *Guardian*, a left-leaning newspaper that is less corporate than other papers. This suggests that even though the takeover would bring the site to a much wider audience, it would do so in a way that is unlikely to compromise the values of *gal-dem* than appearing in a newspaper that had differing political or business values, such as *The Sun* or *The Daily Mail*.

There are twenty-five articles included in the takeover, including an interview with Diane Abbott, an article about micro-aggressions and interviews with Michaela Coel and Gemma Chan. The inclusion of three interviews with women of colour is unusual and highlights the extent to which *gal-dem* can provide an alternative. This is highlighted further in a feature on the magazine by Afua Hirsch titled '"We are offering something that people didn't get before": inside gal-dem magazine'. The use of a quotation from the collective that highlights their uniqueness reinforces the idea that the mainstream is not covering this. Furthermore, the stand-first for the articles states that the organisation is 'disrupting traditional media – all from their tiny HQ in a London car park'. The explicit mention that they are working from a 'tiny HQ' alludes to the lack of financial resources, reinforcing their independence.

Throughout the article, Hirsch points to the differences between *gal-dem* and other publications. For example, she notes that of the four women in the newsroom when she visits 'none is older than 25'. Similarly, she contrasts the 'garnished' parking spaces of other businesses that operate in the same building as *gal-dem* with the 'miniscule' space that *gal-dem* have. All of this contributes to the sense that *gal-dem* are outsiders. Hirsch notes that whilst the magazine has 'famous women' who are 'keen to collaborate', at the same time, the editor of *gal-dem* Liv Little 'frets about the price of the phone calls required to arrange the next star' and argues that this 'is a marker of the reality of life at this major media disrupter'. As we have already seen throughout this book, there is a contradiction between maintaining independence, whilst on the other hand wanting to grow and engage with high-profile interviewees.

The interrelationship between maintaining independent values and financial security can also be seen in the statement that 'Corporate gigs provide some financial relief from the unpaid work of the gal-dem magazine itself but are not without hazards'. Hirsch quotes Little, who acknowledges that '"It's hard"' since:

The boundaries are constantly shifting. The way media and brands and advertising are set up, it's against people of colour. To find those brands that are not part of that, or that have a good ethos, they are few and far between. We say no to loads of stuff.

A parallel can be drawn between *gal-dem* and the other texts that we have looked at in this book. However, there is also a key difference. When talking about the problems that *gal-dem* has with investment from corporations, the impact on people of colour is highlighted, in contrast to when this was discussed in *Ms.* and *Spare Rib*, where the impact on women of colour specifically was not considered. This highlights the extent to which a magazine that focuses on women of colour is more likely to prioritise the experiences of women of colour. This can be linked to the changes that were seen when the *Spare Rib* collective became more collective.

CONCLUSION

This chapter has identified the ways in which contemporary feminist blogs can be seen as continuations of the feminist media tradition that has been discussed in this book. As this book as a whole has argued, feminist media producers often have a complex relationship with capitalism. For digital feminist media this is intensified as the most visible (Banet-Weiser, 2018) forms of feminism tend to be those that are most amenable to capitalism.

The three case studies that have been included in this chapter demonstrate the extent to which the material contexts of feminist media need to be considered. Whilst *Teen Vogue* has become an increasingly important vehicle for challenging the misogyny of the Trump administration, it must also be noted that the site is still part of publishing conglomerate *Conde Nast*, and arguably this means that the extent to which it can really challenge capitalism is limited.

The analysis of *xoJane* showed a different understanding of the feminist internet. In particular, *xoJane* highlighted the ways that a new intimacy has been curated online (Steenson, 2016). However, following on from criticisms by Thi Nyugen (2012) in the chapter on Riot grrrl, it is important to recognise the problems with cultivating this discourse of intimacy, in so much as it potentially distracts from structural change.

It is also important to note that the first three case studies that were mentioned in this chapter all privilege whiteness, either through a predominantly white workforce or alternatively using mainstream sites of visibility that tend to privilege a white middle-class audience that are seen as most valuable as consumers. The final example used in this chapter, *gal-dem*, is a corrective to this as a site and magazine that is run collectively by women of colour. However, even so, in an article by Afua Hirsch, there is still acknowledgement of the difficulty of maintaining your political principles whilst being able to pay your writers. As the chapters throughout this book have demonstrated, there is often a disconnect between the feminist principles of media producers and the financial realities, which mean that this is not reflected in the pay and conditions of workers. However, *gal-dem* does seem to be bucking this trend somewhat, with a new internship scheme that pays the London Living Wage and helps provide accessible housing for those outside London (*gal-dem*, 2019). Whilst it still remains to be seen how sustainable this is in the long term, it does suggest an acknowledgement of the need to make workplaces as accessible as possible in a way that feminist media has not always done so.

NOTE

1. Ironically, when looking through old copies of *Spare Rib*, I noted that an 'Anna Wintour' wrote an article about young fashion designers in September 1972. Given that the article is about fashion, I assume it is the same person.

Conclusion

Key to the analysis in this book, whether discussing historical or contemporary feminist media, is an understanding of how the material conditions of each of the magazines had an impact on the kind of topics that they covered and the depth of coverage that they were able to provide. Since *Spare Rib* made a conscious decision to exclude advertising for most mainstream products, it was able to be much more radical in its discussion of capitalism. In contrast, *Ms.* made no secret of the fact that it wanted to reach as wide an audience as possible, and one of the consequences of this is that it was limited in its radicalism. As I have argued, this is in part due to the different contexts between the United Kingdom and the United States, though the different publishing contexts are, I argue, the most important factor.

Similarly, when looking at the ways in which *Spare Rib* and *Ms.* discussed race, working practices are vital to understanding the differences in amount and nature of coverage. *Ms.* was much less likely to substantively represent race and was much more likely to present a Western focus when it did represent race. It is, then, perhaps no coincidence that the magazine also continued to be staffed predominately by white women. This can be contrasted with *Spare Rib*, whose coverage of race in earlier years was also tokenistic and centred on discussions of whiteness. However, the intentional move towards a more representative collective had a substantial impact on the extent to which race was not only a topic for discussion but one that was dealt with in nuanced ways. The oftentimes negative reaction of white *Spare Rib* readers to this change does, however, demonstrate the ways in which whiteness and the interests of white women are more often than not presumed as the norm.

Indeed, as the analysis of advertising in *Ms.* demonstrates, whiteness was generally assumed to be the norm, and the white reader was assumed. It was only once *Spare Rib*'s content changed so that whiteness was no longer assumed that this became evident. The example of the assumed reader in *Spare Rib* and *Ms.*, and the differing ways in which they understood their readers, is instructive in highlighting that change needs to come through changes in who is employed in the magazine (Saha, 2018), whilst it cannot be assumed that this change is going to be welcomed by white readers who feel threatened. This change in focus was possible for *Spare Rib* for a couple of reasons. Firstly, it did not need to rely on advertisers, and therefore did not need to promote an affluent white audience to readers. Secondly, it found that in spite of criticism from some white readers, the move towards inclusivity was supported by women of colour. However, it does need to be noted that *Spare Rib* ceased publication largely because it no longer had the finances to carry on.

The relationship between capitalism and feminist media production is central to this book. In the chapters on 1990s feminist media, the focus was primarily on the ways that *Bitch* and *Bust* moved from zines to magazines. Looking at the books that were produced by the magazines, it is clear that *Bust* presented a version of feminism that did not see a contradiction between the engagement with popular and consumer culture and feminism. However, one of the issues with this is that it meant a more radical and collective feminism was less visible. In contrast, whilst *Bitch* has been critical of the extent to which contemporary feminist media has been dominated by capitalist media companies, the corporate material that is sent to advertisers that is discussed in this book makes it clear that the magazine sees its readers in relation to their economic potential. This gestures towards the key issue with feminist media: how can you, on the one hand, maintain ideological integrity, whilst at the same time acknowledging the compromises that need to be made.

This is an issue that has only intensified with the rise of digital feminist media, which was the focus in the final part of this book. On the one hand, the feminist status of *Teen Vogue* is complicated by the fact that it is an imprint of *Vogue*, and owned by *Condé Nast*, and therefore very much exists within the capitalist system. On the other hand, it is clear that the content of the website in particular has become increasingly progressive in its politics. I have argued that *Teen Vogue* represents a particularly popular feminism that has become increasingly hegemonic in the last decade (Banet-Weiser, 2018). However, it is important to acknowledge the limitations of this feminism, given that it essentially depends on your ability to be a consumer. The inclusion of advertisements for beauty products alongside scathing indictments of the president is indicative of this mix. However, this is nothing new, as the use of celebrity and advertising in *Ms.* demonstrates. The visibility of popular feminism suggests that feminism has become increasingly accepted, but there are questions about the extent to which this popular feminism can be truly transformative. As Banet-Weiser (2018) argues, popular feminism is the most dominant in part because it is the only representation of feminism that is non-threatening enough to remain visible. In some respects, the tension between maintaining visibility and having meaningful ability to change the status quo seems like an intractable problem. However, as I hope that this book has demonstrated, understanding the ambiguity inherent in the production of feminist media is important when considering the extent to which such media can ever be revolutionary.

xoJane, founded by *Sassy* and *Jane* founder Jane Pratt, exemplifies, even more so than *Teen Vogue*, the movement towards the confessional. To a certain degree, this mirrors the 'personal is political' ethos of the second wave, though the interaction between the confessional and capitalism means that they need to be read as potentially transactional forms of emotional labour. However, this conflict between capital and feminism is again no new thing, and the aim of this book was to identify the ways in which feminist media, from past and present, has always been implicated deeply with capitalism, almost by definition. We are at a crossroads. On the one hand, it is easy to dismiss the popular feminism that is evident in both *Ms.* and *Teen Vogue*. It is deeply problematic that the employment practices of *xoJane* do not match up with the rhetoric coming from the site. On the other, these are media products that have to some greater or lesser degree espoused feminism to a much wider audience than zine makers have access.

The final part of this book outlined some of the sites that are perhaps working within a more collective framework. It is perhaps unsurprising that these organisations such as *gal-dem* are produced by women of colour who have been historically marginalised within the media industry. The collaboration between *gal-dem* and *The Guardian* arguably shows one way that established news organisations can help promote independent feminist media. However, the issue of funding persists, and the continual dilemma for feminist media organisations will be whether to 'sell out' and potentially compromise your values or continue producing work under precarious conditions. As the chapter on *Spare Rib* and *Ms.* suggests, as well as the discussion of zines and blogs shows, such an approach will inevitably privilege those who are able to support themselves with alternative funds, whilst also having enough hours to also devote to the production of the media.

Whilst a young woman wearing a 'this is what a feminist looks like' t-shirt is better than her not being a feminist at all, this expression of empowerment is limited in its effectiveness if the t-shirt was made in a sweatshop by employees with few rights. My aim with this book has been to ensure that any discussion of feminist media is also a discussion about capitalism, because capitalism has an impact on the kind of content that is produced, who can produce and how many people will get to read it.

Bibliography

Abbott, D. (2018) 'Diane Abbott: 'Before going to bed, I wrap my hair and have a cup of camomile tea'. *The Guardian*, www.theguardian.com/lifeandstyle/2018/aug/14/diane-abbott-before-going-to-bed-i-wrap-my-hair-and-have-a-cup-of-camomile-tea, accessed 10/02/2020.

Adams, K. H., and Keene, M. L. (2007) *Alice Paul and the American Suffrage Campaign*, Champaign: University of Illinois Press.

Anderson, W. (2002) *The Cultivation of Whiteness: Science, Health and Racial Destiny in Australia*. Durham: Duke University Press.

Andrews, D. (2012) 'Toward a More Valid Definition of "Pornography"'. *The Journal of Popular Culture*, 45(3), pp. 457–477.

Ani. (2016) 'Goodbye, xoJane. No Love Lost There'. *The Story of A*, www.thestoryofa.com/goodbye-xojane-no-love-lost/, accessed 12/02/2020.

Anon. (2013) '10 Celebrities Who Say They Aren't Feminists'. *Huffington Post*, https://www.huffpost.com/entry/feminist-celebrities_n_4460416, accessed 12/01/2020.

Anon. (1992) 'Malcolm-Rebel Without a Pause'. *Spare Rib* (London), May 1992, pp. 28–29.

Anon. (1992) 'War Ina Babylon'. *Spare Rib* (London), June 1992, pp. 10–16.

Arneil, B. (1999) *Politics and Feminism*. Oxford: Blackwell.

Attar, D. (1983) 'An Open Letter on Anti-Semitism and Racism'. *Trouble and Strife* (Winter), pp. 13–16.

Atton, C. (2002) *Alternative Media*. London: Sage.

Aziz, R. (1997) 'Feminism and the Challenge of Racism: Deviance or Difference'. In Mizra, H. S. (ed.) *Black British Feminism: A Reader*. London: Routledge, pp. 70–80.

Bailey, C. (2003) 'Bitching and Talking/Gazing Back: Feminism as Critical Reading'. *Women and Language*, 26(2), pp. 1–8

Banet-Weiser, S. (2012) *Authentic™: The Politics of Ambivalence in a Brand Culture*. New York: NYU Press.

Banet-Weiser, S. (2018) *Empowered: Popular Feminism and Popular Misogyny.* Durham: Duke University Press.

Bashevkin, S. (1998) *Women on the Defensive: Living Through Conservative Times*. Chicago: University of Chicago Press.

Bates, L. (2014) *Everyday Sexism*. London: Simon and Schuster.

Bazin, V. (2017) 'A New Kind of Trade': Advertising Feminism in *Spare Rib*'. In Smith, A. (ed.) *Re-reading Spare Rib*. New York: Springer, pp. 197–212.

BBC News. (2017) 'Gaslighting: The Perfect Romance that Became a Nightmare'. *BBC News*, www.bbc.co.uk/news/stories-41915425, accessed 12/01/2020.

Beckett, C., and Deuze, M. (2016) 'On the Role of Emotion in the Future of Journalism'. *Social Media+ Society*, 2(3), pp. 1–6.

Beetham, M. (1996) *A Magazine of Her Own? Domesticity and Desire in the Woman's Magazine*. London: Routledge.

Bell, L. (2013) 'Trigger Warnings: Sex, Lies and Social Justice Utopia on Tumblr'. *Networking Knowledge: Journal of the MeCCSA Postgraduate Network*, 6(1).

Bellos, L. (1982) 'Backlash'. *Spare Rib* (London), September 1982, p. 16.

Benjamin, W. (1969) *Illuminations*. New York: Schocken.

Benn, M. (1987) 'What's in a Vote?' *Spare Rib* (London), May 1987, pp. 18–22.

Bhavnani, K. K. (1982a) 'Racist Acts'. *Spare Rib* (London), February 1982, pp. 49–52.

Bhavnani, K. K. (1982b) 'Racist Acts'. *Spare Rib* (London), April 1982, pp. 24–27.

Bhavnani, K. K. (1982c) 'Racist Acts: Racism and Racialism in Britain in the 1980's'. *Spare Rib* (London), March 1982, pp. 25–27.

Bhavnani, K. K., and Talcott, M. (2011) 'Interconnections and Configurations: Toward a Global Feminist Ethnography'. In Hesse-Biber, S. N. (ed.) *Handbook of Feminist Research: Theory and Praxis*. Thousand Oaks: Sage, pp. 176–186.

Bitch (n.d.) 'Advertise with Bitch, Become a Sponsor'. *Bitch*, www.bitchmedia.org/sponsorship, accessed 10/02/2020.

Blake, C. (1982) 'Citizenship, Law and the State: The British Nationality Act 1981'. *The Modern Law Review*, 45, pp. 179–197.

Bouchier, D. (1983) *The Feminist Challenge: The Movement for Women's Liberation in Britain and the United States*. Basingstoke: Macmillan.

Bourdieu, P. (1986) 'The Forms of Capital'. In Richardson, J. E. (ed.) *Handbook of Theory of Research for the Sociology of Education*. Westport: Greenword Press, pp. 241–258.

Boston Women's Health Book Collective. (1973) *Our Bodies, Ourselves: A Book by and for Women*. New York: Simon and Schuster.

Boycott, R. (1984) *A Nice Girl Like Me*. London: Chatto and Windus.

Bracx, A. (1977)'A Meeting of Small Capitalists'. *Spare Rib* (London), July 1977, p. 39.

Bradley, P. (2003) *Mass Media and the Shaping of American Feminism 1963–1975*. Jackson: The University Press of Mississippi.

Brownmiller, S. (2013 [1975]) *Against Our Will: Men, Women and Rape*. New York: Open Road Media.

Brownmiller, S. (2000) *In Our Time: Memoir of a Revolution*. New York: Delta.

Bryson, V. (2003) *Feminist Political Theory: An Introduction*. Basingstoke: Palgrave Macmillan.

Buchanan, P. D. (2011) *Radical Feminists: A Guide to an American Subculture*. Santa Barbara: ABC-CLIO.

Carby, H. V. (1997) 'White Woman Listen! Black Feminism and the Boundaries of Feminism'. In Mizra, H. S. (ed.) *Black British Feminism: A Reader*. London: Routledge, pp. 45–53.

Carr, D. (2003) 'Coming Late, Fashionably, Teen Vogue Joins a Crowd'. *New York Times*, www.nytimes.com/2003/01/13/business/media-coming-late-fashionably-teen-vogue-joins-a-crowd.html, accessed 12/02/2020.

Chambers, D., and Worrall, R. (2017) 'The Frontiers of Sisterhood: Representations of Black Feminism in Spare Rib (1972–1979)'. In Smith, A. (ed.) *Re-reading Spare Rib*. New York: Springer, pp. 159–178.

Chambers, D., Steiner, L., and Fleming, C. (2004) *Women and Journalism*. London: Routledge.

Cochrane, K. (2013) 'The Great Feminist Revival'. *The Guardian*, www.theguardian.com/lifeandstyle/2013/may/14/feminism-slutwalks-spare-rib, accessed 10/02/2020.

Cohen, R. (2012a) Marie-Therese McGivern, interviewed by Rachel Cohen. *Sisterhood and After: The Women's Liberation Oral History Project*.

Cohen, R. (2012b) Sue O'Sullivan interviewed by Rachel Cohen. *Sisterhood and After: The Women's Liberation Oral History Project*.

Collins, P. H., and Bilge, S. (2016) *Intersectionality*. Hoboken: John Wiley & Sons.

Colman, F. (2010) 'Notes on the Feminist Manifesto: The Strategic use of Hope'. *Journal for Cultural Research*, 14(4), pp. 375–392.

Comedia (1984) 'The Alternative Press: The Development of Underdevelopment'. *Media, Culture, Society*, 6(2), pp. 95–102.

Coote, A., and Campbell, B. (1982) *Sweet Freedom*. Oxford: Blackwell.

Cottom, T. M. (2019) *Thicc*. New York: The New Press.

Coward, R. (1982) 'What Is Pornography? Two Opposing Feminist Viewpoints'. *Spare Rib* (London), June 1982, pp. 52–55.

Crenshaw, K. (1989) 'Demarginalizing the Intersection of Race and Sex: A Black Feminist Critique of Anti-discrimination Doctrine, Feminist Theory and Anti-Racist Politics'. *University of Chicago Legal Forum*, 139, pp. 139–167.

Critchlow, D. T., and Stachecki, C. L. (2008) 'The Equal Rights Amendment Reconsidered: Politics, Policy, and Social Mobilization in a Democracy'. *Journal of Policy History*, 20(1), pp. 157–176.

Cronin-Wohl, L. (1982) 'Watch on the Right: The New Danger – A Three Step Antiabortion Plan'. *Ms.* (NY), February 1982, pp. 87–88.

Cronin-Wohl, L. (1982) 'Rise in Antiabortion Terrorism'. *Ms.* (NY), November 1982, p. 19.

Cunningham, A., and Haley, E. (1990) 'A Look Inside the World of Advertising Free Publishing: A Case Study of *Ms* Magazine'. *Journal of Current Issues and Research in Advertising*, 22(2), pp. 17–30.

Dahlerup, D. (1986) *The New Women's Movement Feminism and Political Power in Europe and the USA*. London: Sage.

Daileader, C. R. (1997) 'The Uses of Ambivalence: Pornography and Female Heterosexual Identity'. *Women's Studies: An Interdisciplinary Journal*, 26(1), pp. 73–88.

Daniels, J. (2013) 'Race and Racism in Internet Studies: A Review and Critique'. *New Media & Society*, 15(5), pp. 695–719.

Daniels, J. (2015) 'The Trouble with White Feminism: Whiteness, Digital Feminism and the Intersectional Internet'. *Digital Feminism and the Intersectional Internet*, https://academicworks.cuny.edu/cgi/viewcontent.cgi, accessed 10/02/2020.

Davies, M. M., and Mosdell, N. (2006) *Practical Research Methods for Media and Cultural Studies: Making People Count*. Athens: University of Georgia Press.

Dean, J. (2010) 'Feminism in the Papers: Contested Feminisms in the British Quality Press'. *Feminist Media Studies*, 10(4), pp. 391–407.

Deem, M. (2003) 'Disrupting the Nuptials at the Town Hall Debate: Feminism and the Politics of Cultural Memory in the USA'. *Cultural Studies*, 17(5), pp. 615–647.

D'enbeau, S. (2011) 'Sex, Feminism, and Advertising: The Politics of Advertising Feminism in a Competitive Marketplace'. *Journal of Communication Inquiry*, 35(1), pp. 53–69.

Dicker, R. (2016) *A History of US Feminisms*. New York: Seal Press.

Doueihi, M. (2011) *Digital Cultures*. Cambridge: Harvard University Press.

Dow, B. J. (2014) *Watching Women's Liberation, 1970: Women's Pivotal Year in the Network News*. Chicago: University of Illinois Press.

Downes, J. (2010) *DIY Queer Feminist Subcultural Resistance in the UK*. Doctor of Philosophy, University of Leeds.

Drisko, J., and Maschi, T. (2015) *Content Analysis*. Oxford: Oxford University Press.

Duca, L. (2016) 'Donald Trump Is Gaslighting America'. *Teen Vogue*, December 10, 2016, https://www.teenvogue.com/story/donald-trump-is-gaslighting-america, accessed 10/02/2020.

Duca, L. (2017a) Harvey Must Be a Turning Point in the Way We Respond to Climate Change. *Teen Vogue*, August 30, 2017, www.teenvogue.com/story/harvey-houston-texas-climate-change-thigh-high-politics-lauren-duca, accessed 10/02/2020.

Duca, L. (2016) 'Hillary Clinton Encourages Hope and Determination Among Supports in the New Year'. *Teen Vogue*, December 31, 2016, www.teenvogue.com/story/hillary-clinton-new-years-message, accessed 10/02/2020.

Duca, L. (2017b) 'Lauren Duca Sounds Off on Why Pop Culture and Politics Are so Intertwined'. *Teen Vogue*, May 23, 2017, www.teenvogue.com/story/lauren-on-why-pop-culture-and-politics-are-so-intertwined, accessed 10/02/2020.

Duca, L. (2017c) 'To Trolls, With Love'. *Teen Vogue*, January 10, 2017, www.teenvogue.com/story/lauren-duca-internet-trolls-online-harassment, accessed 10/02/2020.

Duca, L. (2017d) We Have to Stop Pretending We Can't Do Anything About Gun Violence. *Teen Vogue*, October 2, 2017, www.teenvogue.com/story/las-vegas-shooting-guns-thigh-high-politics-lauren-duca, accessed 10/02/2020.

Duggan, L., and Hunter, N. D. (2006) *Sex Wars: Sexual Dissent and Political Culture*. Abingdon: Taylor & Francis.

Duncombe, S. (2008) *Notes from Underground: Zines and the Politics of Alternative Culture*. Bloomington: Microcosm Publishing.

Dworkin, A. (1989 [1981]) *Pornography: Men Possessing Women*. New York: Plume.

Easton, S. M. (1994) *The Problem of Pornography: Regulation and the Right to Free Speech*. Abingdon: Taylor & Francis.

Echols, A. (1989) *Daring to Be Bad: Radical Feminism in America 1967–1975*. Minneapolis: University of Minnesota Press.

Edmonds, L., and White, R. (2017) 'What Did It Mean?' A Generational Conversation. In Smith, A. (ed.) *Re-reading Spare Rib*, New York: Springer, pp. 23–40.

Edmunds, L. (1987) 'Barbara Mikulski: US Senator'. *Ms.*, January 1987, pp. 63, 94.

Elias, A. S., and Gill, R. (2018) 'Beauty Surveillance: The Digital Self-Monitoring Cultures of Neoliberalism'. *European Journal of Cultural Studies*, 21(1), pp. 59–77.

Ellis, K., O'Dair, B., and Tallmer, A. (1990) 'Feminism and Pornography'. *Feminist Review*, (36), pp. 15–18.

Everett, A. (2004) 'On Cyberfeminism: High Tech Mediations of Feminism's Discontents'. *Signs*, 30(1), pp. 1278–1286.

Fairclough, N. (2003) *Analysing Discourse: Textual Analysis for Social Research*. London: Routledge.

Fakhry, M. (1992) 'Libya: Gadhafi Human Rights Award'. *Spare Rib*, July 1992, pp. 46–47

Faludi, S. (1991) *Backlash: The Undeclared War Against Women*. New York: Crown.

Farrell, A. E. (2011). 'From a Tarantula on a Banana Boat to a Canary in a Mine: *Ms* Magazine as a Cautionary Tale in a Neoliberal Age'. *Tulsa Studies in Women's Literature*, 30, 393–405.

Farrell, A. E. (1998) *Yours in Sisterhood: Ms. Magazine and the Promise of Popular Feminism*. Chapel Hill: The University of North Carolina Press.

Felski, R. (1998) '3 On Confession. In Smith, S., and Watson, J. (eds.) *Women, Autobiography, Theory: A Reader*. Madison: University of Wisconsin Press, 83–95.

Ferguson, J. H., Kreshel, P. J., & Tinkham, S. F. (1990) 'Ms.: Sex Role Portrayals of Women in Advertising'. *Journal of Advertising*, 19(1), pp. 40–51.

Ferguson, M. L. (2010) 'Choice Feminism and the Fear of Politics'. *Perspectives on Politics*, 8(1), pp. 247–253.

Ferguson, M. (1983) *Forever Feminine: Women's Magazines and the Cult of Femininity*. London: Heinemann Educational.

Forster, L. (2016) 'Spreading the Word: Feminist Print Cultures and the Women's Liberation Movement'. *Women's History Review*, 25(5), pp. 812–831.

Foss, S. K. (1979) 'Equal Rights Amendment Controversy: Two Worlds in Conflict'. *Quarterly Journal of Speech*, 65(3), pp. 275–288.

Fraser, D. (2009) *The Evolution of the British Welfare State: A History of Social Policy Since the Industrial Revolution*. Basingstoke: Palgrave.

Frazer-Carroll, M. (2018) 'Gemma Chan: 'Is It Better to Give or to Receive? Are we Talking About Oral Sex?' *The Guardian*, www.theguardian.com/lifeandstyle/2018/aug/11/q-and-a-gemma-chan, accessed 10/02/2020.

Freeman, J. (1975) *The Politics of Women's Liberation: A Case Study of an Emerging Social Movement and Its Relation to the Policy Process*. Philadelphia: David McKay.

Friday, N. (1973) *My Secret Garden*. New York: Rosetta Books.

Friedan, B. (1963) *The Feminine Mystique*. London: Penguin.

Gal-Dem (2019) About *gal-dem*, http://gal-dem.com/about/, accessed 10/02/2020.

Gelb, J. (1989) *Feminism and Politics: A Comparative Perspective*. Berkeley: University of California Press.

Gilheany, B. (1998) 'The State and the Discursive Construction of Abortion'. In Randall, V., and Waylen, G. (eds.) *Gender, Politics and the State*. London: Routledge, pp. 58–79.

Gill, R. (2007) *Gender and the Media*. Cambridge: Polity Press.

Gill, R. (2010) '"Life Is a Pitch": Managing the Self in New Media Work'. In Mark Deuze (ed.), *Managing Media Work*. London; Sage.

Gill, R. (2011) 'Sexism reloaded, or, it's time to get angry again!.' Feminist Media Studies, 11(01), 61–71.

Gill, R. (2017) 'The Affective, Cultural and Psychic Life of Postfeminism: A Postfeminist Sensibility 10 Years on'. *European Journal of Cultural Studies*, 20(6), pp. 606–626.

Gillespie, M. A. (1987) 'Personal Words: My Gloves Are Off Sisters-Power Racism and That "Domination Thing"'. *Ms.* (NY), April 1987, pp. 19–20.

Gillis, S., Howie, G., and Munford, R. (eds.) (2004) *Third Wave Feminism: A Critical Exploration*. Basingstoke: Pan Macmillan.

Gillis, S., and Munford, R. (2004) 'Genealogies and Generations: The Politics and Praxis of Third Wave Feminism'. *Women's History Review*, 13(2), pp. 165–181.

Gilman, L. (2007) 'Beyond the Shadow: Rescripting Race in Women's Studies'. *Meridians: Feminism, Race, Transnationalism*, 7(2), pp. 117–141.

Glenn, P. (2015) 'I Am Not Nearly as Cool with Having Christmassess as I Thought'. *xoJane*, December 31, 2015.

Glick, E. (2000) 'Sex Positive: Feminism, Queer Theory, and the Politics of Transgression'. *Feminist Review*, 64(1), pp. 19–45.

Godard, B. (2002) 'Feminist Periodicals and the Production of Cultural Value: The Canadian Context'. *Women's Studies International Forum*, 25(2), pp. 209–223.

Gough-Yates, A. (2012) '"A Shock to the System" Feminist Interventions in Youth Subculture—The Adventures of Shocking Pink'. *Contemporary British History*, 26(3), pp. 375–403.

Gough-Yates, A. (2003) *Understanding Women's Magazines: Publishing, Markets and Readerships*. London: Routledge.

Greene, G. (1991) 'Feminist Fiction and the Uses of Memory. *Signs: Journal of Women in Culture and Society*, 16(2), pp. 290–321.

Griswold, C. 'The Best Gift Ideas for Mom and Dad'. *Teen Vogue*, November 28, 2018., www.teenvogue.com/gallery/best-parents-holiday-gift-ideas, accessed 10/02/2020.

Groeneveld, E. (2016) *Making Feminist Media: Third-Wave Magazines on the Cusp of the Digital Age*. Waterloo: Wilfrid Laurier University Press.

Grow, J. M. (2008) 'The Gender of Branding: Early Nike Women's Advertising as a Feminist Antenarrative'. *Women's Studies in Communication*, 31(3), pp. 312–343.

Hall, S. (2001) 'The Spectacle of the Other'. In Wetherall, M., Taylor, S., and Yates, S (eds.) *Discourse Theory and Practice: A Reader*. London: Sage, pp. 324–344.

Hamad, H., and Taylor, A. (2015) 'Introduction: Feminism and Contemporary Celebrity Culture'. *Celebrity Studies*, 6(1), pp. 124–127.

Hamling, W. (1972) 'Patience Is a Vice'. *Spare Rib* (London), October 1972, p. 7.

Hanna, K. (1991) *Bikini Kill*, www.artzines.info/bikini-kill/, accessed 10/02/2020.

Harris, A. (2003) 'gURL Scenes and Grrrl zines: The Regulation and Resistance of Girls in Late Modernity'. *Feminist Review*, 75(1), pp. 38–56.

Harris, A. (2008) 'Young Women, Late Modern Politics, and the Participatory Possibilities of Online Cultures'. *Journal of Youth Studies*, 11(5), pp. 481–495.

Harrison, B. (1972) '*Midge Decter's "Bible of the Backlash"'*. *Ms.* (NY), December 1972, pp. 5, 30–35.

Harvey, D. (2007) *A Brief History of Neoliberalism*. Oxford: Oxford University Press

Helmbrecht, B. M., and Love, M. A. (2009) 'The BUSTin' and Bitchin' of Third-Wave Zines'. *College Composition and Communication*, 61(1), pp. 150–169.

Hemmings, C. (2011) *Why Stories Matter: The Political Grammar of Feminist Theory*. Durham: Duke University Press.

Henry, A. (2001) *Not My Mother's Sister: Generational Conflict and Third Wave Feminism*. Bloomington: Indiana Press.

Hermes, J. (1995) *Reading Women's Magazines*. Cambridge: Polity.

Higgins, M. (2015) 'I Has an Absurd Period Accident in Front of a High School Softball Team'. *xoJane*, November 25, 2015.

Hill, C., Corbett, C., and St Rose, A. (2010) *Why so Few? Women in Science, Technology, Engineering, and Mathematics*. Washington: American Association of University Women.

Hirsch, A. (2018) 'We Are Offering Something People Didn't Get Before': Inside gal-dem magazine'. *The Guardian*, www.theguardian.com/lifeandstyle/2018/aug/10/offering-something-people-didnt-get-meet-gal-dem-team, accessed 10/02/2020

Hirsch, M., and Smith, V. (2002) 'Feminism and Cultural Memory: An Introduction. *Signs*, 28(1), pp. 1–19.

Hollows, J. (2012) 'Spare Rib, Second Wave Feminism and the Politics of Consumption'. *Feminist Media Studies*, 13(2), pp. 268–287.

Hooks, B. (1987) *Ain't I a Woman: Black Women and Feminism*. London: Pluto Press.

Hornaday, A. (1987) 'Executive Assistants: Is There Power Behind the Throne'. *Ms.* (NY), October 1987, pp. 28–32.

Hovitz, H. (2016) 'I Had a Halloween Experience so Scary that I got Sober'. *xoJane*, October 28, 2016.

Hsieh, H. F., and Shannon, S. E. (2005) 'Three Approaches to Qualitative Content Analysis'. *Qualitative Health Research*, 15(9), pp. 1277–1288.

Humm, M. (ed.) (1992) *Feminisms: A Reader*. London: Harverster Wheatsheaf.

Hunter, J. E. (1990) 'A Daring New Concept: The Ladies Home Journal and Modern Feminism'. *NWSA Journal*, 2(4), pp. 583–602.

Hyman, P. (1997) *Jewish Feminism Faces the American Women's Movement: Convergence and Divergence*. Ann Arbor: Jean and Samuel Frankel Center for Judaic Studies.

Irish Women's Group in London. (1982) 'Blood Sisters'. *Spare Rib* (London), February 1982, p. 41.

Jackie (1982) 'Sheffield Women's Conference (on Race and Class), July 3rd and 4th'. *Spare Rib* (London), September 1982, p. 18.

Jacques, A. (2001) 'You Can Run but You Can't Hide: The Incorporation of Riot Grrrl into Mainstream Culture'. *Canadian Woman Studies*, 21(1),pp. 46–50.

Jervis, L., and Zeisler, A. (2006) *BITCHFEST*. New York: Farrar, Straus and Giroux.

Johnson, S. (2007) 'Why Should They Care'. *Journalism Studies*, 8(4), pp. 522–528.

Johnson, E. (2018) 'Lauren Duca became an internet star overnight. Now, she says she's "fireproof"'. *Vox*. https://www.vox.com/2018/2/22/17037234/lauren-duca-donald-trump-gaslighting-tucker-carlson-fox-news-peter-kafka-recode-media-podcast [Accessed 02/05/2020].

Jolly, M. (2008) *In Love and Struggle: Letters in Contemporary Feminism*. New York: Columbia University Press.

Jolly, M. (2019) *Sisterhood and After: An Oral History of the UK Women's Liberation Movement, 1968-present*. Oxford: Oxford University Press.

Jordan, J. (1977) 'Forum: Second Thoughts of a Black Feminist'. *Ms.* (NY), February 1977, pp. 113–115.

Jordan, T. (2010) 'Branching Out: Second-Wave Feminist Periodicals and the Archive of Canadian Women's Writing'. *ESC: English Studies in Canada*, 36(2), pp. 63–90.

Kahn, R., and Kellner, D. (2007) 'Oppositional Politics and the Internet: A Critical Reconstructive Approach'. *Cultural Politics*, 1(1), pp. 75–100.

Karp, M., and Stoller, D. (1999) *The Bust Guide to the New Girl Order*. New York: Penguin.

Keller, J. (2015) *Girls' Feminist Blogging in a Postfeminist Age*. London: Routledge.

Keller, J., and Ringrose, J. (2015) 'But Then Feminism Goes Out the Window!': Exploring Teenage Girls' Critical Response to Celebrity Feminism'. *Celebrity Studies*, 6(1), pp. 132–135.

Kelly, K. 'What "Capitalism" Is and How It Affects People'. *Teen Vogue*, 2018, www.teenvogue.com/story/what-capitalism-is, accessed 10/02/2020.

Kim, J. (2018) '6 Non-Boring LBDS for When You Have Nothing to Wear to your Holiday Party'. *Teen Vogue*, November 29, 2018, www.teenvogue.com/gallery/best-holiday-lbd-under-200, accessed 10/02/2020.

Kinser, A. E. (2010) *Motherhood and Feminism: SealStudies*. New York: Seal Press.

Kort, M. (1987) 'Entrepreneurs: Making a Healthy Business out of Fitness'. *Ms.* (NY), April 1987, pp. 14, 16–17.

Kreps, J., and Leaper, J. R. (1977) 'The Secretary of Commerce on the Future for Working Women'. *Ms.* (NY), March 1977, p. 6.

Krynski, S. (1982) 'Sex Objects'. *Spare Rib*, March 1992, pp. 6–7.

Laing, A. C., and Sutton, L. A. (eds.) (1999) *Reinventing Identities: The Gendered Self in Discourse*. Oxford: Oxford University Press.

Lake, C. (1992) 'State of the Economy'. *Spare Rib*, August–September 1992, p. 43.

Lazar, M. M. (2005) 'Feminist Critical Discourse Analysis: Gender, Power and Ideology in Discourse'. Basingstoke: Palgrave.

Lesniak, K. (2017) 'Cashing in on Feminism: The Bustle Edition'. *Bitch*, www.bitch media.org/article/bustlecashinginfeminism, accessed 10/02/2020.

Leung, L. (1997) 'The Making of Matriarchy: A Comparison of Madonna and Margaret Thatcher'. *Journal of Gender Studies*, 6(1), pp. 33–42.

Levine-Rasky, C. (2011) 'Intersectionality Theory Applied to Whiteness and Middle-Classness'. *Social Identities*, 17(2), pp. 239–253.

Lind, A. C. (2013) 'Heteronormativity and Sexuality'. In Walyen, G., Celis, K., and Weldon, S. L. (eds.) *The Oxford Handbook of Gender and Politics*. Oxford: Oxford University Press.

Lindgren, J. (1993) 'Defining Pornography'. *University of Pennsylvania Law Review*, 141(4), pp. 1153–1275.

Loomes, P. (2016) 'I thought yoga, meditation and Instagram could save me from PTSD after I was raped'. *xoJane*, October 21, 2016.

Lovink, G. (2008) *Zero Comments: Blogging and Critical Internet Culture*. London: Routledge.

Lowell, T. (ed.) (1990) *British Feminist Thought: A Reader*. Oxford: Blackwell.

Mackinnon, C. A. (1985) 'Pornography, Civil Rights, and Speech'. *Harvard Civil Rights-Civil Liberties Law Review*, 20, p. 1.

Mackinnon, C. A., and Dworkin, A. (1997) *In Harm's Way: The Pornography Civil Rights Hearings*. Cambridge: Harvard University Press.

Macleish, J. (2018) 'Jughead's Dad Is up to Something on Riverdale and It's Probably Totally Bad'. *Teen Vogue*, November 29, www.teenvogue.com/story/riverdale-recap-season-3-episode-6, accessed 10/02/2020.

Mann, S. A., and Huffman, D. J. (2005) 'The Decentring of Second Wave Feminism and the Rise of the Third Wave'. *Science and Society*, 69(1), pp. 56–91.

Marciano, L. (1980) *Ordeal*. New York: W.H Allen.

Marcus, S. (2010) *Girls to the Front*. New York: Harper Collins.

Martin, C. E., and Valenti, V. (2013) '#Femfuture: Online Revolution'. *New Feminist Solutions*, 8, http://bcrw.barnard.edu/wp-content/nfs/reports/NFS8-FemFuture-Online-Revolution-Report.pdf, accessed 10/02/2020.

McCracken, E. (1993) *Decoding Women's Magazines from Mademoiselle to Ms*. Basingstoke: Macmillan.

McIntosh, P. (1990) 'White Privilege: Unpacking the Invisible Knapsack'. *Independent School*, Winter, www.racialequitytools.org/resourcefiles/mcintosh.pdf, accessed 10/02/2020.

McManus, A. (1987) 'From Liberation to Confirmation'. *Spare Rib* (London), August 1987, p. 7.

McNamara, B. (2018) 'This Is How to Stay Healthy When You Travel'. *Teen Vogue*, November 29, 2018, www.teenvogue.com/gallery/how-to-stay-healthy-when-you-travel, accessed 10/02/2020.

McRobbie, A. (2009) *The Aftermath of Feminism: Gender, Culture and Social Change*. London: Sage.

McRobbie, A. (ed.) (1997) *Back to Reality? Social Experience and Cultural Studies*. Manchester: Manchester University Press.

McRobbie, A. (2013) 'Feminism, the Family and the New "Mediated" Maternalism'. *New Formations*, 80, pp.119–137.

McRobbie, A. (2015) 'Notes on the Perfect: Competitive Femininity in Neoliberal Times'. *Australian Feminist Studies*, 30(83), pp. 3–20.

Mendes, K. (2011) *Feminism in the News: Representations of the Women's Movement Since the 1960s*. Basingstoke: Palgrave Macmillan.

Mendes, K. (2015) *Slutwalk: Feminism, Activism and Media*. Basingstoke: Palgrave Macmillan.

Mendes, K., Ringrose, J., and Keller, J. (2019) *Digital Feminist Activism: Girls and Women Fight Back Against Rape Culture*. Oxford: Oxford University Press.

Mennel, B. (2010) 'Feminism's Sex Wars and the Limits of Governmentality the Female Body'. In Reed, L., and Saukko, P. (eds.) *Governing the Female Body: Gender, Health, and Networks of Power*. Albany: SUNY Press, pp. 253–270.

Mennel, B. (2016) *The Representation of Masochism and Queer Desire in Film and Literature*. New York: Springer.

Milloy, J., and O'Rourke, R. (1991) *The Woman Reader: Learning and Teaching Women's Writing*. London: Routledge.

Monem, N. K. T. (ed.) (2007) *Riot grrrl: Revolution Girl Style Now!* London: Black Dog Publishing.

Morgan, R. (1977) 'Alice Paul: Mother of the ERA'. *Ms.* (NY), October 1977, p.112.

Morgan, R. (ed.) (1970) *Sisterhood Is Powerful: An Anthology of Writings from the Women's Liberation Movement*. New York: Vintage.

Ms. (1972) 'The Bulletin Board: Memo for Election Day'. *Ms.* (NY), November 1972, pp. 108–109.

Ms. (1982) 'No Comment'. *Ms.* (NY), July/August 1982, p. 265.

Mulvey, L. (1989) *Visual and Other Pleasures*. New York: Springer.

Muñoz, J. E. (1999) *Disidentifications: Queers of Color and the Performance of Politics*. Minneapolis: University of Minnesota Press.

Murray, S. (2004) *Mixed Media: Feminist Presses and Publishing Politics*. London: Pluto Press.

Neff, G. (2012) *Venture Labor: Work and the Burden of Risk in Innovative Industries*. Cambridge: The MIT Press.

Nguyen, M. T. (2012) 'Riot grrrl, Race, and Revival'. *Women & Performance: A Journal of Feminist Theory*, 22(2–3), pp. 173–196.

Onwurah, C. (1987) 'Sexist, Racist and Above All Capitalist: How Women's Magazines Create Media apartheid'. In Davies, K., Dickey, J., and Stratford, T. (eds.) *Out of Focus: Writings on Women and the Media*. London: The Women's Press, pp. 74–81.

Oosthuizen, A., Fazan, C. (1977) 'Women Talk About Why They Marched'. *Spare Rib* (London), January 1977, pp. 26–28.

Orbach, S. (1978) *Fat Is a Feminist Issue*. London: Arrow.

O'Reilly, J. (1987) 'A Global Click!' *Ms.* (NY), July 1987, pp. 60–61, p.188.

O'Sullivan, S. (1996) *I Used to Be Nice: Sexual Affairs*. London: Cassell.

Paige, C. (1982) 'Watch on the Right: The Amazing Rise of Beverly LaHaye'. *Ms.*, February 1982, pp. 24–28.

Phillips, A. (1972) 'The Aftermath of the Bosom Boom'. *Spare Rib* (London), July 1972, p. 32.

Phillips, A. (1977) 'Secret Deal.' *Spare Rib*, December 1977, p. 13.

Phillips, E. B. (1978) 'Magazine heroines: Is Ms. Just Another Member of the Family Circle?' In Tuchman, G., Daniels, A., and Benit, J. (eds.) *Hearth and Home: Images of Women in the Mass Media.* Oxford: Oxford University Press, pp. 116–129.

Piepmeier, A., and Zeisler, A. (2009) *Girl Zines: Making Media, Doing Feminism.* New York: New York University Press.

Pindado, E. '7 Portraits of Young People Traveling in the Migrant Caravan'. *Teen Vogue*, November 26, 2018, www.teenvogue.com/gallery/7-young-people-in-the-migrant-caravan, accessed 10/02/2020.

Pogrebin, A. 'How Do You Spell Ms?' *New York Magazine*, 2011, http://nymag.com/news/features/ms-magazine-2011-11/, accessed 10/02/2020.

Poletti, A. (2005) 'Self-Publishing in the Global and Local: Situating Life Writing in Zines'. *Biography*, 28(1), pp. 183–192.

Pruchniewska, U. M. (2018) 'Branding the Self as an "Authentic Feminist": Negotiating Feminist Values in Post-feminist Digital Cultural Production'. *Feminist Media Studies*, 18(5), pp. 810–824.

Radway, J. (2016) 'Girl Zine Networks, Underground Itineraries, and Riot grrrl History: Making Sense of the Struggle for New Social Forms in the 1990s and Beyond'. *Journal of American Studies*, 50(1), pp. 1–31.

Radway, J. A. (2009 [1982]) *Reading the Romance: Women, Patriarchy, and Popular Literature.* Chapel Hill: University of North Carolina Press.

Randall V. (2012) 'Gender, Feminism and the State: An Overview' In Randall, V., and Waylen, G. (eds.) *Gender, Politics and the State.* London: Routledge.

Randall, V., and Waylen, G. (eds.) (2012) *Gender, Politics and the State.* London: Routledge.

Rasool, A. 'This Platform Is Trying to Stop Fashion Magazines from Appropriating Black Culture'. *Teen Vogue*, 2018,www.teenvogue.com/story/every-stylish-girl-interview-black-women-in-media, accessed 10/02/2020.

Rearick, L. 'How to Make Alessia Cara's Runny Eye Makeup Work for Your Next Holiday Party'. *Teen Vogue*, 2018, www.teenvogue.com/story/fenty-beautys-priscilla-ono-shared-tips-for-wearing-alessia-caras-runny-eye-makeup, accessed 28/05/2019.

Renninger, B. J. (2015) '"Where I Can Be Myself . . . Where I Can Speak my Mind": Networked Counterpublics in a Polymedia Environment'. *New Media & Society*, 17(9), pp. 1513–1529.

Retallack, H., Ringrose, J., and Lawrence, E. (2016) '"Fuck Your Body Image": Teen Girls' Twitter and Instagram Feminism in and Around School'. In Coffey, J., Budgeon, S., and Cahill, H. (eds.) *Learning Bodies: The Body in Youth and Childhood Studies.* New York: Springer, pp. 85–103.

Rivers, N. (2017) *Postfeminism (s) and the Arrival of the Fourth Wave: Turning Tides.* New York: Springer.

Rodgerson, G., and Wilson, E. (1991) *Pornography and Feminism: The Case against Censorship by Feminists Against Censorship.* London: Lawrence &c Wishart.

Rottenberg, C. (2017) 'Neoliberal Feminism and the Future of Human Capital'. *Signs: Journal of Women in Culture and Society*, 42(2), 329–348.

Rottenberg, C. (2014) 'The Rise of Neoliberal Feminism'. *Cultural Studies*, 28(3), pp. 418–437.

Rowbotham, S. (1973) *Hidden from History: 300 Years of Women's Oppression and the Fight Against It*. London: Pluto.

Rowbotham, S. (1989) 'The Past Is Before Us: Feminism in Action Since the 1960s'. *Feminist Review: Issue,* (33), p. 109.

Rowe, M. (1982) *Spare rib reader*. London: Viking Press.

Rowe, M. (2013) 'Spare Rib Was Born of Grassroots Feminism: It's Not a Brand'. *The Guardian*, 14/03/2013, www.theguardian.com/commentisfree/2013/jun/14/spare-rib-grassroots-feminism-not-brand, accessed 10/02/2020.

Rowe, M., and Boycott, R. (1972) 'Liberation the Lady Said'. *Spare Rib* (London), July 1972, p. 4.

Rubin, G. (1984) Thinking Sex: Notes for a Radical Theory of the Politics of Sexuality. In Schneider, B., and Nardi, P. (eds.) *Social Perspectives in Lesbian and Gay Studies; A Reader*. London: Routledge,pp. 100–133.

Sandberg, S. (2013) *Lean in-Women, Work and the Will to Lead*. London: SAGE Publications.

Sandler, W. A. (1984) 'The Minneapolis Anti-Pornography Ordinance: A Valid Assertion of Civil Rights'. *Fordham Urban Law Journal*, 13, pp. 909–946.

Sandra. (1987) 'When is a Woman not a Woman?' *Spare Rib*, 1987, p. 7.

Sapiro, V. (1986) 'The Gender Basis of American Social Policy'. *Political Science Quarterly*, 101(2), pp. 221–238.

Schilit, K. (2003a) '"A little too ironic": The Appropriation and Packaging of Riot grrrl Politics by Mainstream Female Musicians'. *Popular Music and Society*, 26, pp. 5–16.

Schilit, K. (2003b) '"I'll resist you with every inch and every breath" Girls and Zine Making as a Form of Resistance'. *Youth Society*, 35(1), pp. 71–97.

Schulte, S. R. (2011) 'Surfing Feminism's Online Wave: The Internet and the Future of Feminism'. *Feminist Studies*, 37(3), pp. 727–744.

Schuster, J. (2013) 'Invisible Feminists? Social Media and Young Women's Political Participation'. *Political Science*, 65(8), pp. 8–24.

Scott, A. (1972) 'The Equal Rights Amendment: What's in it for You?' *Ms.* (NY), July 1972, pp. 82–86.

Sedgwick, E. K., and Frank, A. (2003) *Touching Feeling: Affect, Pedagogy, Performativity*. Durham: Duke University Press.

Segal, L. (2014) *Out of Time: The Pleasures and Perils of Ageing*. London: Verso.

Segal, L. (1987) 'Sex and Violence'. *Spare Rib* (London), February 1987, pp. 40–44.

Segal, L. (1999) *Why Feminism*. Cambridge: Polity Press.

Shalala, D. (1982) 'Feminist Notes: Women in Power – An Agenda for the '80s'. *Ms.*, May 1982, p. 96.

Smith, H. (1992a) Capitalism Isn't Working: Britain's Economy Reaches All Time Low. *Spare Rib* (London), February 1992, pp. 38–39.

Smith, H. (1992b) 'A Major Crisis: The British Economy Goes into Free Fall'. *Spare Rib* (London), October–November 1992, p. 46.

Smith, S. E. (2016) 'When I Voted, I Issued the Country an Ultimatum: It's Them or Me'. *xoJane*, November 7, 2016.

Spare Rib. (1992) 'Letter'. *Spare Rib* (London), July 1992, p. 3.

Spare Rib Collective. (1992a) 'Alert for Action'. *Spare Rib* (London), March 1992, p. 49.

Spare Rib Collective. (1992b) 'Annus Horribilis: The State of the Nation'. *Spare Rib* (London), December–January 1992, pp. 46–47.

Spare Rib Collective (1992c) 'Babylon Blues—Exposing Police Brutality: Survivors Tell Their Stories'. *Spare Rib* (London), August–September 1992, pp. 36–41.

Spare Rib Collective. (1992d) 'Cuba: Standing Strong'. *Spare Rib* (London), April 1992, p. 46.

Spare Rib Collective. (1992e) Editorial. *Spare Rib* (London), January 1992, p. 4.

Spare Rib Collective. (1983) 'Sisterhood is Plain Sailing'. *Spare Rib*, July 1983, pp. 24–27.

Spare Rib Collective. (1987) 'Where We've Been'. *Spare Rib* (London), July 1987, pp. 38–40.

Spare Rib Collective. (1977) 'Women's Liberation 1977—the National Women's Liberation Conference'. *Spare Rib* (London), May 1977, pp. 6–16.

Spence, J. T., and Helmreich, R. L. (1979) *Masculinity and Femininity: Their Psychological Dimensions, Correlates, and Antecedents*. Austin: University of Texas Press.

Stadtmiller, M. (2016) 'xoJane: My Former Website's Death Was A Blessing'. *The Daily Beast*, www.thedailybeast.com/xojane-my-former-websites-death-was-a-blessing, accessed 28/05/2019.

Steenson, S. (2016) 'The Intimization of Journalism'. In Witschge, T, Anderson, C. W., and Hermida, A. (eds.) *The SAGE Handbook of Digital Journalism*. London: Sage, pp. 113–127.

Steinem, G. (1977) 'If the Shoe Doesn't Fit, Change the Foot'. *Ms.* (NY), 1977, pp. 76, 85–86.

Steinem, G. (2012) *Outrageous Acts of Everyday Rebellion New* York: Open Road Media.

Steinem, G. (2013) 'Op-ed: On Working Together Over Time'. *The Advocate*, www.advocate.com/commentary/2013/10/02/op-ed-working-together-over-time, accessed 10/02/2020.

Steinem, G. (1972a) 'A Personal Report from Ms. *Ms.* (New York), July 1972, pp. 4–7.

Steinem, G. (1977) 'Pornography – Not Sex But the Obscene Use of Power'. *Ms.* (NY), August 1977, pp. 43–44.

Steinem, G. (1995 [1990]) 'Sex, Lies & Advertising'. In Hovland, R., Wolburg, J., and Haley, E. (eds.) *Readings in Advertising, Society and Consumer Culture*. London: Routledge, pp. 180–192.

Steinem, G. (1972b) 'Women *Voters Can't Be Trusted*'. *Ms.* (NY), July 1972, pp. 47–51, 131.

Stephens, E., and Ades, R. (1977) Mice in Manchester. *Spare Rib* (London), July 1977, pp. 10–13.

Stringer, P. (2018) 'Finding a Place in the Journalistic Field: The pursuit of recognition and legitimacy at BuzzFeed and Vice'. *Journalism Studies*, 19(13), pp. 1991–2000.

Strub, W. (2011) *Perversion for Profit: The Politics of Pornography and the Rise of the New Right*. New York: Columbia University Press.

Sunstein, C. R. (1986) Pornography and the First Amendment. *Duke Law Journal*, 1986(4), pp. 589–627.

Sweet, C. (1987) 'Who Pays for Pregnancy?' *Spare Rib*, January 1987, pp. 12–17.

Tarvis, C. (1982) 'What's Your P. Q' '. *Ms.* (NY), December 1982, pp. 49–50, 95.

Tasker, Y., and Negra, D. (eds.) (2007) *Interrogating Post-Feminism: Gender and the Politics of Popular Culture*. Durham: Duke University Press.

Taylor, A. (2016) *Celebrity and the Feminist Blockbuster*. New York: Springer.

Thom, M. (1997) *Inside Ms: 25 Years of the Magazine and the Feminist Movement*. New York: Henry Holt.

Thom, M. (1987) *Letters to Ms. Magazine, 1972–1987*. New York: Henry. Holt.

Thomas, B. (1982) 'Falklands "Brides and Sweethearts" Bite Back'. *Spare Rib*, August 1982, pp. 24–27.

Thomas-Flannery, K. (2005) *Feminist Literacies: 1968–1975*. Chicago: University of Illinois Press.

Thompson, B. (2002) 'Multiracial Feminism: Recasting the Chronology of Second Wave Feminism'. *Feminist Studies*, 28(2), pp. 337–360.

Todd, S. (1999) 'Models and Menstruation: Spare Rib Magazine, Feminism, Femininity and Pleasure'. *Studies in Social and Political Thought*, 1, pp. 60–78.

Tolentino, J. (2017) 'The Personal Essay Boom is Over'. *The New Yorker*, www.newyorker.com/culture/jia-tolentino/the-personal-essay-boom-is-over, accessed 10/02/2020.

Tong, R. (1997) *Feminist Thought: A Comprehensive Introduction*. London: Routledge.

Trachtenberg, J. 'Time Inc. Acquires Websites Aimed at Women'. *Wall Street Journal*, 2015, www.wsj.com/articles/time-inc-acquires-websites-aimed-at-women-1445901445, accessed 10/02/2020.

Travis, T. (2008) The Women in Print Movement: History and Implications. *Book History*, 11(1), pp. 275–300.

Triggs, T. (2010) *Fanzines*. London: Thames and Hudson.

Tuchman, G. (1978) *Making News: A Study in the Construction of Reality*. New York: Free Press.

Tuchman, G. (1979) 'Women's Depiction by the Mass Media'. *Signs*, 4(3), pp. 528–542.

Tyler, I. (2008) '"Chav mum chav scum" Class disgust in Contemporary Britain'. *Feminist Media Studies*, 8(1), pp. 17–34.

Van Gelder, L. (1982) 'Burn Out: What Happens When the World Won't Change'. *Ms.* (NY), May 1982, pp. 60–62, 84.

Vinen, R. (2010) *Thatcher's Britain: The Politics and Social Upheaval of the Thatcher Era.* London: Simon and Schuster.

Wahl Jorgenson, K. (2006) Letters to the Editor in Local and Regional Newspapers: Giving Voice to the Reader. In Franklin, B. (ed.) *Local Journalism and Local Media: Making the News Local.* London: Routledge, pp. 231–241.

Walker, N. A. (ed.) (1998) *Women's Magazines 1940–1960: Gender Roles and the Popular Press.* Boston: Bedford/St Martin's.

Wallsgrove, R. (1977) Pornography: Between the Devil and the True Blue Whitehouse. *Spare Rib* (London), December 1977, 44–46.

Waters, M. (2016) 'Yours in Struggle': Bad Feelings and Revolutionary Politics in Spare Rib'. *Women: A Cultural Review*, 27(4), pp. 446–465.

Watney, S. (1997) *Policing Desire: Pornography, AIDS and the Media.* London: A&C Black.

Weinberg, M. S., Williams, C. J., and Moser, C. (1984) 'The Social Constituents of Sadomasochism'. *Social Problems*, 31(4), pp. 379–389.

Welch, M. S. (1982) 'Is God for the ERA'. *Ms.* (NY), May 1982, p. 6.

Wheeler, E. (1977) 'Guess who's for the ERA? The ERA? Mary Kay Place and Bruce Solomon'. *Ms.* (NY), April 1977, 78–79.

White, C. (1970) *Women's Magazines 1693–1968.* London: Michael Joseph.

White, P. (1972) 'The Edible Present'. *Spare Rib* (London), December 1972, pp. 32–33.

Whitlock, M. J. (1987) '5 More Years of Desolation', *Spare Rib*, July 1987, p. 15.

Willis, E. (1993) 'Feminism, Moralism, and Pornography'. *New York Law School Law Review*, 38, pp. 351–358.

Wilson, A. (1997) 'Finding a Voice'. In Mizra, H. S. (ed.) *Black British Feminism: A Reader.* London: Routledge, pp. 31–35.

Winship, J. (1987) *Inside Women's Magazines.* London: Pandora.

Withers, D. (2015) *Feminism, Digital Culture and the Politics of Transmission: Theory, Practice and Cultural Heritage.* London: Rowman & Littlefield International.

Wikipedia (n.d.) 'Gloria Steinem', https://en.wikipedia.org/wiki/Gloria_Steinem, accessed 10/02/2020.

Wohl, L. C. (1977) 'A Mormon Connection?: The Defeat of the ERA in Nevada'. *Ms.* (NY), July 1977, pp. 68–70, 80–85.

Wolf, N. (1991) *The Beauty Myth: How Images of Beauty Are Used Against Women.* New York: Random House.

Woodard, A. (2016) 'I'm Alfre Woodard and this is #whyI'mwithher''. *xoJane*, November 2, 2016.

Wright, J. (1977) 'Letter'. *Ms.* (NY), December 1977, p. 4.

Zarnow, L. (2010) 'From Sisterhood to Girlie Culture: Closing the Great Divide between Second and Third Wave Cultural Agendas'. In *No Permanent Waves: Recasting Histories of US Feminism.* New Brunswick, Rutgers University Press pp. 273–304.

Zeisler, A. (2016) *We Were Feminists Once: From Riot Grrrl to Cover Girl, The Buying and Selling of a Political Movement*. New York: Public Affairs.

Zimmerman, A., and Dahlberg, J. (2008) 'The Sexual Objectification of Women in Advertising: A Contemporary Cultural Perspective'. *Journal of Advertising Research,* pp. 48, 71–79.

Zobl, E. (2009) 'Cultural Production, Transnational Networking, and Critical Reflection in Feminist Zines'. *Signs: Journal of Women in Culture and Society*, 35(1), pp. 1–12.

Index

advertising, 4–5, 17, 33–34, 40–55, 62,
   75–76, 94, 110, 119, 139, 145, 147,
   160, 168, 171, 173, 175–76
alternative media, 129
archives, 1–2, 13, 15, 27, 29, 155

Bhavnani, Kum Kum, 59, 61–62,
   66–69, 75
Bikini Kill, 127, 133–36, 134
Bitch, 11, 19–20, 40, 123, 127, 129,
   131, 138–40, 141, 143–48, 168, 176
Boycott, Rosie, 6–7, 26, 42
Brownmiller, Susan, 21, 81, 89, 91–92,
   98, 136, 152
Bust, 11, 19, 20, 123, 127, 129, 131,
   137–44, 146, 148, 168, 176
Bustle, 168

capitalism, 2–5, 11, 17, 20, 40–41,
   50–52, 55, 76, 93, 101, 103, 108, 110,
   113, 118–19, 121–23, 131, 134,
   144–46, 148–49, 153–54, 160,
   165–68, 170, 173, 175–77
celebrity, 13, 106–8, 129, 145–46,
   151–52, 159–63, 165, 175
congress, 101, 102, 104–5, 111
Conservative Party, 114, 115, 117,
   122

content analysis, 13, 15–16, 20, 43–45,
   60–61, 65–66, 82, 100–101, 148, 162
Cosmopolitan, 27, 108, 153

Democrat party, 105, 114, 117
DIY, 19, 130, 135
Duca, Lauren, 134, 151, 160, 162–66,
   168
Dworkin, Andrea, 80, 81, 83–84, 85, 87,
   89, 91, 93, 95, 99

elections, xi, xii, 105, 120, 122, 153,
   155, 157, 160, 162, 164, 165
Equal Rights Amendment (ERA), 9, 19,
   102, 104–8, 112, 123–24

Family Circle, 4
feminism: backlash against, 8, 15–17,
   19, 36–37, 100–103, 107, 110–12,
   119–20; black feminism, 33, 59,
   60–62, 67; digital feminism, 144,
   149–74; histories of feminism, 11–12;
   liberal feminism, 9, 47, 52, 55,
   107–8, 110, 119, 152, 165; popular
   feminism, 120, 134, 152, 159, 160,
   164–65, 176–77; post-feminism, 12,
   19, 76, 101, 103, 112, 119–20, 123,
   146, 152; radical feminism, 3, 10,

195

Lightning Source UK Ltd.
Milton Keynes UK
UKHW011948231020
372129UK00001B/18

9 781786 610416